Paul Lebowitz's 2009 Baseball Guide

A Complete Guide to the 2009 Baseball Season

Paul Lebowitz

iUniverse, Inc.
New York   Bloomington

Paul Lebowitz's 2009 Baseball Guide
A Complete Guide to the 2009 Baseball Season

iUniverse books may be ordered through booksellers or by contacting:

iUniverse
1663 Liberty Drive
Bloomington, IN 47403
www.iuniverse.com
1-800-Authors (1-800-288-4677)

Because of the dynamic nature of the Internet, any Web addresses or links contained in this book may have changed since publication and may no longer be valid. The views expressed in this work are solely those of the author and do not necessarily reflect the views of the publisher, and the publisher hereby disclaims any responsibility for them.

ISBN: 978-1-4401-2817-2 (pbk)
ISBN: 978-1-4401-2818-9 (ebk)

Printed in the United States of America

iUniverse rev. date: 3/2/2009

Contents

American League East
1.　New York Yankees
2.　Boston Red Sox *
3.　Tampa Bay Rays
4.　Baltimore Orioles
5.　Toronto Blue Jays

* Denotes predicted Wild Card winner.

New York Yankees
2008 Record: 89-73; Third Place, American League East

2008 Recap:

For the first time since 1993, the playoffs did not include the New York Yankees. The reasons for this event are as follows, in order: they relied too heavily on their vaunted trio of rookie pitchers Joba Chamberlain, Phil Hughes and Ian Kennedy; they were unable to withstand injuries to key players in Jorge Posada, Hideki Matsui, Chien-Ming Wang, Chamberlain and Hughes; the Rays were made an unanticipated leap into contention right over both the Yankees and Red Sox; they were trying to transition smoothly from former manager Joe Torre to the young, inexperienced and drastically different Joe Girardi; and their bench was undermanned and unable to pick up the slack effectively for the missing stars.

Considering everything they had to endure and that the world seemed to end because they missed the playoffs, it's easy to forget that they still managed to win 89 games. In an ordinary season, with the Rays not improving so drastically, the Yankees would probably have made the playoffs again, and their issues wouldn't have been so glaring.

Girardi experienced a rough transition into the Bronx Zoo on and off the field. Veterans that were used to Torre's ways—even if they didn't like him personally—at least knew what to expect. Realistically, with all the injuries, the season probably would've ended in a similar fashion had Torre been there, but since Girardi was the main difference between then and now, he took the brunt of the blame; in fact, it was likely the injuries that saved his job.

Mike Mussina stepped into the breach created by the injuries to Wang, Chamberlain and Hughes and won 20 games for the first time. Both Robinson Cano and Melky Cabrera had terrible seasons; Cano appeared as if he was disinterested and going through the motions for a big chunk of the season and Cabrera lost his starting job. Even with the flurry of deals that GM Brian Cashman pulled off to fill the Yankees holes with established players Xavier Nady and Ivan Rodriguez, their deficit was too great; their lineup stunningly shaky; and their injuries too much to overcome to reach the playoffs again.

2009 ADDITIONS: LHP C.C. Sabathia signed a 7-year contract.
RHP A.J. Burnett signed a 5-year contract.
1B Mark Teixeira signed an 8-year contract.
OF/1B Nick Swisher was acquired from the Chicago White Sox.
SS Angel Berroa signed a minor league contract.
RHP Kanekoa Texeira was acquired from the Chicago White Sox.
C Kevin Cash signed a minor league contract.

2009 SUBTRACTIONS: RHP Mike Mussina retired.
RHP Carl Pavano was not re-signed.
1B/DH Jason Giambi was not re-signed.
C Ivan Rodriguez was not re-signed.
OF Bobby Abreu was not re-signed.
INF Wilson Betemit was traded to the Chicago White Sox.
RHP Jeff Marquez was traded to the Chicago White Sox.
RHP Jhonny Nunez was traded to the Chicago White Sox.
RHP Darrell Rasner was sold to Japan.
C Chad Moeller was not re-signed.
RHP Chris Britton was released.

2009 PROJECTED LINEUP: C-Jorge Posada; 1B-Mark Teixeira; 2B-Robinson Cano; 3B-Alex Rodriguez; SS-Derek Jeter; LF-Johnny Damon; CF-Brett Gardner; RF-Xavier Nady; DH-Hideki Matsui

2009 PROJECTED STARTING ROTATION: C.C. Sabathia; A.J. Burnett; Chien-Ming Wang; Andy Pettitte; Phil Hughes; Joba Chamberlain (?)

2009 PROJECTED BULLPEN: Mariano Rivera; Jose Veras; Damaso Marte; Edwar Ramirez; Brian Bruney; Jonathan Albaladejo; Phil Coke; Alfredo Aceves; Joba Chamberlain (?)

2009 BENCH: OF/1B/DH-Nick Swisher; C-Jose Molina; INF-Angel Berroa; OF-Melky Cabrera; INF-Cody Ransom

2009 EXTRA PITCHERS/PROSPECTS: Ian Kennedy; Humberto Sanchez; David Robertson; Anthony Claggett; Eric Hacker; Dellin Betances

2009 EVERYDAY PROSPECTS: Juan Miranda; Chris Malec; Seth Fortenberry

ASSESSMENTS:
MANAGEMENT:

Hank Steinbrenner bloviated throughout the season and nothing much was done to follow through on his ranting; his father George would've been firing people left and right during and after the season had he been running things as his $200+ million roster was falling behind the Rays and Red Sox in the last season at Yankee Stadium. More and more, it's becoming clear that Hank is little more than a nuisance who explodes, bullies, threatens…and does nothing to follow through on his emotional reactions. His brother Hal is more levelheaded and deferent to the baseball people in their decisions and the Steinbrenners still spend money to put a superior product on the field.

General Manager Brian Cashman re-signed to stay with the Yankees after the season—a season in which Cashman's vision of having *his* manager Girardi; *his* prospects in the young pitchers; and *his* desire to be given similar credit that other GMs like Theo Epstein and Billy Beane receive for their work—ended in a Yankee-level disaster (as far as 89 wins can be called a disaster) by missing the playoffs. The charade was over as soon as the season ended; the Yankees were going to do what the Yankees do and that's spend, spend, spend to fill their holes.

The perception is obviously that the Yankees and Cashman are throwing money at their problems and are therefore increasing their league-high payroll even further, but with the departures of the likes of Pavano, Mussina and Jason Giambi, the Yankees payroll should be, at most, the same as it was last season. That reality isn't going to change the implication that Cashman's ideas and goals of being feted as a "genius" on the level of other GMs is being soiled by the failures of his young players; the change in philosophy from development to imports; and that he had little choice but to sign players to fill the holes that *his* misjudgments created. Cashman's safe in his job, but his image is taking a big hit and no amount of winning is going to bring it back because it's a return to business as usual with the Yankees.

Manager Joe Girardi will begin the 2009 season on the hot seat, and rightfully so. Girardi made the obvious types of mistakes that a young manager will make in terms of strategy and personnel, but that paled in comparison to the stories that were coming out of the Yankees clubhouse that the veterans couldn't get used to the new manager and his cold, aloof manner after so many years with the charming and bigger than life Joe Torre.

Girardi has many attributes that make him look like a solid manager in the future. He's intelligent; well-spoken and will learn from his mistakes as he goes along. It's unlikely that he'll repeat the same errors from last year, at least off the field. On the field, Cashman fired one of Girardi's hand-picked coaches in third base coach Bobby Meacham and that was more than a GM simply making a change to a different third base coach; that Meacham was fired should be seen as a shot over the bow at Girardi because if it were only a matter of Meacham's third base coaching skills, then he could've been moved to first base or to the bench; firing him was a message that Girardi could be next if things don't get better in 2009.

This team spent almost half-a-billion dollars in contracts to bring in Sabathia, Burnett and Teixeira; if they don't perform any better than last season's inconsistent and sniping group, Girardi has to know that he's the one that's going to take the fall. Here's how things are going to go: if the Yankees get off to a slow start—say, 8-12 after 20 games—Hank will start rumbling; if they're around 14-16 after 30 games, Hal and Cashman will start making calls (my guess is to laid back, historically successful veteran managers who can handle the big city like Davey Johnson or Jim Fregosi) and let them know to be on the ready because the team might be making a move; then if they're at or under .500 after 40 games, that'll be a quarter of the season and Cashman will either make the move himself or Derek Jeter will go to the upper management and, speaking for the remaining veterans, say enough's enough with Girardi.

Simply put, I'd strongly suggest that Girardi get the team off to a fast start if he wants to keep his job because if not, he's going to get fired probably before the end of May and will wait a long time before getting another opportunity to manage in the big leagues.

STARTING PITCHING:

After joining the Brewers from the Indians in a mid-season trade, C.C. Sabathia picked the team up and carried them on his broad shoulders into the playoffs. His heroic performances not only made him a folk hero, but made him a *load* of money. Sabathia would have preferred to pitch closer to his childhood home in California and was almost begging any of the West Coast teams to make a reasonable bid so he could turn down the Yankees initial offer of $140 million without drawing the ire of the Players Association for leaving a substantial amount of money on the table. Sabathia even went to the extent of going directly up to Dodgers GM Ned Colletti to solicit an offer; none came. Without any viable alternative other than the Brewers—who were stretching their payroll to come up with an offer of over $100 million—the Yankees increased their offer to $161 million and Sabathia accepted.

The idea that Sabathia was afraid to pitch in New York was silly; he simply preferred to pitch near his family in California. Sabathia has the guts and the ability to dominate wherever he pitches and as he joins the Yankees, he'll be just as good as he was with the Indians over his career; he's a legitimate ace at the top of any rotation and will be contending for the Cy Young Award by season's end.

A.J. Burnett has had three fully healthy seasons in his career. Each and every one of them was the year before he was arbitration eligible or due to be a free agent. Burnett has never shown the ability—and worse—the desire to pitch over 200 innings in any season other than when there was a load of money on the line. All the talk of Burnett "figuring it out" and "putting it together" as he learns how to keep himself healthy is just that, talk. The Yankees signed him to a 5-year, $82.5 million contract without any idea as to what they're going to get out of him, nor any idea whether he's going to suddenly find Steve Carlton-durability from the ages of 32-37 or be another Carl Pavano. Given his history, I can't see any possible way that the Yankees get what a pitcher making that kind of money would be expected to provide. If he delivers anything more than 23-25 starts and doesn't spend a chunk of the season on the disabled list, I'll be stunned. This is the recipe for ridicule of another Cashman pitching mistake and a sigh of relief for the other teams that were pursuing Burnett.

Chien-Ming Wang is ridiculed for what he isn't, but few seem to appreciate what he is. He gobbles innings; he throws strikes; and he wins. The Yankees have, so far, steadfastly refused to sign Wang to a long-term contract even though he won 19 games in 2006 and 2007 and was well on his way to another 15-18 win season when he injured his ankle running around the bases in Houston. Wang is down on the depth chart of the Yankees starting rotation to the third spot, but given Burnett's history, Wang is going to be needed for his 15-18 wins if the Yankees want to have an easier road to the playoffs, and he'll do it because he's a fine pitcher even if he's unappreciated by the Yankees.

Andy Pettitte's negotiation skills leave something to be desired. He took a load of heat because of the apparent hypocrisy in his on-again/off-again retirement contemplation; his insistence that he wanted to play for no team other than the Yankees, then openly flirted with the Dodgers, among others; and was openly insulted as the Yankees tried to keep costs down on a pitcher like Pettitte who had few options other *than* the Yankees, and didn't pitch all that well as the 2008 season wound down. In the end, after a $10 million offer for one season was rejected, Pettitte must've realized that if he wanted to pitch and have any chance of making more than the $10 million offer, he'd have to accept a $5 million base with incentives that would push it to a possible $12 million. Pettitte isn't what he once was and he may be due for a long-term injury since he's been so durable, but as a back-of-the-rotation starter, he's a good buy for that amount of money and the Yankees will happily pay the incentives if he reaches them; and in an important late-season game, I'd bet on Andy Pettitte delivering a solid performance over a guy like Burnett, Wang or even Sabathia, even at nearly 37-years-old.

Vaunted prospect Phil Hughes had a hideous year. He got off to a terrible start with an 0-4 record; 43 hits in 34 innings and a 6.62 ERA; an injured rib put him on the disabled list and he wound up back in the minors where he was almost as bad as he was in the big leagues. His stock was so far down that there was talk that the only reason the Yankees weren't trading him was because it wouldn't have brought back anything worthwhile to justify it. I believe that this is an overreaction. I've said all along that Hughes reminded me of the late Darryl Kile and Kile had many fits and starts in his career before figuring it all out. Hughes is still only 22 and he'll pitch with the diminished expectations of not being relied upon as an integral part of the starting rotation of a team that's gunning for a championship. As cool and poised as Hughes acts, the pressure had to be overwhelming and he failed. Diminished expectations and a group of veteran starters to take the pressure off of him as he flies under the radar should help Hughes regain what it was he lost and help the team as the season moves along.

Now we get to Joba Chamberlain. I've been a staunch advocate of Chamberlain being a starter since the debate began of what to do with the immature righty. It would be interesting to know what's going through the heads of the Yankees braintrust as to whether they think it was a mistake to bring him up to the majors as a set-up man for Mariano Rivera late in the 2007 season. They didn't win the title they thought he'd be a part of and the debate wouldn't be as fierce had he come up as a starter and simply been a starter. Now they're still continuing with the façade of limiting his innings as a starting pitcher to keep him from getting hurt. Eventually they're going to have to make a decision and take the reins off to see what he can actually do; and in case anyone hadn't noticed, with all the caution, all the care and all the monitoring they did last season in the transition from reliever to starter, he *still* wound up on the disabled list with a shoulder problem.

The Yankees starting rotation is so full now, and their bullpen so shaky that they need to put Chamberlain back in the bullpen for this year at least. The arguments have been held; the reasons elucidated, but an important point is being missed: they don't have to leave him in the bullpen for his entire career! Derek Lowe made the transition from starter to reliever, reliever to starter; Braden Looper became a decent starter as well. It can be done and the Yankees don't realize that this constant back-and-forth could be hurting him just as much as leaving him in one spot. Chamberlain's personality also could be the exact type that's going to find trouble (as evidenced by his DUI during the off-season) if he's got too much time to waste between starts. Most importantly, if they shift him to the bullpen, they go from a good team with question marks in the bullpen, to a dominant team with just about no holes and a great bet to win the World Series.

BULLPEN:

Mariano Rivera was another player who was unhappy with Girardi last season. (How does one go about getting Mariano Rivera angry at them? That's like getting into a fistfight with Yoda.) Rivera didn't let if affect him on the mound as he saved 39 games and was his old dominating self as long he wasn't used in tie games. Rivera is 39-years-old and is eventually going to hit a wall of some kind; but if he's used correctly (and the presence of the workhorse Sabathia should help him keep his workload down) he can maintain his effectiveness throughout the year.

If the Yankees insist on keeping Chamberlain in the rotation, then it's possible that Jose Veras could get the job as right-handed set-up man. Veras pitched reasonably well last season; he's big and durable and throws very hard; his strikeout numbers were more than one per inning, but he did give up seven homers in 58 innings, which is a lot. It's going to be a moot point when the playoffs arrive because no matter what they do with Chamberlain during the season, unless he wins 22 games and supplants one of the top four starters in the rotation, Chamberlain and no one else is going to be setting up for Rivera in the big games.

The Yankees had a contract option on Damaso Marte that they declined and they instead gave him a longer term extension. Marte was expected to be a guy who could get out both lefties and righties when he was acquired from the Pirates in the deal that also brought Xavier Nady to the team.

Marte was overworked and misused by Girardi and despite a high ERA, he did strike out almost 12 batters per 9 innings. If he's used correctly and not extended too far or asked to do too much, he should rebound.

Edwar Ramirez pitched well as a middle reliever and his wicked changeup allows him to be able to get out both lefties and righties.

Phil Coke was almost sent to the Pirates in the trade for Nady and Marte, but after the deal was reworked, Coke stayed with the Yankees and they were glad he did. As he pitched in 12 late season games, Coke was "it" again and there were expectations for what he'd do if he were kept on the roster from the beginning of the season. Coke posted a 0.61 ERA in 12 games, with 14 strikeouts in 15 innings. I'd hesitate before getting too excited about Coke repeating that level of work and he's slid into the background as a potential bullpen arm.

Brian Bruney was touted as another Yankee "find" when they acquired him from the Diamondbacks. Bruney throws hard, but he sustained a foot injury that ended his season prematurely. When he did pitch, Bruney was excellent with a 1.83 ERA in 32 games. If he continues that level of work, he'll see substantial work.

Jonathan Albaladejo had pitched well for the Nationals in 2007, but the beefy righty wound up back in the minors for the Yankees after appearing in only seven games; he could win a spot out of the bullpen coming out of spring training.

Alfredo Aceves looked like a find in four late season starts after the disastrous seasons of Hughes and Kennedy, but he may now be relegated to starting at Triple A because he's far down the depth chart and needs to pitch and be ready if and when one of the veterans like Andy Pettitte misses a few starts or if A.J. Burnett continues his career-long trend of not being able to stay healthy.

Ian Kennedy is only being mentioned because he was such a touted prospect and was such a complete disaster on the mound. He angered veterans with his arrogant attitude and his awful performance and he's going to have to work very hard to replenish his image. Of course, I'm also mentioning him because I'd like to gloat about how I nailed Kennedy's 2008 almost exactly in last year's book. Here's the quote:

Ian Kennedy is the third of the Yankees young starters and the one that the team was most willing to trade in deals for a veteran starter the likes of Santana or Haren. I don't think Kennedy is as good as the other two starters and is the most likely to either not make the team out of spring training, or make the team, get pounded and sent back down. He looks to be a finesse pitcher who has been built up by the Yankee propaganda machine and apparently

other organizations feel the same way with their reluctance to take him as the
centerpiece of any deal for one of their veteran starters.

I'm not quoting that in any attempt to toot my own horn, just as an example
that you didn't waste your money in buying this book.

Regarding Kennedy, the talk that he wasn't going to ever pitch in a
Yankee uniform again and statements of that nature was a bit premature.
Just because he's not as good as he was expected to be (in all fairness, very
few pitchers could've lived up to that hype) doesn't mean they should give
him away; worst case scenario, they could keep him at Triple A, let him get
his confidence back and perhaps give him a few starts in the big leagues,
then trade him for value.

LINEUP:

Jorge Posada's shoulder surgery may keep him out for the start of
the season. Posada's injury prevented him from throwing or hitting with
power and at the time of the injury, I thought he was being selfish with his
insistence of being a catcher when there was a chance that he'd be able to
help the team by playing first base or as the DH, but the shoulder problem
was such that he wasn't hitting with any authority. In retrospect, the team
might have been better served if Posada had the surgery earlier in the
season so he definitely would've been ready to start the season. At age 37,
it's a legitimate question of what the Yankees are going to get out of him
offensively and defensively if he's able to play. Posada's a prideful veteran,
but if the equipment isn't working properly, there's not much that can be
done about that and the Yankees are going to have to find themselves a
catcher while still paying Posada a load of money.

Mark Teixeira brings his professionalism and all-around play to the
Yankees. Teixeira was widely expected to either remain with the Angels
or sign with the Red Sox until the Yankees struck like lightning with
their 8-year, $180 million contract and got their first baseman for the rest
of the decade. Teixeira is a great fielder, a consistent power hitter and a
truly serious player who treats his game similarly to the players on the
championship Yankees did.

Robinson Cano was discussed in trade possibilities after a poor and
indifferent campaign in which he looked like he terribly missed Larry Bowa
and his tough-love; Cano needed to be dragged into the manager's office
by his throat and told in no uncertain terms that enough's enough with the
lackadaisical play and prolonged slumps. Occasionally it appears as if Cano
has just accepted that he's a slow starter and doesn't even bother to work to

get out of his slumps. Girardi waited until late in the season to bench and publicly discipline Cano and the leash should be shorter this season. With guys like Sabathia and Teixeira around, I'd expect better behavior and a big year from Cano.

Alex Rodriguez missed time with a strained quad and his numbers were dwarfed by his absurd 2007 MVP season. ARod is still one of the top three players in all of baseball and the distractions of the relationship with Madonna and the sheer nature of *being* ARod don't generally bother him on the field. The divorce; the allegations of being a bush leaguer; the tabloids; and now the book written by Joe Torre with the statements that are going to be seen as derogatory against ARod (especially by those who haven't actually read the text of the book) would distract and diminish the play of most other players, but ARod feeds off of that and the numbers will be there at the end of the season. That was before the steroid allegations that are still ongoing.

After years of vehement denials to allegations that he used performance enhancing drugs, ARod got busted by the revelations of a failed test from 2003 and accompanying stories detailing his guilt. ARod has given numerous accounts of his use of the drugs, when and where he got them; this is going to go on all season long to the point that the playing field will be his sanctuary and I think he's still going to put up massive numbers and be a contender for the MVP.

Derek Jeter's range is declining so rapidly that a decision about what position he's going to play is going to have to be made eventually. For all of his team-oriented rhetoric, the Yankees would probably be a superior defensive team if ARod were to be moved back to shortstop and Jeter to third, but that's going to happen right after the constitution is changed to allow George W. Bush to run for president again in 2012. Jeter's numbers are still there at the plate although his power and on-base numbers are declining as well. Jeter is going to be the man who's going to have to go to management if the team gets of to another bad start under Girardi and let them know that something has to be done; it's his job as the captain of the team.

Johnny Damon had a wonderful year at the plate and was another player who was unhappy with Girardi. In the midst of a blazing hot streak, Damon found himself on a scheduled "rest day" right in the middle of a hot streak in August. It's going to be hard for Damon, at age 35, to repeat the numbers from last season as he hit .303 with 17 homers and 71 RBI with a .375 on base percentage and 29 stolen bases. The main role for Damon is to get on base for ARod and Teixeira to drive him in. If he hits 15 homers and has a batting average of .280+, while coming close to maintaining his

OBP, the Yankees should be happy with that in the final year of Damon's contract.

The Yankees are insisting that they're willing to go with the defense and speed of Brett Gardner in center field. Melky Cabrera was so terrible last season that he wound up back in the minor leagues and drew the ire of Girardi after he misplayed a hit because he was in the middle of waving at the Bleacher Creatures as they chanted his name during their "roll call" of the starting lineup. What got Cabrera to the big leagues and made him a regular player was that he worked so hard to get to that position; once he felt he was entrenched, he took about three steps back both offensively and defensively. Like Kennedy, I'd be reluctant to just give up on Cabrera at age 24, but he's going to have to work his way not just into the lineup, but to make the roster out of spring training.

Gardner is 25-years-old; hit .228 in 127 at bats. He's never shown any power in the minors, but he has been a basestealer and did hit very well at Triple A last season. If they're intent on going with him as their everyday center fielder, their lineup can carry him until they decide to go after a veteran like Mike Cameron. Jim Edmonds is still available as of this writing and he'd be willing to sign a low-level contract to play for a shot at another World Series.

Xavier Nady has been mentioned in trade talks along with Nick Swisher. Nady would be the more likely choice to go because he's going to be a free agent at the end of the season and Swisher is signed to a long-term contract. Nady has good power, has handled New York while with the Mets and over the second half of last season with the Yankees and is well-liked. I'd expect the Yankees to go into the season with both Nady and Swisher because their outfielders are veterans and there's always the injury problems that creep up during the season. Nady has also had injury problems in his career.

Hideki Matsui missed time during the 2008 season with knee problems and as he ages (he's going to be 35), his numbers and famous durability are both on the decline. Matsui was mentioned in possible trade rumors to the Giants or Mariners, but he's still with the Yankees. He'll rotate in the outfield and at DH with Damon and Swisher; Matsui plays the game correctly and is also popular in the clubhouse. 2009 is the last season of his contract as well.

Nick Swisher is the gregarious bon vivant who had a terrible year in his lone season with the White Sox. Despite hitting only .219 and striking out 135 times, Swisher still hit 24 homers and his on base skills raised his OBP to .332, which is no small feat for a guy who batted .219. Swisher's still only 28 and as an ancillary part to the lineup rather than one who's relied upon to be one of the bashers, Swisher can rebound as a backup first baseman, DH, right fielder and, *very* occasional center fielder.

BENCH:

Whoever isn't starting amongst the crew of Nady, Swisher and Matsui will strengthen a major weakness of 2008 for the Yankees: the bench.

Jose Molina is excellent defensively, but had no business playing as much as he did last season. Molina is not a starting catcher and if Posada is unable to catch anything close to 100 games, they're going to have to do something about this problem. Former Red Sox backup Kevin Cash was signed to a minor league contract, but he's not the answer either.

Angel Berroa was the Rookie of the Year for the Royals in 2003, but his career hit the skids since then; he played well for the Dodgers after joining them last season and could be useful as the utility middle infielder.

Cody Ransom is a 33-year-old journeyman who's shown some pop in the minor leagues and can play every infield position. If the Yankees have to rely on him for much of anything, they've got a big problem.

PREDICTION:

As stated before, this team must get off to a good start if only to assuage the questions that surround manager Joe Girardi. The whole ARod mess will actually *help* the newcomers and manager Girardi because no one will be paying attention to them while the whole media feeding frenzy will be going on. With their pitching, even if Burnett winds up on the disabled list (as I expect him to), they have the depth to withstand the loss. Sabathia is going to have a huge year as long as he doesn't put too much pressure on himself; part of the reason he got off to such a terrible start last season was because of his impending free agency and the uncertainty of whether he'd be traded by the Indians. Sabathia will handle the pressure of pitching in New York even if it takes him some time to grow accustomed to everything involved with the city. Even if Chamberlain is in the starting rotation for the first half of the season, I expect him to be in the bullpen for the playoffs.

The lineup is one of the best in baseball; Teixeira is going to fit in perfectly and allow ARod to relax on the field and drive in plenty of runs. Even with the question in center field, GM Brian Cashman has shown the ability to fill the team's holes at mid-season when necessary. The issue with Posada won't be settled until he proves he's healthy, is able to throw and, most importantly, hit with power. No one's going to know if he can do it until he does it.

Even with the questions still surrounding Girardi (he's smart enough to know that he's on the hot seat and will lose his job if the team isn't playing up to expectations), this team is going to be one of the best in baseball. I don't expect them to get off to another poor start; they'll rebound from missing the 2008 playoffs last season by regaining the top spot in the AL East and winning the World Series with Girardi as the manager.

PREDICTED RECORD: 97-65

Boston Red Sox
2008 Record: 95-67; Second Place, American League East; Wild Card Winner
Defeated Los Angeles Angels in ALDS 3 games to 1
Lost to Tampa Bay Rays in ALCS 4 games to 3

2008 Recap:

The season was dominated by injuries, controversy and trades. The Red Sox withstood chunks of time missed due to injury by David Ortiz, Josh Beckett, Mike Lowell and J.D. Drew; and Manny Ramirez finally exhausted the patience of the organization with his petulance, whining, complaining and finally the worst possible sin— faking injuries and not playing hard— to force his way out of Boston. Even with all of that, the team was able to win 95 games and come within one game of a second straight World Series appearance.

Carried by a deep and well-organized bullpen; a fertile farm system able to cover for free agent mistakes; and an uncanny ability to make something out of nothing (they were able to get rid of Manny *and* find a reasonable replacement in Jason Bay—they did pay Manny's salary while he was becoming a folk hero in Los Angeles) to again make the playoffs and make it further than their decimated roster should have. Dustin Pedroia and Kevin Youkilis are the changing-of-the-guard for the Red Sox from the days of Manny, Big Papi and Jason Varitek carrying the team, to the homegrown talent beginning to take the mantle and responsibility. Pedroia won the MVP and Youkilis was a viable candidate (and my choice) for the award; Jon Lester developed into an ace-quality starter; Daisuke Matsuzaka put up gaudy numbers and pitched serviceably in the playoffs and Beckett, whose injuries were worse than was let on judging by his post-season performances, gutted his way through.

The Red Sox farm system continued to produce with Justin Masterson converted to the bullpen and recording big outs in the playoffs; and Jed Lowrie took over for the horrific free agent signing Julio Lugo at shortstop and contributed offensively and defensively. A break here and there and the Red Sox would be celebrating two straight World Series titles and a burgeoning dynasty of three championships in five years.

2009 ADDITIONS: RHP John Smoltz signed a 1-year contract.
RHP Brad Penny signed a 1-year contract.
RHP Takashi Saito signed a 1-year contract.
OF Rocco Baldelli signed a 1-year contract.
C Josh Bard signed a 1-year contract.
RHP Ramon Ramirez was acquired from the Kansas City Royals.
RHP Junichi Tazawa signed a 3-year contract (Japan).
RHP Randor Bierd was acquired from the Baltimore Orioles.
RHP Virgil Vasquez was claimed off waivers from the Detroit Tigers.
RHP Wes Littleton was acquired from the Texas Rangers.
LHP Billy Traber signed a minor league contract.
RHP Michael Gonzalez was selected in the Rule 5 Draft from the Los Angeles Angels.
RHP Enrique Gonzalez signed a minor league contract.
OF Paul McAnulty signed a minor league contract.
LHP Fabian Williamson was acquired from the Seattle Mariners.
OF Chip Ambres signed a minor league contract.

2008 SUBTRACTIONS: RHP Paul Byrd was not re-signed.
RHP Bartolo Colon was not re-signed.
OF Coco Crisp was traded to the Kansas City Royals.
RHP Curt Schilling was not re-signed.
1B Sean Casey retired.
RHP Chris Smith refused assignment to the minor leagues and elected free agency.
C Kevin Cash was non-tendered.
RHP David Aardsma was traded to the Seattle Mariners.
RHP David Pauley was traded to the Baltimore Orioles.
RHP Mike Timlin was not re-signed.

2009 PROJECTED LINEUP: C-Jason Varitek; 1B-Kevin Youkilis; 2B-Dustin Pedroia; 3B-Mike Lowell; SS-Jed Lowrie; LF-Jason Bay; CF-Jacoby Ellsbury; RF-J.D. Drew; DH-David Ortiz

2009-PROJECTED STARTING ROTATION: Josh Beckett; Jon Lester; Daisuke Matsuzaka; John Smoltz; Brad Penny; Tim Wakefield; Clay Buchholz

2009 PROJECTED BULLPEN: Jonathan Papelbon; Hideki Okajima; Justin Masterson; Ramon Ramirez; Manny Delcarmen; Takashi Saito; Junichi Tazawa; Javier Lopez

2009 BENCH: OF-Rocco Baldelli; OF/1B-Mark Kotsay; INF-Julio Lugo; C-Josh Bard; C-George Kottaras; OF-Jonathan Van Every; OF/1B-Jeff Bailey; 1B-Chris Carter

2009 EXTRA PITCHERS/PROSPECTS: Randor Bierd; Enrique Gonzalez; Wes Littleton; Virgil Vasquez; Billy Traber; Michael Gonzalez; Daniel Bard; Michael Bowden

2009 EVERYDAY PROSPECTS: Lars Anderson; Dusty Brown; Jeff Corsaletti; Jorge Jimenez

ASSESSMENTS:
MANAGEMENT:

The Red Sox organization is the best run and most productive in baseball. Of course it helps that they have gobs and gobs of money to cover up for any mistake, but for GM Theo Epstein to be able to get a viable replacement for Manny Ramirez in Jason Bay was an amazing feat. After putting up with Manny being Manny for so long, the Red Sox finally had enough when Manny decided to jog around the field like he couldn't care less about whether the team won or lost and faked an injury so cluelessly that he forgot which knee it was that he said was bothering him when he went for an MRI. Even with all of that and that there was no way to keep Manny and maintain any kind of clubhouse harmony, it takes guts to trade one of the best hitters in the history of the game, and Epstein did it.

Having built up the entire organization from top-to-bottom based on the principles of sabermetrics along with old school scouting and having the courage and money to make drastic maneuvers is a recipe for success year-after-year and despite having the arrogance and self-importance derail the Red Sox briefly early in Epstein's term, he's become one of the best GMs in all of baseball.

Always aggressive and willing to try for what others would deem impossible, the Red Sox watched as the first baseman and lineup replacement for Manny that he wanted—Mark Teixeira—signed with the arch-rival Yankees, and then made a try at one of the best young hitters in baseball in Hanley Ramirez. The Red Sox didn't get him; in fact, they didn't even come close to meeting the Marlins asking price, but the very idea that the Red Sox made such an attempt is a window into the way they run the team; and even without Teixeira, they have a young first baseman in the minor leagues named Lars Anderson who could probably be an everyday player in the majors this year if necessary. With the injury question of Mike Lowell, such depth makes losing out on Teixeira not as much of a tragedy as it would be for a different organization without as much depth. The signings of veteran All Star pitchers John Smoltz, Brad Penny and Takashi Saito, all of whom are coming off of injuries forcing them to take 1-year contracts, is another stroke of brilliance on the part of the Red Sox, far better than paying $82.5 million for a guy like A.J. Burnett as the Yankees did.

Terry Francona is the perfect manager for this Red Sox club. While he's probably not the guy you want running a rebuilding team and getting by a la Tony La Russa based on sheer strategic brilliance, he's found a comfort zone with the Red Sox because of what he is and doesn't try to be something other than that. He allows his veterans to police the clubhouse; the players like and respect him; he handles the media; and for the most part, he makes the right strategic moves during games. Because of his likeable demeanor and great reputation around baseball, one thing the Red Sox never have to worry about is a player not wanting to come to Boston because they're concerned about dealing with the manager.

Having to deal with the Manny mess and coming through without seeing it destroy the team is a subtle and underappreciated accomplishment. The Red Sox were riddled with injuries to important players like Mike Lowell and Josh Beckett and withstood an atrocious year from Jason Varitek to make it to within one game of the World Series and a major part of that is because of Francona's calm guiding hand at handling everything inherent with managing such a high-profile, crisis-a-day group.

STARTING PITCHING:

No one ever came out with any information of what was really wrong with Josh Beckett late last season. Speculation was rampant that it was far more than a strained oblique, and Beckett's uncharacteristically weak performances in the playoffs were an indication that the injury was more serious than the Red Sox let on. After the season, nothing much came of such speculation, so presumably, Beckett is going to be 100% when the season starts. If he's healthy, I'd expect a massive, Cy Young caliber year from Beckett because of his impending free agency and he's always a playoff ace; that he gutted his way through last season with his injury shows how good he is, injured or not.

Jon Lester is right behind Beckett at the top of the Red Sox rotation and is blossoming into an ace in his own right. Lester is becoming one of baseball's best left-handed starters and a star at age 25 and has rebounded from his bout with cancer and should be counted on for his 200 innings and at least 15 wins. It wouldn't be a shock to see Lester win 20 games and contend for a Cy Young Award.

Daisuke Matsuzka had his gaudy numbers downplayed (by myself included) because of his penchant for walking people and taking advantage of a great bullpen and a team that scored plenty of runs. Matsuzaka only pitched 168 innings in 29 starts, which is not a good ratio; but his 18-3 record is what it is. He racks up a lot of pitches because he's wild and is removed from games early because of that issue. Matsuzaka, who came to the States with a reputation for big game pitching, has been excellent in the post-season for the Red Sox and as far as a middle of the rotation starter, teams could do much worse than having someone like Matsuzaka. Many pitchers are put into a great situation in order to succeed, but don't; Matsuzaka has and there's nothing wrong with that.

If Brad Penny had had a similar season in 2008 as he had in 2006 and 2007 (he won 16 games in both years), he would've gotten at least a similar contract to what Ryan Dempster got from the Cubs in the $50-60 million range, maybe more since Penny's a year younger. The Red Sox brought Penny in hoping that he'll return to form and they're only paying him for one year which makes him a great gamble. In fact, if he's healthy, Penny could win 15 games easily given how deep the Red Sox bullpen and lineup are.

The Braves off-season went from hellish to a near disaster when John Smoltz spurned their lower guaranteed offer of $2 million for the Red Sox $5.5 million. The Red Sox caught the Braves napping, pure and simple, and stole one of the best pitchers in the history of the franchise. Smoltz is so self-confident (bordering on overtly arrogant) that he still thinks he can pitch as well as he did in his prime when he was not only a similar post-season hero to Beckett, but was also devastating during the regular season. Smoltz's injury history and that he's coming off of shoulder surgery makes it a question as to what he's got left, but no one is ever going to question the desire of John Smoltz; if he's able to come back and pitch, he'll drag himself out onto the mound to do it. The idea of Smoltz being such a risk to the Braves was somewhat ridiculous since they've seen him come back from so many different injuries and roles to return to form that his word should've been good enough for the Braves to give him the base salary that the Red Sox did. The money was also a convenient excuse for Smoltz to say that the Braves didn't show the commitment that he wanted; but it could've been that Smoltz wants another chance to strut his stuff in the playoffs and he wasn't going to get that with the Braves, and he likely will with the Red Sox. The Red Sox will use him cautiously and if he and Penny are healthy, they could combine to be a devastating combination at the back of the rotation.

Tim Wakefield will return for another season and, as a knuckleballer, will be able to fill any role the Red Sox need from him. If Clay Buchholz is able to regain his form and health and pitch out of the fifth spot in the rotation, Wakefield can be a spot starter and injury replacement for the veterans; if he needs to be in the rotation, he can do that; and if he's needed out of the bullpen, that's fine too. Wakefield's had some injury problems in the past few years in his shoulder and back, and his time in the big leagues could be coming to a close sooner rather than later.

The aforementioned Buchholz was the subject of trade rumors during the off season. Buchholz's stock has dropped a bit because he was injured and awful last season and if Jason Varitek hadn't re-signed, it's very possible that Buchholz would've been trade bait for a young catcher like Miguel Montero of the Diamondbacks; or Jarrod Saltalamacchia or Taylor Teagarden from the Rangers; in fact, he still might be because despite Varitek's return, the Red Sox are going to have to find an eventual replacement and one spot in which their organization hasn't been able to find a hot young prospect is behind the plate. Buchholz's over the top motion concerns me for the long-term health of his shoulder and I'd absolutely try to replenish his value early in the season and then include him in a trade for a catcher or power bat.

BULLPEN:

Jonathan Papelbon's time to get paid is coming. He made a supreme sacrifice financially when he went to the Red Sox and solved the closer problem (of their own making) in 2007 and singlehandedly saved their season that resulted in their second World Series win in four years. Papelbon's right in not taking one penny less than he feels that he's earned for that lack of selfishness and the Red Sox are going to have to pay him. Papelbon is the heir apparent to Mariano Rivera as the best closer in baseball (if he isn't already) and he's one of the main reasons the Red Sox are contenders on an annual basis.

Hideki Okajima's sophomore season in the majors wasn't as great as his rookie year was and no matter what the Red Sox say regarding the signing of Okajima, he was signed essentially because he's a lefty and to be Matsuzaka's friend. This shows the occasionally odd nature of finding players; Okajima's 2007 performance was a pleasant surprise and he was very good last season as well.

Justin Masterson is another example of the Red Sox taking a young pitcher, getting him acclimated to the big leagues and then sticking him into the fire and having him succeed. Masterson got a few starts in the majors due to the injury-ravaged rotation and then, with the idea that he could be a solid set-up man for Papelbon, they sent him down to the minors so he could get accustomed to relieving, and he did. Masterson's long-term future is probably as a starting pitcher, but his success as a reliever could give the Red Sox pause before allocating a load of money for Papelbon on a long-term contract because given the way he adjusted to the bullpen, the Red Sox would probably have no problem using Masterson to close if necessary.

I've always thought that veteran Takashi Saito was an underrated closer for the Dodgers. Saito has a quirky motion, but throws hard, throws strikes and doesn't give up many homers while striking out a load of hitters. The Dodgers non-tendered him after his elbow put him on the disabled list and he lost his closing job to Jonathan Broxton, but I wouldn't have let Saito go. The Red Sox jumped on him and he's another former All Star that they got amazingly cheaply for how good he's been in the past. Saito is 38-years-old, but the players from the Far East tend to keep themselves in exemplary condition, so his injuries and age shouldn't be as much of a concern, and if he doesn't do the job, well, they've only got him on a 1-year contract.

Ramon Ramirez was acquired from the Royals for Coco Crisp. Ramirez struck out almost a batter per inning setting up for Joakim Soria and had an excellent season. Getting him for a journeyman player like Crisp was a brilliant trade by Epstein.

Manny Delcarmen throws very hard and has become a stalwart of the Red Sox bullpen. There was talk that he might be available in a trade and presumably, he could go with Buchholz in a deal for a catcher or a bat. Delcarmen was effective against both lefties and righties and also strikes out a batter per inning.

Javier Lopez was the Red Sox lefty specialist and had a solid enough season in that role.

Junichi Tazawa was signed from Japan. He's 22 and said to have a power fastball, good curve and a slide, but just like all Japanese imports, who knows how he'll do in the majors?

LINEUP:

The off-season was rife with the back-and-forth about whether or not Jason Varitek was going to return to the Red Sox. The Red Sox offered Varitek arbitration and, in what can only be called a decision of greed and/or stupidity, Varitek and his agent Scott Boras turned it down. Boras had said that he thought Varitek was worth a similar contract that the Yankees gave Jorge Posada a year before; that argument was hurt not only by Varitek not being anything close to the hitter that Posada is, but by Posada getting hurt and missing most of the 2008 season. Varitek's "leadership" was touted as so important that he warranted a multi-year contract at over $10 million per year. This was after Varitek was nothing short of atrocious at the plate in 2008 and his declining skills made it a question if the Red Sox should just move forward without even trying to re-sign him.

In the end, the Red Sox got Varitek back on a 1-year, $5 million contract with a dual option for 2009 in which the Red Sox exercising it would pay Varitek $5 million, or Varitek exercising it would cost $3 million. The Red Sox offer of arbitration was said to have prevented other teams from signing Varitek because it made no sense to give up a first round draft pick for a catcher who's about to turn 37 and looks like he can't hit anymore; these factors may have been enough for the Red Sox to let Varitek go. Known for their coldblooded analysis and sheer ruthlessness that has made them the envy of the rest of baseball, the Red Sox appeared to let a fear of the effect of Varitek's departure and how it would affect the team cloud their judgment and bring him back when they probably should've moved on. I doubt Varitek will be as bad as he was at the plate in 2008, but there's every possibility that he's really finished and they're going to have to make a deal to bring in a replacement by June. In retrospect, I think the Red Sox may regret bringing Varitek back when they could've moved on and no one would've held it against them.

Kevin Youkilis showed the versatility that helps make a team into a championship contender. Youkilis played a Gold Glove first base; moved to third when Mike Lowell got hurt; and also played some outfield. Had the Red Sox been able to sign Teixeira, Youkilis might have moved permanently to third base or to the outfield. Youkilis was an MVP contender and was actually my choice at the end of the season over his teammate Dustin Pedroia. There's nothing that Youkilis doesn't do on the field. He hits; hits for power; plays hard and plays great defense at a number of positions and he hits in the clutch. He's a guy for the Red Sox to build around.

Dustin Pedroia is the epitome of the player who was told by everyone that he'd never achieve his goals of making it to the big leagues because he was too small; he wasn't good enough; he was this, he was that, he wasn't this, he wasn't that, blah, blah, blah, but in his first two years in the big leagues, Dustin Pedroia has a Rookie of the Year, and a MVP. He's a great fielder; he's tenacious; he's loud and irritates the opponents with his hard-nosed play. He's a superstar who, like Youkilis, does everything to help his team win.

Mike Lowell is coming off of hip surgery and is a question whether he's going to be ready to start the season. Part of the reason the Red Sox pursued Teixeira so avidly was because of the injury to Lowell, but if he's healthy, Lowell can still hit, hit for power and play great defense. Worst case scenario, if he's unable to start the season, the Red Sox can move Youkilis to third until Lowell is ready and make do with Mark Kotsay and young Lars Anderson at first base.

Jed Lowrie took over for the injured and terrible Julio Lugo and played solid defense and had some big post-season hits. Lowrie may not be the long-term answer at shortstop, especially since the Red Sox offense may be a bit short with the struggles of Varitek, the age and durability questions beginning to surround Lowell and David Ortiz and that Manny's no longer there. Something may have to be done about that situation, which explains why they tried to get Hanley Ramirez from the Marlins.

Jason Bay did everything the Red Sox asked him in replacing Manny. I questioned how Bay would perform in meaningful games for the first time in his career and he was excellent, especially in the playoffs. Having the look of a guy who was let out of prison (in a way he was after getting away from the Pirates), Bay hit clutch homers and played great all-around baseball. He's a free agent at the end of the season and had they signed Teixeira, he might have been trade bait. Bay's likely to have a big season with the bat, but he's no replacement for Manny in the lineup over the long term.

I have some concerns that Jacoby Ellsbury is never going to hit for enough power to justify being an everyday player in the big leagues; it's not just that he doesn't hit the ball out of the park, but that he only had 38 extra base hits out of his 155 hits. He's got great speed; plays excellent defense and has a sweet swing; but the sweet swing won't do any good if he doesn't hit for some more power. The Red Sox traded their security blanket in center field in Coco Crisp and Ellsbury's the guy now. I was under the impression that had they gotten Teixeira and Lowell was healthy, that J.D. Drew might end up playing a lot of center field and Youkilis would find himself in right field. That may still happen and if the Red Sox have to formulate a package around the likes of Ellsbury and Buchholz to get a bat, I think they'll do that if their offense is faltering.

J.D. Drew has become a clutch post-season player and despite his ragged injury history, I doubt anyone would want to get rid of the contract with what he's provided in the playoffs for the Red Sox. Drew was on his way to a great season when he got hurt again, but he was ready for the playoffs and hit as well as he usually does in the biggest games. As mentioned before, Drew may end up playing some center field if Ellsbury doesn't hit or is traded, but when he reported to Red Sox camp, he said his troublesome back is still bothering him, so he might not even be healthy enough to play right, let alone center.

David Ortiz's wrist injury was the second punch in the combination that hurt the Red Sox offense drastically. Ortiz and Manny were the lifeblood of the lineup in the two championship seasons and if Ortiz is starting to break down physically, the Red Sox could have big problems. Ortiz was hideous against lefties and his numbers across the board have taken a nosedive. If he's supposedly healthy when the season starts and he's still declining, it's going to be a big question of whether this is a predictable fall for a veteran player and the Red Sox are going to have trouble scoring runs.

BENCH:

Mark Kotsay was acquired from the Braves and he can play center field, providing excellent defense; but he also filled in at first base last season and provided some big hits. Kotsay is a very good player when he's healthy, but has had a recurring back problem that prevents him from being an everyday player.

Julio Lugo has two years remaining on one of the worst free agent contract signings in baseball history. Lugo had a quad injury in 2008, but he didn't play all that well when he was supposed to be healthy. He was better than he was in 2007, but I could've hit better than he did in 2007. There was talk that the Red Sox were talking about trading him to a team like the Tigers in exchange for one of their terrible contracts like Dontrelle Willis, but nothing came to pass. I'd expect them to give Lugo away by mid-season if he's not providing anything as a backup/utility player.

Rocco Baldelli is from Rhode Island and the Red Sox are taking a chance on bringing him in despite his blood disorder preventing him from playing regularly; it was said during the off-season that the problem isn't as bad as initially feared, but who knows? Baldelli had some big hits in the playoffs for the Rays, but I'd keep my expectations low.

Josh Bard and George Kottaras are the backup catchers behind Varitek and both may get more playing time than expected if Varitek continues to age poorly. Bard can hit, but he isn't great defensively; Kottaras has shown some pop in the minor leagues. Presumably, Kottaras will be the one to catch Wakefield's knuckleball since it was Bard's trouble with that one assignment that precipitated another horrible decision by Epstein in trading Bard and Cla Meredith to the Padres to bring back Doug Mirabelli.

Jeff Bailey is a veteran first baseman/outfielder who can hit the ball out of the park and gets on base at a good clip. Jonathan Van Every is a veteran backup outfielder who can also hit the ball out of the park, but he's little more than organizational depth.

Chris Carter is a 25-year-old first baseman who has some power and put up good solid numbers across the board in Triple A Pawtuckett last season, but if the Red Sox are going to go with a youngster at first base, it's more probable that it'll be Lars Anderson. Anderson's 21-years-old and split the majority of last season between Single and Double A; Anderson puts up huge on-base numbers and his power should improve much like Youkilis's did. The Red Sox have never had any fear of taking a young player and giving him a chance to play, so if Lowell is still hurt and their offense is hurting, they might just give Anderson a chance to play.

PREDICTION:

The Red Sox offense *is* a concern. That they so avidly pursued Teixeira and Hanley Ramirez shows that they know this might be an issue that will need to be addressed, but one thing Epstein is usually good at (aside from the lost season of 2006) is filling his team's holes during the season. If Varitek continues his slide; if Ortiz, Lowell and Drew are hurt; if Lowrie and Ellsbury don't hit enough, there might be a blockbuster type of trade with the likes of Ellsbury, Buchholz and Masterson going elsewhere.

The Red Sox are lucky in the American League that the Rays are unlikely to have as many lucky breaks—especially with their relievers—as last season and the rest of the league isn't good enough to overtake them. Their starting pitching and bullpen is so deep and so good that they'll account for any lack of offense early in the season, and Epstein will do something to fix the problem with an available power bat like Jermaine Dye or Dan Uggla or someone completely out of the box that I'm not even thinking of. He'll do something about the catching situation sooner rather than later if Varitek still looks weak at the plate.

The Red Sox and Yankees are going to be back to the normal course of business of battling for the division throughout the season with the Yankees coming out on top this time and the Red Sox taking the Wild Card.

PREDICTED RECORD: 94-68

Tampa Bay Rays
2008 Record: 97-65; First Place, American League East
Defeated Chicago White Sox in ALDS 3 games to 1
Defeated Boston Red Sox in ALCS 4 games to 3
Lost to Philadelphia Phillies in World Series 4 games to 1

2008 Recap:

The Rays rode a combination of their number one draft picks blossoming; a series of lucky and smart acquisitions via free agency and trade; and a newfound low tolerance policy for misbehaving players who were part of the problem and would never be part of the solution.

2008 wasn't only the Rays first trip to the post-season, but it was the first time they won more than 70 games in a season. It had become an annual ritual of the Rays: few fans; little success; and a relegation to the bottom of their division. The Rays turnaround began as the front office finally stopped allowing players who were either violent, potential felons like Elijah Dukes; or insolent, short-tempered high draft picks like Delmon Young to behave any way they wanted without repercussions from the organization. Nothing was going to change until the Rays took a hard line against bad behavior on and off the field. In dumping both Dukes and Young, the Rays sent the message that if players weren't going to adhere to certain baseline standards, they could take their act elsewhere.

Coming out of nowhere to leapfrog over both the Red Sox and Yankees to win the American League East, the Rays got previously unheard of performances from unknown and unappreciated players like Grant Balfour; J.P. Howell; Edwin Jackson; and Gabe Gross. Their young players all came together at once and were led on and off the field by Rookie of the Year Evan Longoria. Their veterans Cliff Floyd, Carlos Pena and Troy Percival showed their teammates how to act professionally while standing up for one another and despite everyone who couldn't believe their eyes as the Rays won, won and won some more, they never collapsed and fell out of the playoff race and made it all the way to the World Series before they finally ran out of gas.

With their youth and depth in the pitching department, the Rays are in position to be a solid team for the next several years even as they operate under a budget.

2009 ADDITIONS: DH/OF Pat Burrell signed a 2-year contract.
OF Matt Joyce was acquired from the Detroit Tigers.
RHP Joe Nelson signed a 1-year contract.
2B Adam Kennedy signed a minor league contract.
OF Gabe Kapler signed a 1-year contract.
RHP Lance Cormier signed a 1-year contract.
LHP Brian Shouse signed a 1-year contract.
RHP Derek Rodriguez was selected in the Rule 5 Draft from the Chicago White Sox.
RHP Jason Isringhausen signed a minor league contract.

2009 SUBTRACTIONS: OF/DH Rocco Baldelli was not re-signed.
OF/DH Cliff Floyd's contract option was declined.
LHP Trever Miller's contract option was declined.
OF Jonny Gomes was non-tendered.
OF/1B/3B Eric Hinske was not re-signed.
RHP Edwin Jackson was traded to the Detroit Tigers.
1B Dan Johnson was released.

2009 PROJECTED LINEUP: C-Dioner Navarro; 1B-Carlos Pena; 2B-Akinori Iwamura; 3B-Evan Longoria; SS-Jason Bartlett; LF-Carl Crawford; CF-B.J. Upton; RF-Matt Joyce/Gabe Kapler; DH-Pat Burrell

2009 PROJECTED STARTING ROTATION: Scott Kazmir; James Shields; Matt Garza; Andy Sonnanstine; David Price

2009 PROJECTED BULLPEN: Troy Percival; Dan Wheeler; Grant Balfour; J.P. Howell; Chad Bradford; Jason Hammel; Joe Nelson; Brian Shouse

2009 BENCH: C-Shawn Riggans; OF-Gabe Gross; INF-Willy Aybar; OF/INF Ben Zobrist; OF-Fernando Perez; OF-Justin Ruggiano; 2B-Adam Kennedy

2009 EXTRA PITCHERS/PROSPECTS: Lance Cormier; Jeff Niemann;

Derek Rodriguez; Mitch Talbot; Chad Orvella; Scott Dohmann; Wade Davis; Steve Andrade; James Houser; Ryan Reid

2009 EVERYDAY PROSPECTS: Reid Brignac; Chris Nowak

ASSESSMENTS:
MANAGEMENT:

The situation of the Tampa Bay Rays is a case study of how fleeting perception is in the world of professional sports and, by proxy, is a microcosm of how quick and easy it is in society on the whole for one to go from wearing the equivalent of a public dunce cap to being feted as a genius.

The Rays endured well-earned status as a laughingstock before 2008. First there were the annual last place finishes and celebrations if they came close to winning 70 games; then there were the well-documented and well-intentioned "changes" to the organization. Former GM Chuck LaMar tried to build with veterans and free agency and that didn't work; then they brought in a veteran, successful manager in Lou Piniella and that didn't work; then, when original owner Vince Naimoli sold the club to Stuart Sternberg, Sternberg brought in some of his investment banking buddies who were fluent in rotisserie baseball and sabermetrics in Andrew Friedman and Matthew Silverman and that didn't work either...until 2008.

For the first two years of his tenure, Friedman was in so far over his head that not even David Hasselhoff in his Mitch Buchanan, *Baywatch* glory could've saved him. The Rays were clueless and there was no indication that anything was ever going to change. Elijah Dukes was a violent time bomb waiting to explode; Delmon Young had the terrible combination of being a baby and having the status as a number one draft pick keeping the team from dumping him for his behavior; Josh Hamilton had a well-documented drug and alcohol problem; pitching coach Jim Hickey drove drunk and crashed his truck into the car belonging to another Rays employee. They deserved and received no respect because they didn't know what they were doing, plain and simple.

Then, as if by magic, the Rays stopped putting up with the same crap they always had. They dumped both Dukes and Young; they made some pickups of talented, but underperforming pitchers like Grant Balfour; they tightened up the defense with Jason Bartlett; the number one draft picks began to mature and play well in the big leagues; and they were very, very lucky in some acquisitions like Eric Hinske, Carlos Pena and Gabe Gross. All of a sudden, Friedman and company went from not having the faintest idea of what he was doing to having his "blueprint" copied around baseball.

Everything worked out for the Rays in 2008 and if they're going to continue getting credit, they have to at least play well in 2009; a sudden fall back to earth will put the front office back into flux as to whether their system is viable for the long haul or whether it was just everything falling into place at once in the right place at the right time. Just remember, anyone can be lucky; it's repeating the feat that's hard.

Joe Maddon won Manager of the Year, but he was just as lucky as Friedman was in my opinion. Although the Rays players seem to like their manager, it's hard to know how much of that affinity translates into respect. Closer Troy Percival openly challenged Maddon's decision to remove him from a game because Percival looked hurt and with a young, immature team, things can blow up very quickly if things don't go as smoothly as they did in the previous year.

Maddon made some hideous strategic gaffes that could've cost the Rays the ALCS (he left Grant Balfour in to pitch to J.D. Drew as the Rays blew a massive lead in game 5 of the series) and watched helplessly as the Red Sox rose from the dead and almost stole the ALCS from the Rays in games 5, 6 and 7. In game five of the World Series, the weather related suspension allowed Maddon to have two days to think about what he was going to do for a pitcher as the sixth inning began with the score tied and he inexplicably left Balfour in to pitch and watched as the Phillies jumped on him to take the lead. Rookie David Price had closed out the ALCS against the Red Sox with an above-and-beyond the call performance and should've been in the game to start the sixth inning once game 5 resumed; instead, Maddon stayed with Balfour and blew the game and the series.

I was open in my disgust with Maddon and if I were in charge, my first reaction would've been to consider firing him; there was no excuse for his gaffes. After some reflection, I would probably have brought Maddon back, but had a better and more experienced bench coach to sit beside him and help him along with his strategic shortcomings; instead the Rays are bringing back bench coach Dave Martinez. Maddon has been in baseball for so long that he should've known better; and what made the whole situation confounding is that he's worked for some great strategic managers in Mike Scioscia and spent a great deal of time watching Gene Mauch from his time with the Angels; what's worse is that he had *two days* to think about his strategy for the conclusion of game 5 and still screwed it up so completely. Maddon's job is safe because despite the accolades doled out to the Rays front office, they're not going to have the guts to fire Maddon even if it's necessary.

STARTING PITCHING:

Scott Kazmir is never going to have the stamina nor will he be able to keep his pitch counts reasonable enough to be anything more than a six-inning pitcher at best. Kazmir went 12-8 in 27 starts last season, but his innings count of 152 is ridiculously low for the supposed number one starter as he missed his annual five starts with arm problems. The Rays will never have the guts to do it, but Kazmir should be made into the closer. They have a few prospects that could take the spot in the rotation that Kazmir occupies and eventually, David Price is going to supplant him at the top of the rotation anyway. Kazmir is difficult to hit, but is so small and racks up so many pitches early in the game that he's completely unreliable and will tax the bullpen in every game he starts. It's not that he doesn't have the stuff to be a top starter; it's that he's too small, too fragile and he throws too many pitches; he needs to be moved to the bullpen.

James Shields is the leader of the staff on and off the field. He's tough; he throws strikes; he goes out to the mound every fifth day and he pitched well in the playoffs. Shields is the guy the Rays count on as the slump-buster instead of Kazmir because he'll do whatever the team needs on that particular day. If any pitcher on the staff is ready to bust out and blossom into an 18-20 game winner, it's the hard throwing, gutty Shields.

Matt Garza brought his temper and up-and-down performances along with him from the Twins. Garza went 11-9 in 30 starts for the Rays and one of the reasons the Twins traded him was because his concentration was so easily lost when things started to go sourly for him. Garza almost came to blows several times with catcher Dioner Navarro, but if he were to lose some of that intensity, there's a good chance that it would affect him negatively on the mound; the bridling of that intensity is just as important as the control of his wicked array of power pitches. If Garza matures and keeps his emotions under control, he could also turn into a big 15-18 game winner.

Andy Sonnanstine was bandied about in trade talks, but he'll return to the Rays. Sonnanstine went 13-9 and gives up a pretty large number of hits and home runs, but as a complement to the rest of the Rays rotation of hard throwers, Sonnanstine has a slingshot motion and battles his way through games. To me, he's about a .500 pitcher who's never going to be much better than he was in 2008, but as a back of the rotation starter, he's a useful starter to have around.

Lefty David Price came out of nowhere to become a household name because of his maturity in the highest of high-pressure games in the ALCS (there's even more pressure in the championship series than there is in the

World Series); Price throws very hard and if his work in the post-season after having only a few big league appearances during the season is any indication, he's going to be the Rays ace before long. Price was the top pick in the draft and has a power fastball that has the potential to dominate opposing lineups starting as early as this season. He's a future Cy Young Award contender.

BULLPEN:

If anyone knows what the Rays are going to get out of Troy Percival, I'd like to hear it. It's hard to imagine that he's going to be closing games for them this season, but he's under contract and I'm not even going to venture a guess as to what's going through the head of Maddon. Percival predictably got hurt last season, but he did rack up 28 saves; he also had a bloated 4.53 ERA and allowed 9 homers, which for a closer is unacceptable. It wouldn't be surprising to see Percival retire in spring training or early in the season as a less-embarrassing alternative to him being released.

Dan Wheeler is a workhorse in the bullpen who took over as closer when Percival got hurt; he can do the job as the closer, but doesn't have that one dominant pitch to make him a prototype. He throws strikes and guts his way through with a slider and good command, but he has a penchant for giving up homers as he did to David Ortiz in game 5 of the ALCS.

J.P. Howell came out of nowhere to become an imperative part of the Rays bullpen. A lefty with a quirky motion, Howell had never had the success he had last season at any time in his career whether it was with the Royals or the Rays. Howell was brilliant all season long against both lefties and righties and racked up more than a strikeout an inning to go along with a 2.22 ERA. One thing that I'd be concerned about with both Howell and Grant Balfour is that neither has had any level of success that they did in 2008 and they're ripe for a fall; they're not going to sneak up on anyone in 2009.

Intense Aussie Grant Balfour had always had a power fastball in his time with the Twins and Brewers, but had never done much of anything but get shelled in his numerous opportunities to pitch in the big leagues. In 2008, he became a power pitcher who blew away batters as he came out of the bullpen. Balfour was brilliant and dominating, but as mentioned before, there's always a chance that the Cinderella ride can come to an end as quickly as it began. I'd expect Balfour to get a chance as the closer if Percival can't be counted on.

Chad Bradford was acquired from the Baltimore Orioles for the stretch run and helped the Rays by adding depth to their bullpen and a different look with his submarine junk. Bradford was offered around in trades in the off-season, but he's making a lot of money and he's a pure contact pitcher who's just turned 34 and has had back problems and is now going to miss the first 3 months after having elbow surgery.

Jason Hammel is a big righty who gave up a lot of home runs out of the bullpen, but racked up a couple of important saves as the Rays were feeling their way through without their veteran closer Percival. Hammel is not a strikeout pitcher and his control isn't anything to write home about.

Joe Nelson had an excellent year as a scrap-heap pickup for the Marlins and signed a 1-year contract with the Rays. Nelson has never been as good as he was last season and the Marlins are great at finding pitchers like him, getting as much use out of them as possible, then letting them leave; I don't know that I'd expect him to do as well in the AL East as he did in the NL East.

Brian Shouse is a soft-tossing, sidearming lefty who was the Brewers lefty specialist. He replaces the departed Trever Miller and is good in that role.

Veteran Jason Isringhausen was signed to a minor league contract; he had a terrible year with the Cardinals last season, but perhaps he can find a spot with the Rays as another veteran reclamation projcect.

LINEUP:

Dioner Navarro's most important job last season was handling the young starting rotation; the unproven middle relievers; and the veteran late inning relievers, and he did all of that while finally hitting enough to justify his everyday presence in the lineup. Navarro batted .295 with some occasional pop (7 homers, 27 doubles); drove in 54 runs and posted a reasonable .349 on base percentage. He played a very good defensive catcher and his years of being a top prospect and bouncing from team-to-team (the Yankees and Dodgers gave up on him) as he struggled to fulfill his promise ended. He's just turned 25 and his days bouncing from starting lineup to the bench to the minors appear to be over.

Carlos Pena's numbers fell from the MVP-level they stunningly reached in 2007 to something more normal given the journeyman nature of his career. Pena was hideous against lefties, only batting .190; his power numbers dropped to 31 homers and 102 RBI. Pena can't be much worse against lefties this season than he was last and if he is, he may find himself platooning with Willy Aybar before long. 25-30 homers is pretty much what the Rays should expect from Pena.

Akinori Iwamura was excellent defensively as he made the move from third base to second and was a tough, inspirational player all season long and provided some big hits. Iwamura can run, gets on base, has occasional pop and does all the little things well.

Evan Longoria was a touted prospect and he lived up to the hype when he was recalled from the minors early in the season. He has a lightning fast bat; great power and a maturity that belies his age of 23. Longoria got off to a blazing hot start in the playoffs and looked oblivious to pressure until he collapsed in the World Series. He won the Rookie of the Year and is expected to be a linchpin to the Rays offense for the next decade. He returned from a broken wrist and barely missed a beat late in the season. One thing I'd be concerned with is his sophomore slump. After the pitchers adjust to Longoria, will he be able to return the favor and deal with the different ways they're going to pitch to him? He's a star in the making, but isn't quite at elite status yet and it may take him three or four years to achieve the moniker of superstar even though some have anointed him as such already.

Jason Bartlett was acquired in the trade that also brought Garza with the dual benefit of shoring up the Rays defense and getting rid of Delmon Young. Bartlett played excellent defense and was credited as one of the main reasons for the Rays improvement. I've never really thought much of Bartlett and think that his season in 2008 may have been a highlight rather than the norm. Bartlett was mentioned as possible trade bait and the strange part was that the Twins and Rays were discussing Bartlett for… Delmon Young. If I were the Rays, I would want no part of Young again, but I'd be willing to move Bartlett if the right deal came along. He's one of the players for the Rays that may be in for something of a statistical correction and not come anywhere close to the player he was last season.

Carl Crawford went from the star that no one knows to being an ancillary piece in the Rays lineup. Crawford may be trade bait as his contract option for 2010 comes up and he becomes more and more expensive. He missed a chunk of time with a hand injury and returned for the playoffs. Crawford is an all-around player who can hit for power and average; run; and play good defense. All of his numbers took a bit of a dive in 2008.

B.J. Upton may not be ready for the start of the season after shoulder surgery, but he had what amounted to a coming out party in the playoffs with an impressive display of power and bat speed. Upton is going to be a flat-out superstar who can do anything on the field. There were some minor discipline issues with manager Joe Maddon because Upton wasn't running hard to first base (one wasn't so minor in that it happened in the World Series), but as he matures and the veterans get him to understand the importance of running hard, he'll stop with such behaviors and become an even better player.

The plan is apparently to platoon the newly acquired Matt Joyce and

Gabe Kapler in right field. Joyce came over from the Tigers for Edwin Jackson. He's 24 and has shown some all-around hitting ability in the minors with some decent power. Kapler went from an injury-prone favorite of the ladies (his nickname's Gabe the Babe) to playing in Japan; to being a popular member of the Red Sox; to managing in their minor league system in 2007; to making a comeback with the Brewers and hitting well enough to get a contract from the Rays for slightly over $1 million. Kapler murdered lefties last season, but I'd hesitate before expecting too much from him given his injury history.

Pat Burrell was one of the productive free agents who was most negatively affected by the poor economy and reluctance of teams to spend a load of money. Burrell had turned down what looked like a perfunctory, take-a-hike kind of offer from the Phillies of 2-years at $22 million; he was right to do it under the impression that he'd get more years and more money elsewhere, but the market dried up with the number of outfielder who were similar to Burrell like Bobby Abreu and Adam Dunn and Burrell jumped on the 2-year, $16 million offer from the Rays before he wound up with even less elsewhere.

Burrell's streaky; he strikes out too much and has failed in the clutch; but he's durable; his numbers are generally consistent and he should be better off if he doesn't have to play the field and can DH regularly in the American League. He's a major upgrade over the group of names the Rays used at DH last season like Cliff Floyd, Fernando Perez, Aybar and Eric Hinske, and at $8 million a year, he's a bargain from what he normally would've cost.

BENCH:

Shawn Riggans is the backup catcher to Navarro and if he has to play for a significant amount of time, the Rays are going to have a problem because Riggans can't hit.

Willy Aybar was a jack-of-all-trades last season and played well at third base in the absence of Longoria. Aybar has some pop and should get his 250-300 at bats as a utility player and perhaps in a platoon situation with Pena if Pena continues to struggle against lefties.

Ben Zobrist was a washout as a top infield prospect since the Rays got him from the Astros, but he found a new life as a backup outfielder and utility infielder. Zobrist contributed some big hits and had 12 homers in 62 games.

Gabe Gross showed an ability to hit that he never showed before in his time with the Blue Jays or Brewers. He hit 13 homers for the Rays after coming over in a mid-season trade and has always been excellent defensively. Given his career history, it's hard to imagine him coming anywhere close to repeating those numbers over a full season.

Fernando Perez is a backup outfielder with great speed and little home run power.

Justin Ruggiano is also a backup outfielder who's shown some pop in the minors and is more of a player who provides organizational depth than anything else.

Reid Brignac is a hot prospect who's expected to be a solid big league shortstop. He didn't hit much at all in Triple A and may need more seasoning, but the Rays could give him some at bats if Bartlett falters.

Veteran Adam Kennedy signed a minor league contract after the Cardinals released him before spring training. He's got post-season experience and a little pop in his bat.

PREDICTION:

Even though the Rays took such a gigantic leap into the World Series last season, much of that was due to career seasons from such heretofore unexpected sources like Howell, Balfour, Gross and Bartlett. Unsung heroes are great, but they can't be counted on to repeat that status two years in a row. The addition of Burrell will beef up the offense, but I wouldn't expect all that much from the right field platoon they have planned. With the way *everything* worked for the Rays, it would be outright stupid to think that's all going to happen again. The improvement of the Yankees and the way the Red Sox are so good year-after-year makes it an even tougher assignment for the Rays to repeat or come anywhere close to last season's 97 wins. Kazmir is a serious arm injury waiting to happen. The bullpen is again going to be an issue since I can't imagine Howell and Balfour being as good as they were last season and I'd expect nothing from Percival. Then there's the issue of Maddon's bizarre strategic decisions and new age managerial style; eventually the issue could extend to the players wondering if the manager knows what he's doing as they age and learn more about the game themselves. Having two consecutive seasons like the Rays had in 2008 is a dream and they're going to fall back to where they belong: behind the Yankees and Red Sox and just over the .500 mark.

PREDICTED RECORD: 82-80

Baltimore Orioles
2008 Record: 68-93; Fifth Place, American League East

2008 Recap:

    The Orioles were well on their way to a very respectable season before they completely collapsed in August and lost, lost and lost some more to go from hovering around .500 to a 68-93 finish and familiar place at the bottom of the standings. Given how terrible the Orioles finished, under normal circumstances in Baltimore, it would be hard to find some positives, but now things are different. Despite their atrocious starting pitching and shaky lineup, the Orioles are starting to produce some young talent due to the smart trades that owner Peter Angelos is allowing Andy MacPhail to make as he clears out declining veterans and infuses the organization with much-needed youth.

    There's finally hope in Baltimore. With a young outfield of Nick Markakis and Adam Jones; the solid second baseman Brian Roberts; veterans Aubrey Huff and Melvin Mora; closer George Sherrill; and young starter Jeremy Guthrie along with more youth on the way, the Orioles are going to improve as long as MacPhail can prevail on Angelos the need to be patient. On the surface, 2008 may have looked like another in the string of losing seasons for the once-proud Orioles, but in reality it was another step on the road to respectability.

2009 ADDITIONS: INF Ty Wigginton signed a 2-year contract.
OF Felix Pie was acquired from the Chicago Cubs.
LHP Rich Hill was acquired from the Chicago Cubs.
RHP Koji Uehara signed a 2-year contract (Japan).
SS Cesar Izturis signed a 2-year contract.
C Gregg Zaun signed a 1-year contract.
INF Chris Gomez signed a minor league contract.
LHP Mark Hendrickson signed a 1-year contract.
INF Ryan Freel was acquired from the Cincinnati Reds.

INF Brandon Waring was acquired from the Cincinnati Reds.

INF Justin Turner was acquired from the Cincinnati Reds.

RHP David Pauley was acquired from the Boston Red Sox.

C Lou Palmisano was claimed in the Rule 5 Draft from the Milwaukee Brewers.

C Chad Moeller signed a minor league contract.

RHP Brad Hennessey signed a minor league contract.

2009 SUBTRACTIONS: OF Jay Payton was not re-signed.

LHP Garrett Olson was traded to the Chicago Cubs.

1B/OF/DH Kevin Millar was not re-signed.

C Ramon Hernandez was traded to the Cincinnati Reds.

1B/OF Adam Loewen was released.

RHP Daniel Cabrera was non-tendered.

RHP Lance Cormier was non-tendered.

RHP Randor Bierd was traded to the Boston Red Sox.

INF Brandon Fahey was released.

2009 PROJECTED LINEUP: C-Gregg Zaun/Matt Wieters; 1B-Ty Wigginton; 2B-Brian Roberts; 3B-Melvin Mora; SS-Cesar Izturis; LF-Luke Scott; CF-Adam Jones; RF-Nick Markakis; DH-Aubrey Huff

2009 PROJECTED STARTING ROTATION: Jeremy Guthrie; Chris Waters; Koji Uehara; Radhames Liz; Mark Hendrickson; David Pauley; Rich Hill

2009 PROJECTED BULLPEN: George Sherrill; Jamie Walker; Chris Ray; Dennis Sarfate; Matt Albers; Kam Mickolio; Jim Miller; Danys Baez; Brad Hennessey

2009 BENCH: C-Guillermo Quiroz; INF/OF-Ryan Freel; OF-Felix Pie; INF-Chris Gomez

2009 EXTRA PITCHERS/PROSPECTS: Al Simon; Brad McCrory; Brad Bergesen; Jason Berken; David Hernandez; Chris Tillman; Jake Arrieta; Brandon Erbe

2009 EVERYDAY PROSPECTS: Mike Costanzo; Nolan Reimold; Brandon Snyder

ASSESSMENTS:
MANAGEMENT:

The most stunning thing that Andy MacPhail's been able to do (and he's been able to stick to the plot) has been in convincing notoriously impatient and impetuous owner Peter Angelos to hold off on continuing with the same losing trend of bringing in fading veterans and trying to compete with the Yankees and the Red Sox on a dollar-by-dollar basis. The Orioles are starting the see the fruits of that labor with the young pitching that's just about ready to reach the big leagues; the impressive and enthusiastic young outfield he's formulated while dispatching losing players like Erik Bedard. The package that the Orioles heisted from the Mariners for Bedard is going to go down as one of the worst trades in recent memory since they got center fielder Adam Jones, hot young pitching prospect Chris Tillman and their closer (who may himself get traded as he's blossomed into an All Star despite not having All Star caliber stuff) George Sherrill. Then there was the package MacPhail got from the Astros for Miguel Tejada in Luke Scott (who's showing his teammates how to behave professionally); and young slugger Michael Costanzo along with the pitcher Dennis Sarfate and Matt Albers.

The Orioles have brought in veterans who play the game correctly and behave the right way. This season they've signed the slick fielding Cesar Izturis, who can't hit, but is a former Gold Glove winner; Mark Hendrickson can start or relieve and will do whatever he's asked; and Gregg Zaun is perfectly willing to hold the catching position until top prospect Matt Wieters is ready. Nick Markakis has been locked up into an affordable long-term deal and all of the positive things that are apparent in Baltimore is a direct result of the skills and experience of MacPhail in finding players frugally and who play within a winning system.

Manager Dave Trembley surprised me last season. I had thought that he would be a casualty of the fact that the team wasn't very good and his lack of professional playing experience would wound his standing in the clubhouse, but the team responded well to Trembley as they played far over their heads into August before their lack of talent caught up to them and they collapsed. That being said, if the Orioles are going to take the next step as quickly as possible, they're probably not going to have Trembley as their manager past this season.

Angelos has been patient, but Tony La Russa's situation in St. Louis has become so rancid that I don't see any chance that he's there past this season. La Russa has the cachet to attract players to *want* to play with the Orioles and Angelos has the money to both pay La Russa and his pitching coach Dave Duncan and bring in free agents and turn things around to the point that the Orioles are legitimate playoff contenders within the next 2-3 years. La Russa, at age 65, will want to have one more chance to win; Angelos with the burgeoning young talent on his club will be willing to spend to expedite matters; and MacPhail's smart enough to find the pieces that La Russa's going to need. Trembley's earned respect and a spot in the majors somewhere, but it's not going to be in Baltimore after the 2009 season unless they pull a Rays-style turnaround, and that's not going to happen.

STARTING PITCHING:

Jeremy Guthrie's 10-12 record last season was somewhat misleading because he had a fine year. Guthrie's hits/innings pitched ratio was an excellent 176/191, and he deserved a better fate in his record. Guthrie's had so many fits and starts in his career that I was under the impression that he's younger than he is, but he's 30-years-old. He's not a typical top-of-the-rotation starter, but he's pitched well for the Orioles in rejuvenating a flagging career.

Lefty Chris Waters isn't all that young either as he'll be 28 late in the season, but he pitched adequately in 11 starts in 2008. He doesn't strike out many and he can be wild, but he is a lefty and should hold down one of the spots until the young pitching is ready to join the rotation and supplant him or relegate him to the back of the rotation or bullpen.

Koji Uehara was signed to a 2-year contract from Japan.

Former Red Sox prospect David Pauley was acquired for Randor Bierd and presumably, he'll receive every possible chance to finally pitch in the big leagues and stay. There was no way he'd receive such an opportunity with the veteran depth the Red Sox have built. Pauley had an excellent statistical year in Triple A Pawtuckett last season with a 14-4 record. He's a right-handed contact pitcher.

Radhames Liz started 17 games for the Orioles last season and got pounded. He gave up a lot of hits and a lot of home runs; he's put up big strikeout numbers in the minors, so possibly if he gets comfortable in the big leagues, he can be of some use.

Mark Hendrickson is a tall (6'9") soft-tossing, lefty journeyman who had a decent year as a starter and reliever for the surprising Marlins last season. Hendrickson got off to a 5-1 start, but as he reverted to that which he really is (a barely mediocre veteran), he ended the season with a 7-8 record and in the bullpen. He does have some use as a reliever/spot starter.

Former Cubs prospect Rich Hill was acquired for a player to be named later. Hill has excellent stuff, but he came down with a borderline case of Steve Blass/Rick Ankiel disease and lost the strike zone. The player to be named later is conditional and the hope is that pitching coach Rick Kranitz who worked with Hill before can straighten him out; this is a low risk acquisition with a massive reward if he can be straightened out.

BULLPEN:

Former fat, independent league pitcher George Sherrill was a throw-in designed to be veteran filler when he wound up as the Orioles closer and made the All Star team. Sherrill is more of a bulldog than a dominating-type closer, but there's nothing wrong with that if he gets the job done. The Orioles were willing to discuss Sherrill in trades after maximizing his value as their closer, but the workload over the season sent Sherrill to the disabled list late in the season. I'd expect him to be available again sometime this season, although I wouldn't trade him unless I was getting good value for him because he's a pretty good pitcher and a guy you like to have because he always takes the ball.

Chris Ray was the hard-throwing closer before he required Tommy John surgery and he's expected back this season. I'd work him in slowly, but he could return to the closer's role as B.J. Ryan did for the Blue Jays last season after having Tommy John.

Veteran lefty Jamie Walker had an atrocious year in 2008, but he'd been very solid over the past couple of seasons and the way relievers fluctuate in their performance, I wouldn't be surprised to see Walker rebound if he's healthy.

Veteran Danys Baez is also returning from surgery and there was talk that he may have been converted into a starter. That's not something to automatically dismiss out of hand, but if he can contribute out of the bullpen, he's been a solid reliever before.

Big righty Dennis Sarfate pitched serviceably in 57 games last season and struck out 86 in 80 innings. (He also walked 62, so that's something to watch.) Jim Miller struck out a batter an inning in Triple A Norfolk and in eight games with the Orioles, so he could provide some help.

6'9" Kam Mickolio struck out a batter per inning over three levels in the Orioles organization and has potential.

LINEUP:

Gregg Zaun is a veteran who's hung around far longer than anyone could possibly have expected after his rough first couple of years as manager Jim Leyland's whipping boy with the Marlins. Zaun spent a long time with the Blue Jays and, no matter how many times they tried to replace him with one guy after another, Zaun ended up being the main catcher. Now the veteran has agreed to hold the catching spot until whenever hot prospect Matt Wieters is ready.

Wieters is considered not only one of baseball's best catching prospects, but one of the best prospects overall. The numbers he put up in Double A Bowie were borderline ridiculous with a .365 batting average; .460 OPB; 12 homers and 51 RBI in 61 games. He's very big for a catcher (6'5", 230), so he might eventually have to be moved out from back there, especially if he's such a great hitter, but for now, at age 22, he's the catcher of the future. Unless there's some hiccup, Wieters may be the Orioles starting catcher by June and won't have to look over his shoulder at a disgruntled, usurped veteran because Zaun knows and accepts the deal.

Hard-nosed veteran Ty Wigginton was signed to a 2-year contract to, presumably, play first base. He's a tough player who leads in the clubhouse; murders left-handed pitching; hits the ball out of the park and gets on base at a solid clip (.350 OBP last season). Wigginton can play first base, second base and third base and is a good, ancillary player to help teach the younger players how to act off the field and play hard on it.

Brian Roberts has signed a contract extension to forego free agency. He's a durable veteran; a fine fielder; has some pop and great speed.

Melvin Mora is still hanging around at third base for the Orioles and he can still play and play well. He had a fine season in 2008 with 23 homers and 104 RBI and is still an excellent fielder. Mora might be trade bait, but he keeps himself in excellent shape and if the Orioles are able to turn things around in the next couple of years, Mora can either still be the third baseman or become a roving-type player because he's also a fine defensive outfielder.

Veteran Cesar Izturis was signed to fill the hole at shortstop and while he can't really hit, he's an excellent defensive shortstop. Izturis hit about as well as one could expect last season with the Cardinals with a .263 average. The Orioles should know not to expect too much from him at the plate.

Luke Scott had a very good, professional year at the plate with 23 homers. He's probably better off being a bench/part time player at this point in his career, but he's a good example of how a big leaguer should behave and would be a solid roving outfielder/DH as youngsters Felix Pie and Adam Jones are worked into the starting lineup.

Adam Jones showed great potential after coming over from the Mariners in the Erik Bedard trade. As a top prospect, it was a good idea to get Jones the 500 at bats and grow accustomed to the big leagues. Eventually, he'll be a 15-20 homer man with speed and excellent defense.

Nick Markakis is a homegrown Oriole who signed a long term contract this off season to stay with the team. Markakis plays the game correctly and does everything a manager could want; he hits the ball out of the park; gets on base; and plays great defense. He'll be a major part of an Orioles turnaround.

The underrated Aubrey Huff had an excellent year at the plate with a .304 batting average; 32 homers; 108 RBI; and a .360 OBP. If a team in need of a solid lefty bat came calling for Huff, the Orioles should probably explore the possibility of trading him for a solid group of youngsters.

BENCH:

Veteran utility man Ryan Freel was acquired in the trade that sent Ramon Hernandez to the Reds. Freel is the type of player that any manager loves to have because he's willing to play any position, can hit and plays the game with a reckless abandon that almost got him killed as he nearly broke his neck running into the wall while playing with the Reds; that's not what you want, but if he's willing to go to those lengths to win a game, that can't help but tell his teammates that they should play in a similar fashion.

Felix Pie was a victim of Cubs manager Lou Piniella's impatience with young players. If Piniella gives a youngster a chance to play, he doesn't have the time or inclination to nursemaid him; Pie has put up excellent power/speed numbers in the minors, but that didn't translate to his opportunity in the big leagues. This isn't to imply that Piniella threw him out there and sent him back to the minors after two weeks; Pie played for over a month before he was sent out in favor of veterans Reed Johnson and Jim Edmonds. Pie's only 24 and he's going to get a chance to play with the Orioles and show what he can really do without a raving lunatic hovering over him and waiting to send him out in favor of a veteran.

Guillermo Quiroz is a backup catcher who's either going to be a third stringer or not play at all other than early in the season because once Wieters arrives, there's not going to be room for Quiroz.

Veteran utility player Chris Gomez was signed to a minor league contract and could stick as a backup infielder.

PREDICTION:

The Orioles are developing for a not-too-distant future. If the young players they've accrued—especially Chris Tillman—arrive in the majors at some point and perform well, the Orioles could be far better than anyone expects them to be. They have the bats to score enough runs to win a few games; their bullpen has some power arms and they're working on their starting rotation. There will be growing pains, but as long as they continue down the road they're on, this patience will bear fruit sooner rather than later. With the American League East being as impossible as it is with the Yankees, Red Sox and Rays, the Orioles will be lucky to surpass their win total of 68 from 2008, but the Blue Jays are going to be horrible and the Orioles could surprise a few people and play far better than expected as they prepare for the next stage in their development. I believe the Orioles will improve on paper and will be managed by Tony La Russa in 2010 and be legitimate contenders soon after that.

PREDICTED RECORD: 71-91

Toronto Blue Jays
2008 Record: 86-76; Fourth Place, American League East

2008 Recap:

The Blue Jays had another predictable season: they were expected to contend; they got off to a terrible start; they endured a load of injuries to their pitching staff; GM J.P. Ricciardi had his usual disagreements with players (inside and outside his organization); bickered with fans; fired his manager; made some trades; the team played excellent ball for a chunk of the second half to wind up with a respectable record and make everyone think that they might possibly be turning the corner from perpetual also-ran into legitimate contender.

Their offense was atrocious; their pitching was, for the most part, quite good and the team responded to the veteran manager (and two time World Series winner with the Blue Jays) Cito Gaston. Roy Halladay and A.J. Burnett provided the team with two aces at the top of the rotation; the bullpen was deep and organized; and if they had any kind of offense at all, they would've been in contention for a playoff spot. 2008 was another in a long line of "woulda, coulda, shoulda" for the Blue Jays with no forward progress; just a case of running in place.

2009 ADDITIONS: 1B/DH Kevin Millar signed a minor league contract.
RHP Bryan Bullington was claimed off waivers from the Cleveland Indians.
RHP Dick Haghurst was claimed off waivers from the San Diego Padres.
SS Angel Sanchez was claimed off waivers from the Kansas City Royals.
INF/OF Brandon Fahey signed a minor league contract.
RHP Matt Clement signed a minor league contract.
OF Jason Lane signed a minor league contract.
1B/OF Adam Loewen signed a minor league contract.

2009 SUBTRACTIONS: RHP A.J. Burnett was not re-signed.
C Gregg Zaun was not re-signed.
OF Kevin Mench refused a minor league assignment and elected free agency.
LHP Les Walrond was released.

2009 PROJECTED LINEUP: C-Rod Barajas; 1B-Lyle Overbay; 2B-Aaron Hill; 3B-Scott Rolen; SS-John McDonald; LF-Adam Lind; CF-Vernon Wells; RF-Alex Rios; DH-Travis Snider

2009 PROJECTED STARTING ROTATION: Roy Halladay; Dustin McGowan; Jesse Litsch; David Purcey; Casey Janssen; Brett Cecil; Shaun Marcum

2009 PROJECTED BULLPEN: B.J. Ryan; Scott Downs; Jason Frasor; Jeremy Accardo; Brandon League; Shawn Camp; Brian Tallet; Jesse Carlson; Brian Wolfe

2009 BENCH: C-Curtis Thigpen; INF-Jose Bautista; INF/OF-Joe Inglett; INF-Marco Scutaro; INF/OF Brandon Fahey; OF-Jason Lane

2009 EXTRA PITCHERS/PROSPECTS: Bryan Bullington; Dirk Hayhurst; Kelvin Jimenez; Matt Clement; Brad Mills; Zach Dials; Celson Polanco; Tim Collins; Edgar Estanga; Marc Rzepczynski

2009 EVERYDAY PROSPECTS: Scott Campbell; Brad Emaus; Cory Patton

ASSESSMENTS:
MANAGEMENT:

I'll ask this question as simply and as bluntly as possible: how is GM J.P. Ricciardi still there?

The Blue Jays organization has run its course with Ricciardi in charge. He's been there since late 2001 and despite his bold proclamations of how financially sound and productive the club would be on and off the field, they've never once—not once—been in any kind of realistic contention while Ricciardi's been running the club. They've been mostly above .500; they've been one of the better teams in the American League; they've won enough games to be considered respectable; but they've never, ever been contenders. Ricciardi is now on his fourth manager in seven years and, despite his protestations to the contrary, he has a manager that he didn't even want in Cito Gaston. It's not just that the team has never competed with the Red Sox or Yankees for the division crown; it's the other "stuff" that one has to put up with when employing Ricciardi. Every time you think that there couldn't possibly be another incident; another off-field controversy; another series of embarrassing occurrences for which the GM has to explain himself or apologize, something else happens.

Last season, there was the clumsy way in which Ricciardi jumped the gun in releasing DH Frank Thomas. As much as Ricciardi dismisses the claims that he released Thomas because of the contract-kicker that would've been exercised for the 2009 season had Thomas reached a certain number of at bats in 2008, he clearly released Thomas because of it. Ricciardi, as a *Moneyball* proponent, knew what a slow starter Thomas has been throughout his entire career; and the Blue Jays didn't even have a viable replacement for Thomas in the lineup when he was released.

Then there was the call-in radio show Ricciardi hosted after Blue Jays games in which a caller suggested the Blue Jays make a move on then Cincinnati Reds slugger Adam Dunn. Ricciardi ripped into Dunn, saying that he's a guy who doesn't even like playing baseball. Then, Ricciardi had to apologize to Dunn for the comments and, when receiving a call from someone he thought was Dunn, it turned out that Ricciardi was the victim of a prank.

After that, there was the firing of John Gibbons in favor of Gaston, who is clearly not the type of manager that Ricciardi prefers. Gaston is still worshipped in Toronto after winning two World Series as the manager in 1992 and 1993 and Ricciardi wouldn't win any kind of public relations war with the manager; in addition to that, GMs like Ricciardi like having a manager who's going to do what he's told; that is not Cito Gaston.

As far as the on-field product, the Blue Jays withstood more injuries to their pitchers including budding stars Dustin McGowan and Shaun Marcum. Pitching coach Brad Arnsberg has a long history of his pitching charges getting hurt, but while Ricciardi has been very free with replacing his managers, he's kept Arnsberg there despite the in practice evidence that there's something off with the way he handles his pitchers. After the release of Thomas, the Blue Jays offense was hideous. Scott Rolen was acquired before the season for Troy Glaus. Rolen was brought in for his toughness and leadership, but he had a series of injuries that limited him to 115 games. He signed David Eckstein, whose declining range and offensive production was a drag on the lineup; and his "star" center fielder, to whom Ricciardi doled a long-term, $126 million contract continued to be a mediocre player who's untradeable because of that contract.

The Blue Jays did almost nothing in the off-season other than let A.J. Burnett leave via free agency (after another brilliant contractual decision by Ricciardi in which he let Burnett have an out clause after three seasons, although signing the flighty Burnett was a mistake to begin with); and catcher Gregg Zaun signed with the Orioles. They've acquired no one other than the oft-injured Matt Clement; soft-hitting Brandon Fahey; and journeyman castoff Jason Lane. The organization also laid off about 30 workers and the terrible economy is preventing them from doing much of anything to improve the club significantly.

Given how Ricciardi's resume is so shaky, I can't understand why they brought him back for 2009; the very idea that the Blue Jays hot streak that saved them from a record of around .500 or slightly less had anything to do with Ricciardi is skirting the issue of his overall track record. It's time to bring in some fresh blood and I've called for Ricciardi to be replaced over the past several years; once the Blue Jays are mired in last place at mid-season, they should fire him once and for all and begin a wholesale tear down to rebuild, but given how Ricciardi's survived like a cockroach for this long, I don't know if even a 90-loss season is going to cost him his job.

Cito Gaston was the popular manager of the two Blue Jays championship teams of the early 90s and his presence appeared to wake up a slumbering crew in mid-2008. That being said, Gaston didn't do a very good job as the team declined in the mid-90s as that decline and reliance on veterans who didn't pan out eventually led to the hiring of a new voice in Ricciardi. Things have come full circle, but that doesn't mean the Blue Jays are going to return to their former glory. Gaston's a good manager and knows how to handle his players, but the worst thing that could've happened to the organization last season was their hot streak that got them that 86-76 record. Had they completely collapsed and wound up with a reverse record of 76-86 as it looked like they would when Gaston replaced John Gibbons (who was an excellent strategic manager), there would've been a built-in excuse for the team to start over again with a new GM; instead, the hot streak saved Ricciardi's job leaving the club in their current limbo of not being awful enough to make wholesale changes, but not being good enough to be considered a contender. It won't matter what Gaston does in 2009 because the talent isn't there for him to steer the team into contention in that impossible division and since they haven't added anyone to improve that lineup, there's not much hope, Gaston or not.

STARTING PITCHING:

Roy Halladay is a horse at the top of the rotation. He's old-school; he pounds the strike zone; he goes deeply into games; and he never gives in. Halladay won 20 games for the second time in his career and logged 246 innings with an unprecedented (in today's game anyway) 9 complete games. Had Cliff Lee not had such a gaudy record, Halladay would've won his second Cy Young Award, and it's possible that he should've won the award anyway. The Blue Jays only have Halladay signed through 2010 at $15 million per year and he has a blanket no-trade clause; with the way the Blue Jays farm system is almost completely devoid of prospects and that they have no chance whatsoever of competing this season, they should explore trade options for Halladay. Another reason that Ricciardi should've been replaced is for that reason alone; they don't want to leave Ricciardi in charge of the possible trading of Halladay because his record in making trades has been so poor that a deal of such magnitude cannot be left for Ricciardi to make.

Would Halladay be willing to accept a trade to his hometown Colorado Rockies? The Rockies have a load of prospects to deal and he'd launch them into contention in the weak NL West. How about the Angels, who love pitching? The Mets? The Dodgers, whose farm system is loaded with young arms and bats? Halladay isn't young anymore (he's about to turn 32) and he must be getting tired of having no chance to win and being underpaid in comparison to such pitchers as C.C. Sabathia and Johan Santana. If things are going badly in Toronto, I wouldn't be surprised if Halladay asks to be traded and he'd bring back a bounty of youngsters, but Ricciardi can't be allowed to be the one who makes the deal.

Dustin McGowan was emerging into one of the top young starters in all of baseball before he wound up on the disabled list with shoulder problems. Exploratory surgery showed a fraying of the labrum, and he's supposedly going to be ready for the start of spring training, but who knows? McGowan's effectiveness suffered as he was pitching through the discomfort and if he's unavailable or diminished, the Blue Jays are in a lot of trouble since their other top young starter, Shaun Marcum, had Tommy John surgery last season and is unlikely to return until late this season, if at all.

Jesse Litsch showed flashes of excellence in winning 13 games and pitching 176 innings; he throws strikes and is a contact pitcher who is probably not the prototypical number two starter behind Halladay, but if neither McGowan or Marcum are available, that's what Litsch is going to be.

Big lefty David Purcey pitched very well at Triple A last season and was unimpressive in 12 starts for the Blue Jays. His strikeout numbers are impressive enough, but he gave up a lot of home runs and is 26, which is old for a legitimate prospect to be getting his first shot as a member of a team's rotation at the beginning of the season.

Casey Jansson is a career reliever who's getting a chance to start this season out of necessity.

Brett Cecil is one of the few prospects the Blue Jays have. He's lefty, 22-years-old; did excellent work in Double A before being promoted to Triple A and struggling a bit. In their current circumstances, if Cecil pitches reasonably well in the spring, there's no reason not to give him a chance to start the season in the rotation in the big leagues.

BULLPEN:

B.J. Ryan returned from Tommy John surgery as quickly as humanly possible and, after getting off to a slow start, wound up having a solid year. He saved 32 games and while his velocity was down, he still has that funky, stiff-legged, across his body motion (which was probably a main reason that he got hurt to begin with) to deceive hitters. I'm sure the Blue Jays would love to be rid of his contract and as the season moves along, I'd expect him to be moved to a contender.

Veteran lefty Scott Downs had an excellent season as the set-up man. Downs pitched to a 1.78 ERA in 66 games and wasn't simply a lefty specialist; he throws strikes and is a solid reliever.

Righty Jason Frasor appeared in 49 games and while he had a high ERA of 4.18 and loses control of the strike zone, he strikes out nearly a batter per inning.

I keep waiting for flamethrowing Brandon League to blossom and become a useful part of the Blue Jays bullpen, but every year something derails him. League's fastball is up near the 100 mph mark, but he pitched poorly and wound up back in the minors in 2008 and despite throwing so hard, doesn't strike out that many hitters. He had a 2.18 ERA in 31 big league games last season and 2009 might be the year he fulfills his promise.

Lefty Jesse Carlson had a 7-2 record in 69 games with a 2.25 ERA and an excellent hits/innings pitched ratio of 41/60.

Veteran Shawn Camp appeared in 40 games and had a 4.12 ERA; lefties hammered the righty Camp to the tune of a .356 average.

Brian Tallet is a lefty who had a 2.25 ERA in 51 games and a solid hits/innings pitched ratio of 52/56.

LINEUP:

Rod Barajas was another player who got into a public dustup with Ricciardi after the two came to a handshake agreement for Barajas to join the Blue Jays for the 2007 season, and Barajas backed out of the deal to join the Phillies. Ricciardi threw a tantrum and the back-and-forth went on for awhile, then it was a bit of a surprise to see Barajas join the Blue Jays after the Phillies dumped him. Barajas has some pop in his bat and he's going to be the Blue Jays primary catcher with the departure of Zaun.

Lyle Overbay had a solid enough season, as he batted .270 with 15 homers and 69 RBI and a .358 OBP. In a perfect world, the Blue Jays could use more of a power bat at first base, but Overbay is dependable to put up similar numbers on an annual basis.

Aaron Hill played in only 55 games and didn't hit much at all. He batted .263 with 2 homers; 20 RBI; a .324 OBP; no speed and average defense. The Blue Jays could use another second baseman unless Hill regains the form he showed in 2007 when he hit 17 homers.

Scott Rolen isn't suddenly going to suddenly become Benjamin Button and start aging backwards, but that's the only thing that could save the Blue Jays from having to pay the bloated salary of the injury-prone and declining Rolen. All the talk of Rolen's toughness and hard-nosed play being a great addition to the clubhouse was all well and good, but Ricciardi was warned (specifically by me) that Rolen wasn't going to be able to stay healthy enough to justify trading Troy Glaus to get him. Glaus is injury-prone in his own right, but he had a good, predominately healthy season in 2008 (although he's going to miss a chunk of 2009); but the important disparity between the two is their contracts. Rolen still has a lot of money due him through 2010 and he's likely to spend much of that time out with nagging injuries. Acquiring him was a mistake and another reason for Ricciardi to be dismissed.

John McDonald is a feisty player; he's a useful utility player; he plays very hard; but under no circumstances should he receive any more than 100 at bats (if that) during a big league season. McDonald is listed as the shortstop on the Blue Jays depth chart and I can think of at least three pitchers who are bigger threats at the plate than McDonald. The Blue Jays can't expect to compete if McDonald is their starting shortstop.

Adam Lind batted .282 in 88 games with 9 homers and 40 RBI. If he gets a chance to play regularly, he should provide 15-18 homers.

As Vernon Wells began playing well under Cito Gaston and ended with respectable numbers after an injury-riddled and struggling first half, there was again talk that Wells is so talented that he could be a MVP candidate.

The only way that would happen would be if the Blue Jays actually followed through on the talk that they had interest in Manny Ramirez early in the off-season. (The talk resulted in nothing.) Wells had 20 homers, 78 RBI and a .300 batting average; but his OBP was a poor .343 (a big factor in that could be the weakness of the Blue Jays lineup surrounding Wells), but Wells is wilting under the pressure of the absurd $126 million contract that Ricciardi lavished upon him to keep him from exploring free agency. The contract makes Wells all but untradeable and he's never going to be anything more than what he is: an overpaid underachiever.

It's hard to believe now, but the winter before the 2008 season, there was serious talk that the Giants would consider trading Tim Lincecum to the Blue Jays for right fielder Alex Rios. Rios had a very good season in 2007, but he's not a guy who strikes fear in the opposing pitchers and his numbers in 2008 are respectable, but not anything to be overly impressed with. He wound up with 15 homers, 79 RBI, a .291 average, 32 stolen bases and a weak .337 OBP. (Considering how deeply Ricciardi believes in *Moneyball* , wouldn't it make sense for his players to have high OBPs? Especially the centerpieces of the lineup like Wells and Rios?) Rios still has the potential to blossom into a superstar, so I'd hesitate to give up on him as he's just entering his prime years.

Young slugger Travis Snider has a chance to be the run producer the Blue Jays need. Snider is a big (5'11" 245 lbs) beer league type basher who hit 36 homers in Double A, Triple A and in a brief appearance in the big leagues. He strikes out a lot and he's probably going to have to DH, but he's only 21 and his numbers indicate that he'll provide the pop the Blue Jays desperately need.

BENCH:

Marco Scutaro is a veteran utility player who has the penchant for getting clutch hits. Scutaro should get a chance to play shortstop over McDonald if the Blue Jays are unable to fill the position with a big league quality player who can hit a little bit. Scutaro is more of a utility player who wound up with 500 at bats because of the injuries to Rolen, among others. Scutaro has some pop and gets on base at a reasonable rate; he's a solid utility player.

Jose Bautista is a another veteran infielder who has some pop. He joined the Blue Jays from the Pirates and didn't hit in 21 games, but given the Blue Jays circumstances, they may as well keep Bautista around because of his career-long history of being able to hit with some power.

Joe Inglett batted .297 in 109 games and was a useful backup outfielder with some extra base power and speed.

Curtis Thigpen is the backup catcher to Barajas and can't hit at all.

Former Oriole Brandon Fahey was signed and when I first saw him in the Orioles uniform, all I could think of with his skeletal appearance was that he was the second coming of Mark Belanger. Unfortunately, he hits like Mark Belanger and that was fine in the 60s and 70s, but in today's game a team—especially one as offensively challenged as the Blue Jays—cannot carry Fahey in their lineup as anything more than a defensive replacement.

Gregarious veteran slugger Kevin Millar was signed to a minor league contract and with the sad state of the Blue Jays, Millar should make the club; he can still hit the ball out of the park.

PREDICTION:

Even if the Blue Jays were in one of the weaker divisions in baseball, they'd still have no chance at even being respectable unless everything worked out right for them. By everything I mean McGowan and Marcum both being miraculously healthy and winning 13-16 games each; Wells and Rios both blossoming into consistent power threats; Snider contending for Rookie of the Year with similar power to what he showed in the minors; Rolen staying healthy; and the bullpen repeating their stellar work from last season. This organization is in shambles and it was that way before the economic collapse, so if Ricciardi tries to pawn this mess off as an accident of circumstance, he's using a similar type of self-preservation which led him to sign-off on the hiring of a manager he didn't want in Gaston. I'd say that Ricciardi's in trouble once the season gets underway, but I've expected him to be fired for several years now (not for any other reason than that he deserves it), but he's still there. He's the Don Rumsfeld of the baseball world.

It doesn't matter much; Gaston can't save them; this team can't hit and their starting rotation is injury-riddled and short even with one of the top three pitchers in baseball in Halladay; and the bullpen won't be as good as it was last season. In that impossible American League East, the Blue Jays are going to be a punching bag for the bullies and are even going to fall behind the rising Orioles; then perhaps the ownership will wake up and make the change that's needed to be made for years now and find a new GM who won't get his name in the papers for his off-field actions, statements and disagreements with others, but for doing a good job.

PREDICTED RECORD: 70-92

American League Central:
1. Cleveland Indians
2. Minnesota Twins
3. Chicago White Sox
4. Detroit Tigers
5. Kansas City Royals

Cleveland Indians
2008 Record: 81-81; Third Place, American League Central

2008 Recap:

The Indians came within one game of the World Series in 2007 and were widely expected to at least return to the playoffs in 2008. The contract status of C.C. Sabathia and his bad start contributed to the Indians falling out of contention early and the inability to lock up Sabathia long-term precipitated his trade to the Brewers at mid-season.

Injuries and poor performances from such veterans as Travis Hafner; Fausto Carmona; Paul Byrd; Jake Westbrook; Victor Martinez and Joe Borowski counterbalanced a brilliant, Cy Young Award season from Cliff Lee and only a late season hot streak allowed the Indians to finish the season with a .500 record.

2009 ADDITIONS: RHP Kerry Wood signed a 2-year contract.
INF/OF Mark DeRosa was acquired from the Chicago Cubs.
RHP Joe Smith was acquired from the New York Mets.
RHP Carl Pavano signed a 1-year contract.
RHP Tomo Ohka signed a minor league contract.
INF Luis Valbuena was acquired from the Seattle Mariners.
RHP Kirk Saarloos signed a minor league contract.
OF Mickey Hall was acquired from the Boston Red Sox.
RHP Jack Cassel signed a minor league contract.
RHP Matt Herges signed a minor league contract.
RHP Vinnie Chulk signed a minor league contract.
RHP Greg Aquino signed a minor league contract.

2009 SUBTRACTIONS: RHP Tom Mastny was sold to Japan.
OF Franklin Gutierrez was traded to the Seattle Mariners.
RHP Jeff Stevens was traded to the Chicago Cubs.
RHP Chris Archer was traded to the Chicago Cubs.
RHP John Gaub was traded to the Chicago Cubs.
RHP Bryan Bullington was claimed off waivers by the Toronto Blue Jays.
3B Andy Marte was released.

2009 PROJECTED LINEUP: C-Victor Martinez; 1B- Ryan Garko; 2B-Asdrubel Cabrera; 3B-Mark DeRosa; SS-Jhonny Peralta; LF-Ben Francisco; CF-Grady Sizemore; RF-Shin-Soo Choo; DH-Travis Hafner

2009 PROJECTED STARTING ROTATION: Cliff Lee; Fausto Carmona; Carl Pavano; Anthony Reyes; Zach Jackson; Aaron Laffey; Scott Lewis; Jeremy Sowers

2009 PROJECTED BULLPEN: Kerry Wood; Masahide Kobiyashi; Rafael Betancourt; Rafael Perez; Jensen Lewis; Joe Smith; Matt Herges

2009 BENCH: C-Kelly Shoppach; 1B-Michael Aubrey; INF-Jamey Carroll; INF-Josh Barfield; OF-David Dellucci; INF-Luis Valbuena

2009 EXTRA PITCHERS/PROSPECTS: Vinnie Chulk; Jon Meloan; Greg Aquino; Jack Cassel; Kirk Saarloos; Rich Rundles; Tomo Ohka; Zach Jackson; David Huff; Hector Rondon; Josh Tomlin; Kelvin De La Cruz; Josh Judy

2009 EVERYDAY PROSPECTS: Chris Gimenez; Wes Hodges; Matt La Porta

ASSESSMENTS:
MANAGEMENT:

Mark Shapiro is widely regarded as one of the best executives in baseball. Not only does he have the guts to make big moves as he showed when he traded C.C. Sabathia to the Brewers, but he also knows when to strike; when to basically cut his losses in a season that's not going according to plan; and sign players to reasonable, affordable contracts and getting maximum value from them, then dispatching them when they are no longer of use.

Some may scoff at the signings that Shapiro made this winter like Carl Pavano and Kerry Wood, but given the way he's gotten stunning contributions from journeymen like Paul Byrd and Joe Borowski, would it be such a shock if Pavano and Wood at least delivered *something* of use to the Indians in 2009? Pavano has become a laughingstock because of his slapstick tenure with the Yankees, but he's only signed to a one-year deal and as a veteran who may be looking to cash in on one last payday in his career, he's a great gamble. Wood is oft-injured, but he still has the stuff to dominate and more often than not, he got the job done as the Cubs closer.

With the weakness of the American League Central, the Indians are well-poised to hang around at the top of the standings waiting for Jake Westbrook to return from surgery; for Matt La Porta to be ready to contribute in the big leagues; and for the other young pitchers like Scott Lewis, Zach Jackson and Anthony Reyes to take their spots in the rotation and lead the Indians back into the playoffs. All of this is due to the skills of Shapiro finding talented players at bargain prices and giving them a chance to play; and once they can't play, he dispatches them and repeats the scenario all over again. He's one of the best executives in all of baseball.

Eric Wedge won Manager of the Year in 2007 as the Indians almost made it to the World Series (they would've won too had they gotten past the Red Sox); Wedge handles the players well enough and although occasionally making some odd strategic decisions (they stayed with a soft-tossing and injured Borowski far too long as their closer when it was clear there was something wrong with him), he knows his place in the organization. The decisions on the field come from the top (meaning Shapiro), but it's not so overt that the players lose respect for the manager. Wedge was a tough player and he's a tough manager who puts the trust in his players to perform as expected and they generally do.

STARTING PITCHING:

As great as Cliff Lee was on his way to a dominating 22-3 record, great stats across the board and a Cy Young Award, there's very little chance of him being anywhere close to as good in 2009. Lee has been a consistent, double-digit winner when he's been healthy, but never 22-3 good; the Indians must be prepared for some sort of correction with Lee's performance. If he's able to anchor the rotation, repeat his 220+ innings and win 15-18 games as the top starter, they should be happy with that because seasons like 2008 for a guy like Lee—who doesn't have overpowering stuff by any stretch of the imagination—only come along once in a career.

Fausto Carmona got injured early in the season and was unable to follow up on his 19-wins in 2008. Carmona only started 22 games and had an 8-7 record with a 5.44 ERA; he walked 70 and only struck out 58 in 121 innings. The Indians are going to need the Carmona who won 19 games if they're going to contend, especially now that he's going to be counted on as one of their aces without Sabathia.

Ah, where would I be without Carl Pavano? Pavano became the deserved butt of jokes in his disastrous four-year tenure with the Yankees in which he went through numerous agents; numerous girlfriends; absurd injuries that heretofore could only be imagined in the realm of the ludicrous; and derisive comments in his own clubhouse. Pavano was paid $40 million for those four years as Yankees property and now he's trying to rebuild his career with the Indians on a one-year contract. Pavano's a worthwhile gamble as a veteran trying to rejuvenate his reputation (it's almost impossible by this point), but the big problem may not be desire, it may be ability. After Pavano finally got out on the mound for the Yankees late last season, his stuff was horribly diminished from what it once was. His fastball was mediocre at best in both movement and velocity; his slider was below average. It's understandable that Pavano was feeling his way through as he returned from Tommy John surgery and the long layoff *before* the surgery, but unless his stuff is better than what I saw last year, he's going to be Paul Byrd without the dogged determination that allowed Byrd to get by with similar weak stuff; and Pavano has never shown the ability to battle his way through adversity other than when it came to contract time with the Marlins. The Indians know this and I'm sure they realize that if they get 20-25 starts from Pavano and/or 150 innings, they should be happy with that for what they're paying him.

After escaping from the purgatory of Tony La Russa's doghouse with the Cardinals, the once-hot prospect Anthony Reyes looked like was relieved to be freed from his dysfunctional relationship with the Cardinals manager and pitched brilliantly in six starts for the Indians posting a 1.83 ERA. Reyes pitched ten games in relief for the Cardinals and was okay and pitched pretty well in eleven starts in Triple A for both the Cardinals and Indians. Because he pitched well late in the season doesn't mean the 27-year-old Reyes has turned the corner into fulfilling his potential. The one thing he has going for him to start the season for the Indians is that he's away from La Russa.

Scott Lewis was brilliant in four starts going 4-0 with a 2.63 ERA. He's a contact pitcher whose numbers were consistent over three levels in the Indians system. He's 25-years-old, so it's about time for him to stick in the big leagues as a seasonlong starter.

Aaron Laffey was expected to be a stalwart in the rotation, but had a shaky year and wound up in the minors. He wasn't terrible with a 5-7 record in 16 starts, but his ERA was mediocre at 4.23 and he allowed 10 homers in those 16 starts. With the back of the Indians rotation questionable, they're going to need some production from Laffey.

Jeremy Sowers was 4-9 in 22 starts before being sent back to Triple A where he pitched quite well. Sowers is a soft-tossing lefty who has to have his control to be effective.

Zach Jackson was acquired in the C.C. Sabathia trade and made 9 starts for the Indians; he had a 2-2 record with a 5.02 ERA and allowed 7 homers. Jackson is a bit of a project; he was so hideous in Triple A with the Brewers that he was sent to the bullpen and had a bloated ERA of over seven. It's hard to see him starting the season with the Indians and will probably end up back in the minors for more seasoning.

Jake Westbrook had elbow surgery and is expected to be back with the Indians by mid-season. Westbrook got off to a blazing hot start last season after adding a changeup to his repertoire, but he's been a consistent performer in the Indians rotation for a few years and his return at or around the All Star break would be the equivalent of making a trade for a solid veteran starter if he's able to return to form.

BULLPEN:

Kerry Wood made the adjustment to the closer's role quite effectively for the Cubs last season and that he was able to handle closing games for Lou Piniella is a good sign that he'll handle the pressure of a big game. Wood saved 34 games and struck out 84 in 66 innings and stayed healthy for the first time in years. The Indians make a habit of finding veteran closers who've either been dispatched by their former teams; are coming off injuries or poor seasons; or have been squeezed by the market. Wood fits into the first and third categories. For two seasons and $20 million, Wood's a great pickup to close.

Masahide Kobiyashi got a chance to close a few games, but the Japanese import struggled with a 4.53 ERA in 57 games. He's about to turn 35-years-old.

Rafael Betancourt also got a chance to close when Borowski went down and couldn't handle it, having a terrible season overall. Betancourt gave up

11 homers in 69 games and his ERA was bloated to over five. Betancourt has been consistently good for much of his time with the Indians, so he has a good chance to rebound.

Rafael Perez pitched in 73 games and had a solid enough year with a 4-4 record and 86 strikeouts. He was masterful in 2007, but it would've been difficult for him to repeat those numbers. Perez should continue pitching well.

Joe Smith is a sidearmer acquired from the Mets and he was pretty much the only decent reliever the Mets had. Smith was overused by former Mets manager Willie Randolph and he's probably not suited to pitch to too many lefties (they murder him), but he takes the ball and is very tough on righties. Smith is exactly the type of reliever the Shapiro brings to the Indians and gets great production from.

Jensen Lewis pitched well in 51 games with a 3.82 ERA and has performed consistently during his big league career.

The Indians have signed a bunch of veteran names to minor league contract to fill out the bullpen. Greg Aquino; Matt Herges (probably the best of the bunch); Jack Cassel (who pitched serviceably in Triple A for the Astros, but the most interesting part of Cassel's resume is that he's the brother of New England Patriots quarterback Matt Cassel); and veteran Kirk Saarloos. Aside from Herges, most of these pitchers are destined to be at Triple A in case of an emergency.

LINEUP:

Victor Martinez's power disappeared early in the season before he wound up on the disabled list. Martinez used to be a 100-RBI man, but last year, his power was diminished to nothing. Martinez is 30-years-old now and 20 extra base hits—including only 2 homers—in his 74 hits is a cause for concern for what they're going to get out of him this year. Martinez has never been very good defensively and if he can't hit the ball out of the park, there's little use for him behind the plate. One would assume that his injury was a factor in his power drop.

Ryan Garko drove in 90 runs with 14 homers and his numbers diminished from 2007 as well. Garko is not a prototypical slugging first baseman and with the way Kelly Shoppach hit in the absence of Martinez, it wouldn't be surprising (if Martinez starts hitting the ball out of the park again) if Garko is traded and Martinez is moved to first base. Garko's a hard-nosed player and if a team like the Mets falls out of contention and puts a pending free agent like Carlos Delgado on the market, Garko might be a good fit for the Mets. The Giants also need a first baseman and Garko attended Stanford, so that's a possibility as well.

Asdrubal Cabrera was a revelation when he took the starting second base job from the disappointing Josh Barfield late in the 2007 season; in 2008 he struggled to a .259 average and diminished numbers across the board. The Indians still have utilityman Jamey Carroll on their roster and he can fill in adequately at second if Cabrera struggles again; or they could give Barfield another chance.

Mark DeRosa was surprisingly traded by the Cubs for three minor league pitchers to replenish their dilapidated minor league system and clear some salary. I can't imagine that Cubs manager Lou Piniella wanted to trade DeRosa; DeRosa had his career-year offensively, stayed healthy (which has been a problem in his career), and provided clutch hits for the Cubs all season and was a legitimate MVP candidate. DeRosa is going to move to third base to fill a hole for the Indians and while he can't be expected to hit as well as he did in 2008 (.285 BA; 21 homers; 54 extra base hits; and a .376 OBP) while playing adequate defense all over the field. He's also smart and well-liked in the clubhouse.

Jhonny Peralta had his usual type of season; he was in the lineup every day; hit his 20+ homers and drove in 89 runs. There was talk that the best possible defense for the Indians would have Peralta moving to third base, DeRosa to second and Cabrera to short. I doubt that's going to happen; Peralta's consistent and can be counted on to put up the numbers he generally does season-after-season.

Ben Francsico has immense ability and at the age of 26, it's getting to be put up or shut up time for him to fulfill that potential. Francisco had 15 homers and 54 RBI in 121 games and he has to take advantage of the situation if he's given a chance to play every day.

Grady Sizemore is one of the best players in baseball. He does everything that a team could possibly want from their center fielder; he's great defensively; he hits the ball out of the park; he runs well and he plays hard every single day. He's popular in the clubhouse and respects the game. One thing he can improve is hitting against lefties; last season, Sizemore hit .224 vs southpaws and if he can improve that number to, say, .250, he'll be a MVP candidate because his numbers will be massive.

Shin-Soo Choo had an excellent season as a part-time player with 14 homers, 45 of his 98 hits were for extra bases and he had a .397 OBP. Choo murders right-handed pitching and it might not be a bad idea to give him a chance to play every day and see what he can do.

Will Travis Hafner be the player who missed almost the entire 2008 season with shoulder issues, or will he be the basher he was before the 2008 season? Hafner was limited to 57 games and batted an embarrassing .197 with only 5 homers. Before last season, it was Hafner who would stand in the batter's box and wait for the pitcher to dare throw him a fastball (one of his favorite victims was Josh Beckett) and *unload* on it, driving it 500 feet out of the park. Hafner's absence was one of the main reasons the Indians underachieved so badly in 2008 and if he's not going to give them the power they need from the DH spot, they're going to have to find a bat to replace him. He's said to be feeling much better heading into the 2009 season, but the only way we'll know whether he's going to return to form is by him being healthy and hitting. We'll see. One thing he has going for him is that he can't possibly be any worse in 2009 than he was in 2008.

BENCH:

Kelly Shoppach was forced into duty behind the plate when Martinez got hurt and Shoppach delivered 21 homers and played his usual solid defense. Shoppach could get a chance to play more regularly if Martinez is healthy and hitting and Hafner isn't, the DH/ first base spot could be filled by Martinez and Ryan Garko as Shoppach catches relatively regularly.

Jamey Carroll is a solid utility player who can play any infield position. Carroll played a bit more regularly than he normally has in his career. He has little power and batted .277 in 113 games.

David Dellucci is a veteran outfielder with pop who plays solid outfield defense. Dellucci hit 11 homers in 113 games and only hits against right-handed pitchers. He literally put up the triple zero against lefties last season.

What happened to Josh Barfield? Barfield was a Rookie of the Year candidate for the Padres in the 2006 season and was traded to the Indians for a top hitting prospect in Kevin Kouzmanoff. He lost his starting job in the 2007 season to Cabrera and wound up in the minors for almost all of the 2008 season and he didn't hit all that well down there either. Barfield may need a fresh start elsewhere.

Luis Valbuena is a 23-year-old second baseman who was acquired from the Seattle Mariners and has shown some solid hitting ability in the minors. He batted .302 in Triple A Tacoma last season and has some speed.

Matt La Porta is a top power prospect who's put up big home run/on base numbers in the minors. He was the centerpiece of the trade of C.C. Sabathia and at age 23, it wouldn't be a surprise to see him make the club out of spring training especially if the parts of the lineup the Indians are going to need to hit for them to contend don't look like they're going to be able to live up to expectations, it's conceivable that they'll give La Porta a chance to play. My guess is that he'll start the season in Triple A, but he could be in the big leagues early if Hafner still isn't hitting.

PREDICTION:

The Indians have made a habit of making smart, under-the-radar moves with reasonable price tags and seeing them work out. The acquisitions of Wood and Smith shored up the bullpen; the starting rotation will be adequate if they get *something* from Pavano, or if he can just hold down a spot while the young pitchers are growing accustomed to the big leagues and Westbrook gets back. Lee isn't going to be as good as he was last season, but a healthy Carmona should account for however much Lee diminishes. The production of the lineup, especially Martinez and Hafner, is crucial to how far the Indians go in 2009. If they're not hitting, the Indians are going to have problems scoring runs and something's going to have to be done to fix that problem.

The AL Central is a weak division and the Indians are the best and most complete team of the bunch. Even if their hitting isn't up to snuff, they're still good enough to emerge from the division anyway. I expect the Indians to get a solid comeback season from Martinez and to get good production from DeRosa; Sizemore is a star and only getting better. The Indians are going to win the AL Central easily and lose to their old nemesis the Red Sox in the ALDS.

PREDICTED RECORD: 93-69

Minnesota Twins
2008 Record: 88-75; Second Place, American League Central

2008 Recap:

   Having lost Torii Hunter and Carlos Silva to free agency and having traded Johan Santana, the Twins were expected to fall back into mediocrity as they began reloading with young players in another retooling project. Surprisingly, the Twins were able to make it to a one-game playoff with the White Sox for the AL Central title before losing. The Twins young pitching led by Kevin Slowey, Scott Baker, Nick Blackburn and Glen Perkins; a deep bullpen; the fundamentals drilled in by manager Ron Gardenhire and all the way through the organization from top-to-bottom; and an unbelievable ability to hit in the clutch allowed the Twins to come within one game of making the playoffs despite the loss of the aforementioned veterans and stars.

2009 ADDITIONS: 3B Joe Crede signed a 1-year contract.
                  RHP Jason Jones was selected in the Rule 5 Draft from the New York Yankees.
                  RHP R.A. Dickey signed a minor league contract.
                  RHP Bob Keppel signed a minor league contract.
                  LHP Sean Henn signed a minor league contract.

2009 SUBTRACTIONS: SS Adam Everett was not re-signed.
                     LHP Dennys Reyes was not re-signed.
                     DH Randy Ruiz was released.
                     LHP Eddie Guardado was not re-signed.

2009 PROJECTED LINEUP: C-Joe Mauer; 1B-Justin Morneau; 2B-Alexi Casilla; SS-Nick Punto; 3B-Joe Crede; LF-Delmon Young; CF-Carlos Gomez; RF-Michael Cuddyer; DH-Jason Kubel

2009 PROJECTED STARTING ROTATION: Francisco Liriano; Scott Baker; Nick Blackburn; Kevin Slowey; Glen Perkins; Philip Humber

2009 PROJECTED BULLPEN: Joe Nathan; Jesse Crain; Matt Guerrier; Craig Breslow; Sean Henn; R.A. Dickey; Ricky Barrett

2009 BENCH: OF-Denard Span; C-Mike Redmond; INF-Brendan Harris; INF-Steven Tolleson; C-Jose Morales; INF-Brian Buscher; OF-Jason Pirdie; OF-Luis Matos; INF-Matt Tolbert

2009 EXTRA PITCHERS/PROSPECTS: Boof Bonser; Bob Keppel; Brian Duensing; Jose Mijares; Jason Jones; Ben Julianel; Mike Gosling; Pat Neshek; Blair Erickson; Jeff Manship; Anthony Slama

2009 EVERYDAY PROSPECTS: Luke Hughes; Brian Dinkelman; Chris Parmalee; Ben Revere

ASSESSMENTS:
MANAGEMENT:

GM Bill Smith got off to a bad start with his lower than expected return in the trade of Johan Santana. Time will tell if things work out well in the long term with the players they received in that trade. Smith, for some unfathomable reason, put in a waiver claim on Mariners lefty Jarrod Washburn based seemingly on Washburn having a couple of good months amid a mostly terrible last few seasons; and that Washburn is from Minnesota. Luckily for Smith, the Mariners—in an even *more* unfathomable move—pulled Washburn back rather than just give him to the Twins; of course Washburn got hurt later in the season. Smith did literally nothing to improve the club during the season unless you consider dumping the useless free agent Mike Lamb and the fading Livan Hernandez (who did provide innings and a few wins early in the season); Smith hasn't done anything during this off-season either. There was another odd rumor that the Twins wanted to basically re-do the trade of Jason Bartlett for Delmon Young and the Rays actually considered it before sanity prevailed. I question whether Smith is equipped to handle this job based on his actions so far, overachieving team or not.

Ron Gardenhire is one of the best and most unappreciated managers in all of baseball. The team plays a disciplined brand of baseball; their pitchers throw strikes; they field their positions well and are always where they're supposed to be. From the top of the organization on down, the correct way to play—the *Twins* way—is drilled into every player. Gardenhire learned his craft from former Twins manager Tom Kelly and was a more deserving candidate for Manager of the Year than the winner of the award, Rays manager Joe Maddon. No matter how disciplined the Twins are, Gardenhire had no business even coming close to making the playoffs with the group of young pitchers and the veteran stars he'd lost from his starting lineup. No matter the constitution of the Twins roster, they will always be competitive as long as Gardenhire is their manager.

STARTING PITCHING:

Francisco Liriano started the season in the majors after rehabbing from Tommy John surgery and was atrocious; he was sent back to the minors and after adjusting to the mechanical tweaks designed to take the stress off of his surgically repaired elbow, he began dominating Triple A; there was a bit of a controversy because Liriano and his agent claimed that the Twins were keeping Liriano in the minors long enough to prevent him from advancing his service time and becoming a free agent sooner. When they brought Liriano to the big leagues, he began regaining his form that made him so dominant during the 2006 season and he's expected to become their ace this season. Liriano has the ability to be a Cy Young contender if he's healthy with a power fastball and devastating slider.

Young righty Scott Baker went 11-4 in 28 starts with an excellent hits/innings pitched ratio of 161/172 and a 3.45 ERA; he gives up a lot of homers (20 last season), but so what as long as he does it without a lot of runners on base?

Nick Blackburn started the one-game playoff in Chicago and pitched very well under that high-pressure situation; the Twins were unable to score themselves and lost 1-0. Blackburn gave up a lot of hits and home runs (he's a contact pitcher), but his ERA was a reasonable 4.05 and he showed the potential to be a solid middle-of-the-rotation starter.

Kevin Slowey went 12-11 in 27 starts including 3 complete games. Slowey has excellent control and could be an excellent, innings-eating starter.

Glen Perkins racked up a 12-4 record despite a weak hits/innings pitched ratio of 183/151; he gave up 25 homers and got racked around to a .301 opposing average; but he found a way to win 12 of his 16 decisions and hung around in games long enough to keep the team competitive and win. Someone with the stats that Perkins posted may have won those games due to luck and if that's the case, his luck may run out very quickly.

Philip Humber was one of the pitchers acquired from the Mets in the Santana deal and he pitched similarly to the way he did in the Mets organization. At Triple A Rochester, Humber went 10-8 with a 4.56 ERA; he gave up a lot of homers. He averaged seven strikeouts per nine innings, which isn't bad considering his stuff is so mediocre. After watching him with the Mets, I saw little more than a back-of-the-rotation starter/long-man out of the bullpen at best and his record with the Twins indicated he hasn't evolved into much more than that. He's 26-years-old and his Tommy John surgery from a few years ago was considered part of the reason that his progress has slowed; I just don't think he's all that good.

BULLPEN:

Joe Nathan signed a long-term contract to stay with the Twins before last season and is still one of the best closers in baseball. He doesn't get the respect or accolades that his counterparts Mariano Rivera or Jonathan Papelbon do, but Nathan is in their class. He still racks up the strikeouts and saves and the game is in good hands when it's given over to Nathan.

Jesse Crain was a hard-throwing, promising reliever before he needed shoulder surgery and he returned last season to pitch reasonably well out of the bullpen. Crain posted a 3.59 ERA in 66 games out of the pen.

Matt Guerrier struggled last season with a 6-9 record and bloated 5.19 ERA in 76 games. Guerrier has been a workhorse, but he gave up 12 homers last season and his control wasn't all that great. With Pat Neshek out with Tommy John surgery, the Twins are going to need Guerrier to perform as he has in the past.

R.A. Dickey is a knuckleballer who had an up-and-down season with the Mariners in 2008; he could have some use as a long-man/spot-starter/innings eater out of the Twins bullpen.

Sean Henn was brought in to be a lefty out of the bullpen; he's never pitched particularly well in his opportunities with the Yankees, but the Twins have a habit of finding pitchers cheaply and squeezing some production out of them.

Lefty Craig Breslow pitched very well after joining the Twins from the Indians and has been murder on lefties in his career. Last season, lefties only hit .153 against Breslow and he didn't give up any homers and posted a 1.63 ERA after becoming a Twin.

Pat Neshek is a righty with a bizarre, submarine, whip style delivery who underwent Tommy John surgery. Neshek has been an imperative part of the Twins bullpen over the past few years and if he can return late in the season, he'll give the bullpen a boost.

LINEUP:

Joe Mauer might miss the beginning of the season after surgery for a kidney blockage. The Twins *must* have a healthy Mauer if they're going to be competitive at all. Never mind that he handles the pitching staff well behind the plate, but he's the only major threat in the Twins lineup other than Justin Morneau. Mauer was a viable MVP candidate last season as he hit .328; had a .413 OBP and drove in 85 runs. I've said before and still believe that Mauer is eventually going to learn to turn on inside pitches just as Don Mattingly did and hit more homers; if that happens, then he's going to put up massive—possibly triple crown—numbers.

Justin Morneau was also a MVP candidate as he drove in 128 runs. Morneau is putting together a Hall of Fame resume with his offensive stats. He signed a long-term contract to stay in Minnesota and, along with Mauer, is a guy around whom they can build their entire offense for the next ten years.

Alexi Casilla batted .281 in his first season as a full-time big leaguer. In 98 games, the 24-year-old Casilla showed future power potential with 7 homers and 50 RBI; as he gains strength and experience, his homer numbers should reach the mid-to-high double digits; and he's a switch hitter with some speed.

Oft-injured former White Sox third baseman Joe Crede signed a 1-year contract to fill the Twins gaping hole at the position. Crede has been completely unreliable due to back troubles over the past couple of years, but if he can play, he has good power and is a fine defender; he's a low-risk, high-reward gamble.

Nick Punto is an excellent defensive infielder who had a good offensive season with a .284 average in 99 games; he has no power and should share time at shortstop with Brendan Harris.

Delmon Young is getting a bad reputation around baseball as a difficult to handle personality. Young threw several tantrums with the Devil Rays organization and was traded to the Twins in the deal that sent Matt Garza and Jason Bartlett to Tampa. Twins manager Gardenhire was quoted as saying that Young was probably not going to be a starter in the 2009 season, something he later backtracked. Young is a former top draft pick who, it must be remembered, is still only 23-years-old and, once he matures, is going to be a superstar. His maturity is the key. Young only hit 10 homers last season and posted a .336 OBP, but he did hit .290 and has some speed. I'd hesitate before giving up Young if I were the Twins because he has All Star potential and if any organization can handle him, it's the Twins. I think he'll end up being in the lineup regularly.

Carlos Gomez is being feted as a defensive ace with amazing range because of his speed. Gomez's problem with the Mets was his impatience at the plate and it wasn't all that much better with the Twins. Eventually he's going to have to become more patient at the plate if he's going to fulfill that superstar potential. Gomez is 23 and has a quick bat and blazing speed to go along with his defensive brilliance. The Twins aren't a club that's obsessed with on base percentage above all else, but a .296 OBP isn't going to cut it. With some players, I'd say they'll learn to be a bit more selective, but that doesn't appear to be happening with Gomez and it *has* to happen for him to become the player he can be. As of right now, he's still a player who goes up to the plate with one intention: to hack away at the first pitch he sees.

Michael Cuddyer is saved from having to move back to third base with the signing of Crede. Cuddyer had an injury-shortened season in 2008, but is expected to be healthy for this season. He's got good power, gets on base frequently and is a solid all-around player.

Jason Kubel is the primary DH and was one of the few power threats in the Twins lineup. He hit 20 homers last season and 47 of his 126 hits were for extra bases.

BENCH:

Denard Span is a former first round pick who got a chance to play and batted .294 in 93 games; he stole 18 based and had a solid OBP at .387. He hit seven homers and if he's given a chance to play regularly, should hit his 15 homers and he's a good defensive outfielder.

Mike Redmond is a solid veteran backup catcher who has become a good hitter. The key with Redmond is that he's a pure backup who can hit, but is exposed if he's needed for more than 100-150 at bats and if Mauer is hurt, they're going to have to get by with Redmond and Jose Morales, who's a switch-hitter and has shown some hitting ability in the minors.

Brendan Harris is a utility infielder who could play shortstop and third base regularly in a pinch, but isn't really cut out to be an everyday player. Harris batted .265 in 130 games; he has some occasional pop as he hit seven homers last season, but he's a backup infielder who's more suited to rotate around the infield and get his 250-300 at bats.

Matt Tolbert is a switch-hitting backup infielder who batted .283 in 41 games last season; he has no power.

Brian Buscher is another infielder who saw substantial time at third base last season. He batted .316 against righties and probably shouldn't play much more than a bare minimum of, at most, 200 at bats.

Jason Pirdie is a power hitting minor leaguer who also came to the

Twins in the trade that brought Delmon Young. Pirdie could stick with the Twins as a part time DH/outfielder if he has a good spring.

PREDICTION:

The Twins had amazing success with runners in scoring position last season and that was a major reason that they stayed in contention until the day after the season ended and they lost in the one-game playoff. Their young pitching and attention to fundamentals will always keep the team competitive, but the lack of power and strangely comprised lineup is going to be a problem. There's no way for them to repeat that success with runners in scoring position that will diminish the Twins record from the 88 wins to something more in line with their talent level. They're in a weak division, but that's not going to prevent a fallback to around a .500 record. Gardenhire is a brilliant manager and the Twins are a study in what can be achieved by teaching players to do the right things and play the game correctly, but that's not going to save them this time.

PREDICTED RECORD: 82-80

Chicago White Sox
2008 Record: 89-74; First Place, American League Central
Lost to Tampa Bay Rays in ALDS 3 games to 1

2008 Recap:

The White Sox rebounded from their disappointing 2007 season, made some drastic and aggressive changes and won the American League Central division before losing to the Rays in the ALDS. As always, the White Sox rely on their starting pitching to go deeply into games and log 200+ innings and play an aggressive style of offense based on power, aggressiveness and speed. Gavin Floyd was an unheralded acquisition of GM Ken Williams and Floyd blossomed into an ace. Cuban refugee Alexei Ramirez showed superstar potential and impressive flair; and Carlos Quentin overcame the injury bug that had hindered his career with the Diamondbacks and became a MVP candidate with the White Sox. Veteran Jermaine Dye had an excellent comeback year.

2009 ADDITIONS: INF Jayson Nix signed a 1-year contract.
INF Wilson Betemit was acquired from the New York Yankees.
RHP Jeff Marquez was acquired from the New York Yankees.
RHP Jhonny Nunez was acquired from the New York Yankees.
RHP Kelvin Jimenez was claimed off waivers from the Toronto Blue Jays.
C Tyler Flowers was acquired from the Atlanta Braves.
INF Johnny Gilmore was acquired from the Atlanta Braves.
INF Brent Lillibridge was acquired from the Atlanta Braves.
LHP Santos Rodriguez was acquired from the Atlanta Braves.

RHP John Benschoten signed a minor league contract.
INF Dayan Viciedo signed a 4-year contract (Cuba).
INF Eider Torres signed a minor league contract.
RHP Bartolo Colon signed a 1-year contract.
OF Michael Restovich signed a minor league contract.
RHP Ryan Braun signed a minor league contract.
C-Corky Miller signed a minor league contract.

2009 SUBTRACTIONS: OF Ken Griffey Jr's option was declined.
C Toby Hall's option was declined.
OF/1B Nick Swisher was traded to the New York Yankees.
RHP Kanekoa Texeira was traded to the New York Yankees.
RHP Javier Vazquez was traded to the Atlanta Braves.
LHP Boone Logan was traded to the Atlanta Braves.
INF Juan Uribe was not re-signed.
3B Joe Crede was not re-signed.
SS Orlando Cabrera was not re-signed.

2009 PROJECTED LINEUP: C-A.J. Pierzynski; 1B-Paul Konerko; 2B-Chris Getz; 3B-Josh Fields; SS-Alexei Ramirez; LF-Carlos Quentin; CF-Jerry Owens; RF-Jermaine Dye; DH-Jim Thome

2009 PROJECTED STARTING ROTATION: Mark Buehrle; Gavin Floyd; John Danks; Bartolo Colon; Clayton Richard; Lance Broadway

2009 PROJECTED BULLPEN: Bobby Jenks; Octavio Dotel; Scott Linebrink; Matt Thornton; Ehren Wasserman; D.J. Carasco; Mike MacDougal

2009 BENCH: C-Corky Miller; INF-Jayson Nix; INF-Wilson Betemit; INF-Brent Lillibridge; OF-DeWayne Wise; OF-Brian Anderson; OF-Michael Restovich; INF-Dayan Viciendo; C-Donny Lucy

2009 EXTRA PITCHERS/PROSPECTS: Jose Contreras; Randy Williams; Kelvin Jimenez; Brad Salmon; John Benschoten; Ryan Braun; Andrew Sisco; Jon Link; Leroy Hunt; Anthony Carter; Levi Maxwell

2009 EVERYDAY PROSPECTS: David Cook; Brandon Allen; Tyler Flowers; Jon Gilmore

ASSESSMENTS:
MANAGEMENT:

Ken Williams is one of the best and most preemptively aggressive GMs in all of baseball. He has no interest in waiting for his player to either get hurt or begin to decline when he feels he can get longer term value if he trades them. Before last season, Williams, disgusted with the 72 win nightmare his 2005 World Series winner had degenerated into, made a series of deals that netted Nick Swisher, Carlos Quentin, Orlando Cabrera and Gavin Floyd; he signed Cuban refugee Alexei Ramirez and free agent relievers Octavio Dotel and Scott Linebrink. During the season, he fulfilled his longtime wish of acquiring Ken Griffey Jr.

Williams is patient with young players and his explosive manager, Ozzie Guillen. Other GMs would've fired Guillen years ago because of his penchant of insubordination and off-the-wall comments; but Williams sees that Guillen is a fine strategic manager who gets the players to play for him for the most part. Williams was again aggressive this past off season as he dealt away Javier Vazquez to the Braves for a top catching prospect in Tyler Flowers and an infield prospect Jon Gilmore. He brought back veteran starter Bartolo Colon and traded Swisher to the Yankees for infielder Wilson Betemit and two young pitching prospects one of whom, Jeffrey Marquez, who had fallen out of favor in the Yankees organization, but was once one of their top prospects.

The main thing that makes Williams a good GM, aside from his skills at recognizing talent (I don't know who, other than Williams, saw such great potential in Gavin Floyd), is his fearlessness. He simply does not care what anyone says about the way he runs his team; he makes the moves he feels need to be made to give his team the best chance to win and makes them regardless of the public perception. The White Sox may be in the middle of a slight tweaking as they incorporate some more youngsters into their lineup, but knowing Williams it won't be long before they're back in contention.

As far as controversy goes, this was a relatively tame year for manager Ozzie Guillen. Of course there was the incident in which he called out his GM demanding that a move be made to shore up the clubs flagging offense; and he basically laid the blame on their problem scoring runs at the feet of hitting coach Greg Walker; but other than that, Nuclear Ozzie was pretty quiet. There were neither back-and-forth battles with the press, nor confrontations with opposing players, coaches or managers. Guillen followed his usual strategy of pushing his starters over 200 innings and evenly doling out the innings for his relievers. He juggled the lineup as veterans Paul Konerko and Nick Swisher struggled and got production from a journeyman in DeWayne Wise. Guillen is always a threat to explode for no reason and eventually there will be a final explosion that forces Williams to fire him, but until then, he's a solid game manager who handles his clubhouse. The one advantage that he has is that the only way for a manager to last a very long time in one place without having his message ignored is if there's a consistent and drastic turnover in personnel and the White Sox are always bringing in new players on an annual basis; because of that, Guillen is able to maintain a similar style without the players tuning him out.

STARTING PITCHING:

Mark Buehrle is a durable, innings-eating starter who can be counted on to win his 15 games a year and log 220 innings. He's a contact pitcher who gives up a load of hits; doesn't seem to fool anyone with his mediocre left-handed stuff; and finds a way to win. He's not a prototypical ace, but at least a manager doesn't have to worry about him missing starts or asking to be taken out of games, and there's value in that.

Gavin Floyd came out of nowhere to win 17 games and showed the potential to be a dominant starter. How Ken Williams saw the ability in Floyd when he pitched so horribly in every chance he had in the big leagues with the Phillies is amazing. Add in that Floyd didn't pitch all that well in the minors and it's hard to know what it was that made Williams think that Floyd would develop as he did with the White Sox. Floyd not only pitched well enough to win 17 games, but every few starts, he looked like he was about to pitch a no-hitter. He gives up his share of homers, but he throws strikes and pitches deeply into games. There was talk that Williams was willing to trade Floyd after last season, but he's still with the White Sox. I'd be concerned that Williams wanted to trade him if I was an interested party, but it might've been a case that Williams didn't think he'd ever get a better season out of Floyd and wanted to sell high; but if Floyd's anywhere near as good as he was in 2008, he'll be a solid top of the rotation starter.

John Danks also developed into a gutty, solid starter. Acquired from the Rangers before the 2007 season for former top prospect Brandon McCarthy, the 24-year-old Danks went 12-9 with a 3.32 ERA. He pitched brilliantly in the one-game playoff against the Twins showing an ability to pitch in big games and he's expected to be a major factor in the White Sox rotation.

Bartolo Colon returns to the White Sox on a one-year deal after spending last season with the Red Sox. The 36-year-old Colon no longer throws the power fastball he once did, but he pitched reasonably well in seven starts for the Red Sox posting a 4-2 record and a 3.92 ERA and he also pitched well in nine starts at Triple A Pawtucket. He's been injury prone in recent years and has never exactly been a fitness fanatic; if he's able to provide 20+ starts for the White Sox and is effective enough to keep the team in games, they should be happy with that.

Jose Contreras is coming off a ruptured achilles tendon and wasn't pitching all that well before he got hurt.

Righty Lance Broadway is going to get a chance to win a spot in the starting rotation. He appeared in seven games with the White Sox last season, mostly in relief; and pitched to a high 4.66 ERA in 23 starts for Triple A Charlotte; he did win 11 of his 18 decisions in the minors.

Clayton Richard got knocked around in 13 appearances with the White Sox in 2008, but pitched well in the minors in both Double and Triple A. If I had to guess, I'd say it's Richard who wins the final spot in the White Sox rotation this year.

BULLPEN:

Bobby Jenks's name was tossed about in trade rumors in the off-season with the Mets interested, but the market was saturated with closers and it made no sense for Williams to settle for pennies on the dollar for a closer with the successful resume (especially in the post-season) as Jenks. Jenks saved 30 games and his strikeout numbers continue to decline, but just like last year, that seems to be a matter of design. Jenks's fastball is still in the mid-to-upper nineties and is only about to turn 28. That being said, I still think it's possible that Williams will deal Jenks if the right offer comes along.

Octavio Dotel had a solid enough comeback year while still giving up the occasional longball (12 in 72 games is a lot for a short reliever), but Dotel was effective for the most part and he struck out 92 in 67 innings. One thing that should be a concern with Dotel is that he's got such a checkered history of injuries and he was healthy last season, so 2009 might be a year in which he misses a chunk of time due to injury.

Scott Linebrink was the other late inning reliever that Williams signed to shore up the bullpen and he appeared in 50 games for the White Sox, pitching reasonably well. He missed time with a sore shoulder, but as a veteran reliever Linebrink comes into games and throws strikes while continuing his penchant for giving up home runs with eight in those 50 games.

D.J. Carrasco appeared in 31 games in relief, pitching 39 innings and posting a 3.96 ERA.

Ehren Wasserman got knocked around pretty good with an opposing batting average of .333 in 24 games, but interestingly, he didn't give up any homers in the majors and his minor league relief numbers are fantastic which could be an indicator that he'll be an effective reliever in the majors.

Lefty Matt Thornton had a fine year appearing in 74 games with a 2.67 ERA and 77 strikeouts in 68 innings; he's a veteran who should be able to perform somewhat similarly in 2009.

Mike MacDougal throws nearly 100 mph and pitched well in 16 games with the White Sox, and spent a chunk of the season in the minors.

LINEUP:

A.J. Pierzynski's replacement is now in the organization with the trade for catching prospect Tyler Flowers. Pierzynski had his usual offensive numbers with a .281 average and 13 homers; plus he handled the pitching staff and was an obnoxious pest with the opponents as he always is. Depending on how the White Sox season goes, it wouldn't be surprising to see Pierzynski offered up in trades to a catcher hungry team. If Jorge Posada can't come back and catch, or if Jason Varitek doesn't hit any better than he did last season, the Yankees and Red Sox could be vying for Pierzynski's services as the season moves along.

Paul Konerko had a terrible year at the plate and was the subject of trade rumors before and during the season. Konerko had to share time with the equally struggling Nick Swisher and a second half hot streak allowed Konerko's numbers to look respectable with 22 homers and 62 RBI, but the White Sox can't afford to have Konerko have another bad start as he did last year.

The White Sox are moving last season's regular second baseman Alexei Ramirez to shortstop and have a large cast to try to win the second base job for 2009. Prospect Chris Getz had an excellent year at Triple A with a .302 average, 11 homers and 52 RBI; he also only made 3 errors in 62 games at second base. The other candidates are the newly acquired former Braves top infield prospect Brent Lillibridge and newly signed Jayson Nix.

Josh Fields was the semi-regular third baseman in 2007 and hit 23 homers. Last season, when Joe Crede began the season healthy, Fields was relegated to the minors and struggled; he seemed to be affected by having the job taken away from him after performing well the previous year. Manager Guillen called out Fields in what looked like an attempt to motivate him. When Crede got hurt again, Fields wasn't the one to take his place, but veteran Juan Uribe was. The job should be Fields's to lose this season since both Crede and Uribe are gone.

Orlando Cabrera was not re-signed and the young Cuban Alexei Ramirez is going to get the chance to play shortstop. Ramirez showed a flair and wiry power similar to Alfonso Soriano in his first year in the big leagues. Ramirez batted .290 with 21 homers and 77 RBI including a grand slam in an imperative game against the Tigers that forced the one game playoff against the Twins. Ramirez has star potential, but he needs some discipline at the plate (he had a .317 OBP) and on the bases (he stole 13 bases in 22 attempts). I think Ramirez is going to be a perennial All Star and put up big offensive numbers.

Carlos Quentin's broken wrist possibly cost him the American League MVP. Much like the scouting brilliance Williams showed with Floyd, Quentin joined the White Sox and instead of being the injury-prone underachiever he was with the Diamondbacks, he blossomed into a star with the White Sox bashing 36 homers, driving in 100 and posting a .394 OBP with 63 extra base hits in 130 games. Given his history, there's always the chance that Quentin will again be injury-prone and miss substantial time, but he began fulfilling his massive potential last season which proves he can do it if he can stay out on the field.

Jerry Owens was left out in the cold as the White Sox first brought in Nick Swisher in the off-season and Ken Griffey Jr in-season. Owens has speed and can catch the ball in the outfield and with both Swisher and Griffey gone, he's likely to be the man in center field. Owens struggles when in the big leagues and was mediocre in Triple A. He's 28-years-old and if he doesn't take advantage of this possible chance to play regularly, it could be his last chance.

Jermaine Dye was the subject of trade rumors to such destinations as the Reds, Braves or Mets but he's still with the White Sox. Dye's contract has a mutual option with the club for 2010 and he's not young anymore at age 35. He had a fantastic offensive year in 2008 with 34 homers and 77 extra base hits; he's well-liked in the clubhouse and has history of playing well in the post-season. If the White Sox decide to start dealing some veterans, they'll be able to get some decent return on Dye.

Jim Thome is still the two-fisted basher he's always been. He got off to a terrible start, but wound up with his usual 34 homers. His on base numbers dropped to .362 (he's usually up around .400); and he is going to be 38 late in the season. Thome could be trade bait as well as the season moves along and someone needs a DH who can hit the ball out of the park and has an expiring contract. I suggested last season that Thome would be a good fit for the Angels, and he still would be.

BENCH:

Whichever second baseman doesn't win the job should be a backup infielder. Jayson Nix had a terrible season with the Rockies, but put up excellent numbers in Colorado Springs, the Rockies Triple A affiliate. This could be his final shot before being relegated as a guy who hits and plays well at Triple A, but can't make it in the majors.

Brent Lillibridge was once a hot prospect for the Braves, but he was atrocious in Triple A Richmond and in Atlanta. Again, this could be a brilliant salvage job for Williams if he can rehabilitate Lillibridge.

Veteran journeyman DeWayne Wise got a chance to play late in the season and in the playoffs because of the struggles of Swisher and Griffey and delivered some big hits. He's a backup outfielder, but a guy who's always ready to play and can hit and play defense he has great value, journeyman or not.

Corky Miller was a backup catcher with the Braves last season; he rarely played and didn't hit at all when he did.

Brian Anderson is a defensive specialist in the outfield and showed some pop with eight homers in just under 200 plate appearances last season. He's not a very productive hitter overall.

Veteran utility infielder Wilson Betemit was acquired from the Yankees in the trade that sent Swisher to New York. Betemit showed some pop earlier in his career with the Braves, but has been nothing special since then. He did almost nothing in his time with the Yankees and presumably, Betemit will replace the departed Juan Uribe as the backup who can play every infield position.

Dayan Viciedo is another Cuban defector who signed a long-term contract with the White Sox; he's an infielder with some pop in his bat. If they can get anything close to what they got from Ramirez, Viciedo will be a great find, but just like the players from the Far East, no one can know what they're going to get out of a Cuban defector until he performs in the big leagues one way or the other.

PREDICTION:

The White Sox appear to be in the middle of a retooling in which they're trying to incorporate some youngsters in the lineup and are ready to start moving forward from the remaining veterans from their 2005 championship season. Williams is always ready to deal and unless the White Sox get off to a good start and the AL Central appears winnable, I'd expect the veterans to be dangled to contending teams. Dye, Konerko, Jenks, Pierzynski and Thome are presumably all available and it will depend on the White Sox position in the standings at around mid-season before Williams decides what to do.

I expect the White Sox starting rotation to be about as effective as they were last season (although Floyd could take a fallback); the bullpen is solid enough and they'll score their share of runs especially if Quentin can come close to repeating last season and Ramirez develops, but they've got some major holes if their young second baseman and third baseman don't deliver. They'll be a respectable team and possibly hang around the outskirts of contention past the All Star break, but they'll fall out of the race and I expect Williams to start making some blockbuster trades to re-stock the organization even further.

PREDICTED RECORD: 81-81

Detroit Tigers
2008 Record: 74-88; Fifth Place, American League Central

2008 Recap:

After an off-season in which they brought in one big name after another, were widely expected to romp over their competition in their division and contend for the World Series, everything that could've gone wrong for the Tigers did go wrong. The vaunted starting rotation was hideous; Justin Verlander's velocity dropped from its previous highs of the upper 90s and he had a terrible season; Jeremy Bonderman's elbow injury limited him to 12 starts; Kenny Rogers finally began to show his age; Nate Robertson was awful; and Dontrelle Willis couldn't throw strikes and wound up back in the minors. The bullpen was almost as bad with closer Todd Jones pitching terribly and losing his job to Fernando Rodney, who wasn't all that good either. Joel Zumaya missed a chunk of the season as he tried to overcome the injuries that are making his 102 mph fastballs from the 2006 playoffs seem like a distant memory relegated to difficult to believe folklore.

The offense was constantly in flux due to the repeated and overzealous position changes made by manager Jim Leyland. Both Gary Sheffield and Ivan Rodriguez looked ready for retirement; Edgar Renteria was slow in the field and unproductive at the plate; and the vaunted offense which was supposed to be a run-scoring machine, turned out to be slow and apathetic. All of these factors transformed the team from a pre-season favorite into a 74-88, last place laughingstock who instead of contending for a world championship, contended for the moniker of the worst team money could buy.

2009 ADDITIONS: C Gerald Laird was acquired from the Texas Rangers. RHP Edwin Jackson was acquired from the Tampa Bay Rays. SS Adam Everett signed a 1-year contract. RHP Brandon Lyon signed a 1-year contract.

LHP Kyle Bloom was selected in the Rule 5 draft from the Pittsburgh Pirates.

C Matt Treanor signed a 1-year contract.

INF Don Kelly signed a minor league contract.

OF Alexis Gomez signed a minor league contract.

RHP Scott Williamson signed a minor league contract.

RHP Juan Rincon signed a minor league contract.

2009 SUBTRACTIONS: SS Edgar Renteria's option was declined.

RHP Guillermo Moscoso was traded to the Texas Rangers.

RHP Carlos Melo was traded to the Texas Rangers.

OF Matt Joyce was traded to the Tampa Bay Rays.

RHP Aquilino Lopez was non-tendered.

RHP Todd Jones retired.

LHP Kenny Rogers was not re-signed.

C Vance Wilson was not re-signed.

RHP Kyle Farnsworth was not re-signed.

RHP Gary Glover was not re-signed.

RHP Freddy Garcia was not re-signed.

2009 PROJECTED LINEUP: C-Gerald Laird; 1B-Miguel Cabrera; 2B-Placido Polanco; 3B-Brandon Inge; SS-Adam Everett; LF-Carlos Guillen; CF-Curtis Granderson; RF-Magglio Ordonez; DH-Gary Sheffield

2009 PROJECTED STARTING ROTATION: Justin Verlander; Jeremy Bonderman; Armando Galarraga; Edwin Jackson; Dontrelle Willis; Nate Robertson

2009 PROJECTED BULLPEN: Brandon Lyon; Fernando Rodney; Joel Zumaya; Scott Williamson; Freddy Dolsi; Bobby Seay; Macay McBride; Juan Rincon

2009 BENCH: C-Matt Treanor; OF-Marcus Thames; OF-Jeff Larish; OF-Clete Thomas; 1B-Mike Hessman; INF-Ryan Raburn; INF-Ramon Santiago

2009 EXTRA PITCHERS/PROSPECTS: Fu-Te Ni; Kyle Bloom; Casey Fien; Clay Rapada; Chris Lambert; Zach Miner; Alfredo Figaro; Jon Kibler; Rick Porcello

2009 EVERYDAY PROSPECTS: Maxwell Leon; Wilkin Ramirez; Casper Wells

ASSESSMENTS:
MANAGEMENT:

GM Dave Dombrowski had put together what was widely perceived as an unbeatable combination of pitching and power; he had a respected veteran manager and despite the fact that the entire farm system had been decimated by the trades for veterans Edgar Renteria, Miguel Cabrera and Dontrelle Willis, but had those veterans had the years their careers indicated they would, things would've been all right; instead the team got off to an atrocious start and combined with the injuries, things came apart almost before the season started. Dombrowski is a solid baseball man with an eye for talent and there was no way to predict everything that went wrong even in a Tigers fan's worst nightmare.

In the off-season, he took steps to fix the problems of defense and bullpen depth. The signings of catcher Gerald Laird and shortstop Adam Everett added two defensive aces; the bullpen now has veteran Brandon Lyon, but the question has to be asked if they're much better than they were last season even with the new faces. Dombrowski knows how bad things were last season and with the manager Jim Leyland's contract up after this season, there's the potential for an even worse disaster than the 88 losses in 2008. Dombrowski isn't going to waste any time this year; if things begin as poorly as they did last season, I'd expect him to act quickly and start putting some veterans on the market and try to reinvigorate the destitute farm system. We'll know by mid-May which direction Dombrowski's going to head.

Manager Jim Leyland has never been one to hide his emotions, positively or negatively. The Tigers were playing terribly in every aspect when Leyland began moving his players all over the place. Miguel Cabrera started at third base and was moved to first; Carlos Guillen was the first basemen; then became the third baseman; and then the left fielder. Brandon Inge, one of the best defensive third basemen in baseball, was relegated to a utility role and then moved back to his original position of catcher when the unproductive Ivan Rodriguez was traded. The starting rotation was a mess and the bullpen was hideous.

Much of that isn't Leyland's fault, but there was a panicky aspect to Leyland's maneuvers that couldn't have helped the players relax and actually believe that things were going to turn out okay. Leyland's contract is up at the end of the season and he's not happy about not getting an extension; he and Dombrowski have a love/hate relationship going back to their days as the GM/manager with the Marlins. Leyland had the upper hand then because of his relationship with then-Marlins owner Wayne Huizenga; that is no longer the case in Detroit with owner Mike Ilich and if someone goes, it's going to be Leyland. If the Tigers get off to a bad start, Leyland's going to get fired for the first time in his big league managerial career.

STARTING PITCHING:

Is there something physically wrong with Justin Verlander or is it just a matter of his mechanics being out of whack? His fastball lost 5-7 mph in velocity for a reason and his stuff was diminished as well. Verlander was horrible last year with an 11-17 record and a 4.84 ERA. He should be better with an improved defense behind him and a defensive-minded catcher, but there's going to be the question of his velocity if new pitching coach Rick Knapp can help straighten him out. The Tigers *must* have a solid season out of Verlander if they're going to return to contention.

Where would the Tigers have been last season without the solid 13-win season out of longtime minor leaguer Armando Galarraga? Galarraga was a lifesaver with a 13-7 record and an excellent hits/innings-pitched ratio of 152/179. Given the kind of career that Galarraga's had, it's hard to imagine him sneaking up on anyone in 2009, but if he can win 12 games and pitch close to as well as he did last season, the Tigers should be satisfied with that.

Jeremy Bonderman only started 12 games due to elbow problems and he wasn't pitching all that well when he got hurt. Bonderman's a contact pitcher who should also benefit from the Tigers improved defense if he's healthy.

Edwin Jackson was acquired from the Tampa Bay Rays after having a breakout 14-win season. Jackson throws close to 100 mph, but never strikes anyone out; last season could've been seen as benefiting from having a better team with a better defense behind him, but it could also have been a career-year. Jackson was terrible before last season although he's still very young at 25.

Dontrelle Willis is said to have lost weight from last season and it will be up to new pitching coach Knapp to try and unravel Willis's complicated, herky-jerky windup and put it back together so the Tigers get the charismatic, innings-eating ace that Willis was in Florida, and not the guy who couldn't throw strikes and when he did, gave up towering home runs. Willis has to straighten himself out because he signed a lucrative contract with the Tigers and if he can't throw strikes, he could be the next in a long line of pitchers like Rick Ankiel and Adam Loewen to move from the mound to the outfield. His problems appeared mechanical and psychological instead of physical.

Nate Robertson pitched about as poorly as a big league pitcher can pitch. The lefty had a 7-11 record with a 6.28 ERA and a horrible hits/innings-pitched ratio of 218/169, and allowed a whopping 26 homers. I'd consider using him out of the bullpen as a set-up man or even the closer if none of the current possibilities in those roles pan out.

BULLPEN:

Hard throwing veteran Brandon Lyon signed a one-year contract to compete to be the Tigers closer. Lyon throws strikes, but gives up a *lot* of home runs (7 last season) and a *lot* of hits (75 in 59 innings) with the Diamondbacks last season as their closer. The Diamondbacks defense wasn't very good and a contact pitcher like Lyon should benefit from the Tigers improved defense as long as he keeps the ball in the park. I'd expect Lyon to win the closer's job.

Fernando Rodney is another hard thrower who took over as the closer for Todd Jones last season and saved 13 games. Rodney can be wild and has been given the chance to be a closer before and hasn't been able to handle the job over the long term because of injury and ineffectiveness.

Who knows what's going to happen with Joel Zumaya? The Tigers are saying that he's going to be healthy, but he hasn't been healthy since his coming out party in 2006. I said last year that Zumaya might end up being a guy who's discussed on barstools in reverential tones about what he did to the likes of Alex Rodriguez in the 2006 ALDS, but is never able to put it together over a full season. I wouldn't expect anything out of Zumaya and be happy if he's able to pitch.

Injury-prone veteran Scott Williamson was signed to a minor league contract; Williamson has been very good when he's been healthy, but this is a pitcher who's had Tommy John surgery twice and pitches with a stressful overhand motion. If I had to guess, I'd say Williamson gets hurt either in spring training or very early in the season and retires.

Freddy Dolsi has an impressive fastball and posted a 3.97 ERA in 42 games in relief.

Bobby Seay appeared in 60 games as a situational lefty (he got knocked around to the tune of a .303 average *by* lefties), and struck out 58 in 56 innings.

Juan Rincon appeared in 47 games for the Twins and Indians last season and got pounded. He's been a solid and very durable reliever in his career and perhaps he can rebound.

Zach Miner pitched reasonably well in 45 apperances (13 starts); Miner is a contact pitcher who allowed 118 hits in 118 innings and 10 homers. He could be a starter depending on the health and/or effectiveness of Bonderman/Willis/Robertson.

LINEUP:

Gerald Laird is a defensively minded catcher who takes over for the combination of the over-the-hill veteran Ivan Rodriguez and Brandon Inge. Laird was playing in the hitter's paradise of Rangers Ballpark in Arlington and never put up even decent offensive numbers, so I wouldn't expect him to hit at all. If the rest of the Tigers lineup hits, it won't matter how productive Laird is at the plate as long as he handles the pitching staff.

Miguel Cabrera is an offensive machine who's been moved to first base (permanently at least until the DH spot opens up); Cabrera seems to have been around forever even though he's only 26; every year the power numbers are going to go up on the board with 35+ homers; 120+ RBI; a .300 batting average; and a high on base percentage. Cabrera should be an annual MVP candidate as long as he keeps his focus.

Placido Polanco has become a consistent .300 hitter with a little pop and solid defense at second base. Polanco had 178 hits of which 45 were for extra bases. He's also 33-years-old, so he could possibly begin declining in his production starting soon.

Brandon Inge had asked to be traded before the 2008 season started when it looked like there was no room for him to get his at bats; but injuries and unproductiveness got Inge back into the lineup and he surprisingly found himself back behind the plate after Rodriguez was dumped. Inge is an excellent fielding third baseman and has the power to hit his 20+ homers if he gets a chance to play. His .205 batting average probably owed itself more to the way he was bounced around and in and out of the starting lineup. He should be closer to normalcy this season playing third base every day.

Adam Everett is one of the best defensive shortstops in baseball, but he's a black hole in the lineup. With Everett and Laird, that's two outs in the lineup that the Tigers have to deal with and carry. Edgar Renteria's range was non-existent last season, so with Inge and Everett patrolling the left side of the infield, the pitching should improve, but his bat is going to be a problem.

Carlos Guillen started the season at first base, moved to third base and finally to left field. Guillen missed a chunk of time with injuries, but he can still hit at age 33. He batted .286 with 10 homers and a .376 OBP; if things go badly for the Tigers, Guillen could be trade bait.

Curtis Granderson is blossoming into a five-tool star who can literally do everything on the baseball field and has intelligence, a great attitude and personality off the field. Granderson reached double digits in doubles, triples, homers and stolen bases and can play great defense. He's 28 and a player for the Tigers to build their future around.

Magglio Ordonez couldn't have been as great as he was the previous couple of years, but he was still plenty good with a .317 batting average, 21 homers and 103 RBI. Ordonez is 35 and like Guillen, if things go badly for the Tigers, he could be traded to a contender who needs a corner outfield bat like the Mets or Red Sox.

Gary Sheffield had a terrible year at the plate due to injuries and he invited the ire of manager Leyland by essentially calling him a liar when Sheffield claimed he was told that he'd get a chance to play some outfield. Leyland insisted that Sheffield understood when the Tigers acquired him and extended his contract that he was going to be a DH. The Tigers would love to get out from under Sheffield's salary, but unless he proves he can still hit, he's not going anywhere. He did have 19 homers in 114 games, so he can still provide some pop. As the season moves along, Sheffield could be traded because as a veteran down the stretch run, a contending team could use him if he looks like he has anything left. An unhappy Sheffield can cause problems.

BENCH:

Outfielder Marcus Thames forced his way into the lineup by getting into streaks of hitting a lot of home runs. Thames can crush a fastball and had 25 homers in 103 games; he goes up to the plate hacking, but his power and that quick bat makes him worth keeping around.

Catcher Matt Treanor was signed to share the duties with Laird. Treanor's a journeyman who can't really hit.

Veteran minor league power hitter Mike Hessman hit 5 homers in 12 games with the Tigers last season, but he's a guy who can take Triple A pitching deep consistently and hasn't ever gotten a chance to play in the big leagues. He'd hit 20-25 homers if he got a chance to play in the majors.

Backup middle infielder Ramon Santiago batted .282 in 58 games and had an excellent .411 OBP.

Clete Thomas batted .368 against lefties last season and is a solid defensive outfielder.

Jeff Larish batted .260 in 42 games.

Backup infielder Ryan Raburn batted .236 in 92 games and had four homers.

PREDICTION:

I'm somewhat torn with the Tigers. Last year, I had a similar ominous feeling about the San Diego Padres that they were going to collapse and be as bad as they ended up being (this isn't revisionist history, it's true); but I was listening to outside voices saying that the Padres were going to contend; I knew it wasn't the case, but hedged my bets and predicted that they'd finish with a record of 79-83, bad, but not 63-99 bad. I'm getting a similar vibe from these Tigers and am tempted to have them lose nearly 100 games, but considering their division and all the factors, I'll make the following predictions.

In a best case scenario, the situation is going to stabilize for the Tigers due to their improved defense and that their pitching can't possibly be as bad as it was last season. Jim Leyland's contract issue has to be watched closely because if the team gets off to a good start, he's going to want a contract extension; if the team gets off to a bad start, he's going to want a contract extension so he won't be a lame duck and lose his authority in the clubhouse as the players play out the string waiting to get traded. Bottom line, if the Tigers get off to a bad start, the contentious relationship with Dombrowski is going to come to a head and Leyland's going to get fired.

The key to the season is how the Tigers play at the start, and I'd push them to have a solid spring training to get the thought into their minds that the hellish 2008 season is completely behind them and was an accident of circumstance than a signal that the Tigers are going to have to start a rebuilding project. There are so many question marks that it's going to be hard for them to contend even if the starters and guys like Sheffield and Inge rebound. If the starters pitch well and the bats turn things around, the bullpen is so bad that they're going to blow a bunch of games the Tigers should win.

I expect the Tigers to continue playing similarly to how they did last season and I believe that Leyland is going to get fired early in the season; after that, aside from Granderson and possibly Cabrera, no one will be safe from the possibility of being traded. The Tigers are going to have to replenish that empty farm system and if Ordonez, Guillen and the other veterans can facilitate that, then Dombrowski's smart enough to know when things are too far gone to turn around and start cleaning house.

This team is different from the 2008 version, but unless they get better pitching, then what good is the improved defense? If their only consistent, power bats are Cabrera, Granderson and Ordonez, are they actually any better? I don't think they are. The Tigers are going to have a bad year that could wind up with a loss total in the mid-90s if things go completely wrong; I don't think that's going to happen, but at this point, what's the difference between 86 losses and 96?

PREDICTED RECORD: 76-86

Kansas City Royals
2008 Record: 75-87; Fourth Place, American League Central

2008 Recap:

    The Royals were well on their way to another near 100-loss season as their inability to score runs sabotaged any improvement in pitching they've made in recent years, but they played solid baseball over the last couple of months to climb out of the cellar in the AL Central and finish ahead of the expensive and star-laden Tigers.

    New manager Trey Hillman had brought an enthusiasm and history of talent evaluation and success with him, but it didn't translate onto the field early in the season. The Royals got solid performances from starters Gil Meche and Zack Greinke; gained some valuable experience for former top picks Luke Hochevar and Alex Gordon; and had an excellent bullpen. Climbing out of last place and developing some young players pointed things in a positive direction despite a season that ended with a 75-87 record.

2009 ADDITIONS: 1B Mike Jacobs was acquired from the Florida Marlins.
OF Coco Crisp was acquired from the Boston Red Sox.
RHP Kyle Farnsworth signed a 2-year contract.
INF Willie Bloomquist signed a 2-year contract.
RHP Doug Waechter signed a 1-year contract.
OF Jordan Parraz was acquired from the Houston Astros.
LHP Jose Lugo was selected in the Rule 5 Draft from the Minnesota Twins.
LHP Heath Phillips signed a minor league contract.
LHP Lenny DiNardo signed a minor league contract.
RHP Oscar Villareal signed a minor league contract.
OF Tommy Murphy signed a minor league contract.

2009 SUBTRACTIONS: RHP Kip Wells was released. RHP Leo Nunez was traded to the Florida Marlins. RHP Ramon Ramirez was traded to the Boston Red Sox. RHP Ryan Braun was released. LHP Tyler Lumsden was traded to the Houston Astros. 2B Mark Grudzielanek was not re-signed. LHP Jose Lugo was traded to the Seattle Mariners. OF Joey Gathright was non-tendered. INF Jason Smith was non-tendered.

2009 PROJECTED LINEUP: C-John Buck; 1B-Mike Jacobs; 2B-Alberto Callaspo; 3B-Alex Gordon; SS-Mike Aviles; LF-David DeJesus; CF-Coco Crisp; RF-Jose Guillen; DH-Billy Butler

2009 PROJECTED STARTING ROTATION: Gil Meche; Zack Greinke; Kyle Davies; Luke Hochevar; Brian Bannister; Horacio Ramirez; Mike Maroth

2009 PROJECTED BULLPEN: Joakim Soria; Kyle Farnsworth; Ron Mahay; Doug Waechter; Oscar Villareal; Lenny DiNardo; Robinson Tejeda; John Bale; Jimmy Gobble

2009 BENCH: C-Miguel Olivo; INF-Willie Bloomquist; INF/OF/DH-Mark Teahen; 1B-Ryan Shealy; INF-Tony Pena, Jr.; 1B/OF-Ross Gload; INF-Esteban German; OF-Mitch Maier; 1B/DH-Kila Ka'aihue

2009 EXTRA PITCHERS/PROSPECTS: Robinson Tejeda; Franquelis Osoria; Joel Peralta; Jairo Cuevas; Brandon Duckworth; Tim Hamulack; Daniel Cortes; Henry Barrera; Juan Abreu; Danny Duffy; Danny Gutierrez

2009 EVERYDAY PROSPECTS: Joshua Johnson; Cody Strait

ASSESSMENTS:
MANAGEMENT:

Here's the difference between someone like me who's able to take the available information and all of its aspects and come to a conclusion and the difference between those that are so invested in stats and the *Moneyball* concept and won't admit when one of their brethren doesn't know what he's doing based in practice and steadfastly refuses to own up to it based on their attachment to the theory and the idea that if they allow the idea that the numbers don't always fit, they'll be confessing that the numbers don't automatically work out.

I was an ardent supporter of Dayton Moore when he took over as Royals GM. I liked what he was doing. He was bringing in young players and veterans who could help the young players grow; he re-did the scouting staff; brought in a younger and hipper manager and did many positive things to imply that there was a new day dawning in Kansas City; but Moore's gone so far off the path that there's no longer any way to defend what he's doing.

With the *Moneyball* advocates, there are inexplicably still those that will defend former Dodgers GM and soon-to-be former Padres assistant GM Paul DePodesta and insist that he has the aptitude to be a successful big league executive. Facts, which are supposed to be the lifeblood of the theory don't enter in the equation. DePodesta believes what they believe; he has the numbers to back up whatever he does; so it doesn't matter that the teams he's been involved with since leaving the safety of nuzzling at Billy Beane's teat haven't just been bad, they've been atrocious. They've been run arrogantly and cruelly; they've treated the players like chattel and deserved everything they've begotten on the field; but you'd never know it from the stat-geeks who so obsessively pore over numbers as if the building of a team is only a matter of plugging the right numbers into a computer, but it hasn't worked and as long as they continue to tout DePodesta as a possible GM candidate, they're never going to have any credibility. I don't expect that to change—ever.

Moore made some moves this winter that can only be described as inexplicable. Trading two valuable relievers and depleting what had been one of the Royals few strengths in the bullpen for journeymen like Mike Jacobs and Coco Crisp? Signing Kyle Farnsworth, Willie Bloomquist and Horacio Ramirez to 2-year contracts? Not making the conscious decision to give Kila Ka'aihue a chance to play at first base or as the DH despite his offensive numbers in the minors?

There is no explanation for what Moore's done in terms of player moves; this team had appeared as if they were on the slow climb into respectability, but they're now looking like an expansion team and if these are the kinds of moves that Moore is going to be making, I question how much longer he's going to have as the GM of a big league team.

Trey Hillman came in with a sterling pedigree. He'd managed a championship team in Japan; he ran an organization's minor league system in Texas; he's managed in the minors; and he's scouted. His game management skills in his first year in the majors showed some inexperience and aspects that need improvement. What was the purpose of playing Ross Gload at first base instead of bringing up Ka'aihue to see what he could do? How is the team going to get any better as long as veterans like the departed Joey Gathright were playing as often as they were at the expense of building for the future and looking at younger players? The Royals are in flux right now. They've brought in veterans they didn't need and if things are still static and they accrue a win total in the mid-70s, there's a chance that both Moore and Hillman will be shown the door for another management team and it'll be hard to argue with the move.

STARTING PITCHING:

Gil Meche has turned out to be a brilliant signing for Moore. Meche has been an anchor at the top of the rotation who in his two years with the Royals would have won around 16-18 games in each year if he'd had a better team behind him. Having pitched over 200 innings each season with the club, Meche, whose contract was ridiculed when he signed it, has earned every penny. The one thing to be concerned about with Meche is that he had several injury-interrupted seasons with the Mariners and he's been so healthy over the past two seasons with the Royals, it might be a bit much to expect him to have another 200+ inning season. He's due to miss some time due to injury and possibly fall back in his performance, especially with the bullpen depleted as it's been in the deals Moore made to beef up the offense.

Moore was given credit for signing young Zack Greinke to a long-term contract after the months of dismay he inspired with his bizarre trades and free agent signings. I don't see why Moore should receive credit for making such an obvious decision to lock up Greinke. Greinke pitched very well in the 2008 season with a 13-10 record in 32 starts and excellent stats across the board. At age 25, Greinke poised to be a top-of-the rotation starter for a long time.

Kyle Davies finally began to develop into the pitcher the Braves thought they had for years. Davies went 9-7 in 2008 and pitched respectably in 21 starts after being brilliant at Triple A Omaha. The Royals defense may be a bit porous with Mike Jacobs at first base and whichever of the group of journeymen they have vying for second base. Davies is also likely to see much of his good work going to waste because of that decimated bullpen.

Luke Hochevar has brilliant stuff and reminds me of Roy Halladay. Hochevar has star potential even though he struggled in his first big league season. Hochevar went 6-12 and gave up a lot of hits and homers. It was a learning process for the future Cy Young contender and Hochevar is going to learn to pitch in the big leagues sooner rather than later and blossom into a star, possibly as soon as this season.

Brian Bannister got off to a blazing hot start last season and was making the Mets look foolish for trading him after the 2006 season. Bannister was an innings-eating, consistent starter in 2007 which led me to begin questioning my own eyes which told me that he was a mediocre journeyman who was lucky to be in the big leagues. He was wild with an average fastball, slider and shaky mechanics. With every zero that went up on the board, Bannister accumulated more and more fans…then reality set in. Bannister got rocked all over every ballpark after that quick start and was atrocious. Bannister went 9-16, allowed a huge number of hits; gave up 29 homers; and was terrible. If he manages to stay in the rotation all season, it'll only be because of the pitchers who are also vying for the slot in the rotation since Horacio Ramirez and Mike Maroth might actually be worse than Bannister.

For some unfathomable reason, not only did Moore pay Horacio Ramirez to remain with the Royals, but he gave him a 2-year contract for nearly $2 million. Ramirez can't pitch, bottom line, and if the Royals need him as anything more than a veteran long man out of the bullpen (or a mop-up man), then Moore had better start getting his resume ready.

BULLPEN:

The Royals had a solid bullpen last season with closer Joakim Soria and set-up men Leo Nunez and Ramon Ramirez. Both Nunez (traded to the Marlins for Mike Jacobs) and Ramirez (traded to the Red Sox for Coco Crisp) are gone; and Soria is going to have to make do with their replacements. Soria saved 42 games with a 1.62 ERA and 66 strikeouts in 67 innings; he has a good fastball and wicked off-speed curveball.

Kyle Farnsworth was signed to a 2-year contract for $9.25 million. Why? I don't know. Farnsworth was horrible with the Yankees; he was horrible with the Tigers; and for a guy who throws a 100-mph fastball, Farnsworth can't get anyone out. He's going to play an important role for the Royals setting up for Soria, but expect him to blow so many games that the Royals may end up trying him in the starting rotation by the time their dismal season is coming to a close.

Ron Mahay had an excellent season after signing a free agent contract with the Royals. Not only was the lefty Mahay effective against lefties, but he was useful against righties as well. Mahay's a solid, veteran reliever and his career has been a solid one overall. His contract is up at the end of the season and the Royals will be able to get some value for him from a contender during the season.

Doug Waechter was another scrapheap pickup by the Marlins and, as they've done year-after-year, the Marlins rehabilitated the career of a veteran pitcher who became available cheaply. Waechter appeared in 48 games for the Marlins and pitched very well, throwing strikes.

Lefty Lenny DiNardo was signed to a minor league contract and should get a shot as a lefty out of the pen. DiNardo was hideous for both the Athletics and their Triple A farm club and he might not even make the Royals out of spring training if he pitches as poorly as he did with the A's.

John Bale is a veteran journeyman lefty who didn't pitch well last season, was non-tendered by the Royals and signed him to a cheaper contract. Perhaps Bale can have a rebound season that's common with relievers of his type.

Righty Robinson Tejeda pitched reasonably well out of the bullpen for the Royals after coming over for the Rangers. I've seen Tejeda numerous times over the years and have always wondered why someone with his stuff hasn't ever been more successful. Tejeda's a guy who still has the ability to blossom into a useful pitcher.

Veteran righty Oscar Villarreal signed a minor league contract with the Royals after spending last season with the Astros. His numbers weren't particularly good, but in watching Villarreal with the Braves, he could be a useful part of the Royals bullpen.

LINEUP:

The Royals have two catchers to choose from with John Buck and Miguel Olivo. Neither hits for a high average or gets on base; both are decent defensively with Olivo having an excellent arm; both have some pop to hit the ball out of the park. Their numbers combined equaled over 20 homers and nearly 100 RBI, which isn't all that bad if their flaws are accepted as fact before the season starts.

For what possible reason would the Royals make the conscious decision to, number one, play Ross Gload as much as they did at first base last season instead of giving minor league slugger Kila Ka'aihue a chance to play; and now to acquire a one-dimensional player like Mike Jacobs who hits the ball out of the park; strikes out a lot; is a terrible defensive first baseman, and is also due to start making big money in a year or two?

Jacobs is a journeyman; a guy you can find on the waiver wire or cheaply by signing one of the available names who signed minor league contracts like Kevin Millar; to make matters worse, they traded a valuable reliever in Leo Nunez to get Jacobs and weakened one of the few strengths the Royals had by dwindling their bullpen. There was no point to making that trade and now there's also noplace for Ka'aihue to play with Billy Butler prepared to be the DH; and it's not as if Ka'aihue is a 20-year-old kid; he's 25; when's he getting a chance to play?

Second baseman Alberto Callaspo batted .305 in 74 games and stole 14 bases in 16 attempts; with the competition he's facing at second base in Willie Bloomquist, the Royals are going to have a big problem if they have to play Bloomquist instead of Callaspo.

Alex Gordon is a former first round draft pick who spent almost no time in the minors and is still learning to play in the big leagues. He had 16 homers last season and his play has improved slowly although he strikes out a lot. He's eventually going to be a top third baseman and hit between 25 and 30 homers a year.

Mike Aviles came out of nowhere to win the job at shortstop and played very well. Aviles was a non-prospect until he got a chance to play and delivered a .305 average with 10 homers and 51 RBI; he had 41 extra base hits out of his 136 hits and played respectable defense.

Former center fielder David DeJesus moves to left field to accommodate the newly acquired and superior defensively Coco Crisp. DeJesus had a solid year with a .307 average; 12 homers; drove in 73 and had a .366 OBP. He also has some speed with 11 stolen bases.

Coco Crisp was acquired from the Red Sox for another useful reliever in Ramon Ramirez. Crisp is a solid enough player, but he's also a guy you can find relatively cheaply and isn't a difference-maker for a team that won 75 games the previous season to get much better. Jim Edmonds hasn't retired, clearly still wants to play and would put up more power numbers than Crisp will while playing similar defense. Trading for Crisp made no sense for a team like the Royals.

Jose Guillen had his usual bout of problems with teammates, management and coaches and delivered generally what was expected at the plate. He has power; a great arm in the outfield; is a loose cannon waiting to explode. If Guillen can keep his temper in check, I don't think he's such a bad guy to have in a lineup because at the very least, he'll hit his 20-25 homers and drive in close to 100 runs.

Big Billy Butler will get the chance to play regularly as the DH. For a guy like Butler to be as big as he is (6'1", 240), Butler should hit the ball out of the park more than he does with his 11 homers in 124 games. It may be worth it to give Ka'aihue a chance to win the job as the DH because his numbers indicate he's a better prospect than Butler.

BENCH:

Mark Teahen was said to be prepared to move to second base in an attempt to get more playing time. Teahen's game has degenerated from a couple of years ago when he looked like he was blossoming into a power/ on base guy as he was expected to be as a part of the 2002 Billy Beane *Moneyball* draft. Teahen's 27 and is what he is at this point. If he gets his at bats, he'll hit his 15-18 homers and drive in a few runs. The Royals would be well-served to give Teahen a chance to play and then trade him.

Ross Gload was the regular first baseman last season, but he has no power and doesn't do anything to warrant getting more than 150 at bats as a backup.

For some unfathomable reason, Moore gave a 2-year, $3 million to veteran infielder Willie Bloomquist. Moore made some nonsensical statements about Bloomquist being a hustling player who's versatile. Well, I hope Bloomquist is a hustling player because the day he stops hustling is the day he decides that he doesn't want to play baseball anymore because he doesn't do anything to warrant a team keeping him. That amount of money spent on a player like Bloomquist, who had one extra base hit out of his 46 hits (a double) is a fireable offense.

Tony Pena Jr. was the regular shortstop for a while and he batted an embarrassing .169 in 225 at bats. He shouldn't even be in the big leagues, let alone be a player who gets that many at bats.

Ryan Shealy was once a top prospect who was never really given a chance to play regularly either. Shealy had some pop in the minors, but the Royals chose to play Gload at first base instead. Shealy's about to turn 30, so he's probably going to have to go to another organization if he ever wants a chance to play.

Esteban German is a veteran utility player who can play any position adequately, has some speed and can hit a bit. He's a useful guy to have around.

PREDICTION:

I have no explanation for the moves Moore made this off-season; he has no concept of reality if he thinks it was money well-spent to lavish the 2-year deals on the likes of Ramirez, Farnsworth and Bloomquist. Trading useful relievers for Crisp and Jacobs, especially when Ka'aihue deserves at least a *chance* to play in the big leagues was absurd. If they think that Jacobs and Crisp are going to solve the problems the Royals had in scoring runs last season, then they're either living in fantasy world or deluding themselves intentionally. The starting rotation could be pretty good with Meche, Greinke, Hochevar and Davies; but any game in which they pitch pretty well and leave with a lead is very likely to get blown up by Farnsworth if they're using him as their regular set-up man.

There were many positive things happening when Moore first took over, but now he looks like a guy who doesn't really know what he's doing. The Royals don't have any chance to contend and the decisions they've made this past winter are going to be predictable disasters. If the ownership is paying attention, Moore is going to be in trouble as the season winds down and I think there's a great chance he's going to get fired. The Royals are going to be one of the worst teams in the American League and fall to last place in the AL Central.

PREDICTED RECORD: 72-90

American League West
1. Los Angeles Angels
2. Oakland Athletics
3. Texas Rangers
4. Seattle Mariners

Los Angeles Angels
2008 Record: 100-62; First Place, American League West
Lost to Boston Red Sox in ALDS 3 games to 1

2008 Recap:

This was the season in which the Angels went for it all by making the bold, mid-season trade for Mark Teixeira. Teixeira was supposed to support Vladimir Guerrero in the lineup as he added another power bat to a lineup of contact hitters and speedsters. The Angels pitching from top-to-bottom has always been among the most organized and consistent in all of baseball under manager Mike Scioscia and the addition of Teixeira was specifically meant for the playoffs. After winning 100 games, the Angels again ran into their old nemesis the Boston Red Sox and were again dispatched from the playoffs in the first round; their World Series hopes smashed, again wondering what they have to do to get past the playoff-tested Red Sox and cash in on their annual playoff appearances with another championship.

2009 ADDITIONS: LHP Brian Fuentes signed a 2-year contract with club option.
OF Bobby Abreu signed a 1-year contract.
RHP Matt Palmer signed a minor league contract.

2009 SUBTRACTIONS: OF Garret Anderson was not re-signed.
RHP Francisco Rodriguez was not re-signed.
RHP Jon Garland was not re-signed.
1B Mark Teixeira was not re-signed.
RHP Darren O'Day was claimed in the Rule 5 draft by the New York Mets.

2009 PROJECTED LINEUP: C-Mike Napoli; 1B-Kendry Morales; 2B-Howie Kendrick; 3B-Chone Figgins; SS-Erick Aybar; LF-Bobby Abreu; CF-Torii Hunter; RF-Vladimir Guerrero; DH-Juan Rivera

2009 PROJECTED STARTING ROTATION: John Lackey; Ervin Santana; Joe Saunders; Jered Weaver; Nick Adenhart; Kelvim Escobar

2009 PROJECTED BULLPEN: Brian Fuentes; Scot Shields; Jose Arredondo; Justin Speier; Darren Oliver; Kevin Jepson; Rich Thompson

2009 BENCH: OF-Gary Matthews Jr.; INF-Brandon Wood; INF-Maicer Izturis; C-Jeff Mathis; 1B-Robb Quinlan; INF-Freddy Sandoval; OF-Reggie Willits

2009 EXTRA PITCHERS/PROSPECTS: Anthony Ortega; Jason Bulger; Shane Loux; Dustin Moseley; Ryan Aldridge; Jordan Walden

2009 EVERYDAY PROSPECTS: Peter Bourjos; Anthony Norman; Mark Trumbo; Roberto Lopez; Alex Amarista

ASSESSMENTS:
MANAGEMENT:

GM Tony Reagins had learned his job well from former GM Bill Stoneman; the Angels value pitching from a deep starting rotation to a well-organized bullpen. Rarely, under Stoneman, did they ever make an aggressive mid-season move for a superstar-type player, especially one who was due to become a free agent; but it was in mid-season that the Angels under Reagins did just that by trading for Mark Teixeira.

When they made the trade, the Angels already had the division locked up and, in reality, they didn't give up all that much to get Teixeira—Casey Kotchman isn't that good—but the move was designed for the Angels to advance past the first round of the playoffs. Teixeira was everything the Angels had expected when he came over, but they didn't advance past the Red Sox in the first round, so the bottom line is that the trade didn't work. Reagins and owner Arte Moreno made a good faith effort to keep Teixeira, but he had bigger offers from the Red Sox and Yankees and chose the Yankees.

The Angels also allowed closer Francisco (K-Rod) Rodriguez to leave because they weren't about to break the bank for a closer when they have replacements in house who could do the job and the market was saturated with lower cost replacements. They filled the hole with lefty Brian Fuentes who, while not being as good as K-Rod, will still rack up the majority of his save opportunities; he won't save 62 games, but that record set by K-Rod was more of an accident of circumstance and opportunity than any kind of incredible accomplishment.

The Angels made some interesting decisions by not going after any of the big bats available (specifically Manny Ramirez) and deciding to wait out the market and getting someone productive and inexpensive (Bobby Abreu) and filling their first base hole in-house (Kendry Morales). They stick to the plan of having a budget and filling their needs inexpensively and they've always been willing to trade, so they may not be done with their renovating. As of right now, they've stuck to the script that was written by Stoneman and manager Mike Scioscia and is being followed through upon by Reagins.

Manager Mike Scioscia is so entrenched as Angels manager that he signed a contract extension that has the potential to keep him as Angels manager through the *2018* season. That's not just an extension; nor is it a long-term extension; that's a *looooooooong*-term extension.

Scioscia has two of the most important attributes a manager can have: he's supported by upper-management; and he has the respect in and control of the clubhouse. That doesn't diminish the fact that his reputation as a top field manager took a bit of a beating this past season with the way the Angels were bounced from the playoffs again. Scioscia's managing style has always been aggressive. He wants his players to swing the bat; he wants his baserunners to try and steal bases. That's the problem. His teams have always been geared around speed and relying on Vladimir Guerrero to drive home the runs; that should've changed with the acquisition of Mark Teixeira. It wasn't noticeable during the second-half of the season after Teixiera came over, but the Angels continued playing the way they always have and it was a mistake that became evident in the playoff loss to the Red Sox. With Teixeira, it would've been more prudent and strategically sound to ease off on the gas pedal and tone down the aggressiveness if only slightly to give the power bats of Guerrero and Teixeira a chance to drive in some runs. This failed approach became pronounced and rightfully criticized in the playoffs.

In game four of the ALDS, the Angels had a runner on third base with one out; instead of giving the batter a chance to swing the bat to drive the run in and give the Angels the lead in the top of the ninth inning, Scioscia called for a suicide squeeze which the Red Sox had expected (the Angels had done the same thing against the Red Sox previously) and pitched out. The runner was caught in a rundown; the Angels blew their chance to score, win the game and send the series back to Anaheim for a game five and watched as Scot Shields allowed the winning run in the bottom of the ninth to win the series for the Red Sox.

Scioscia is a good manager; but the main thing that is separating him from being a great manager is this clear reluctance to adjust his strategies to his personnel. Earl Weaver was a master at this and his teams won year-after-year despite upheaval in personnel because of Weaver's flexibility. The Angels win because of their organization and Scioscia's overall skills; but they also lost last season because of his dogged adherence to what he believes and it was to his team's detriment in 2008.

STARTING PITCHING:

John Lackey is one of the best pitchers in baseball and doesn't get the attention he deserves for that fact. He missed the beginning of the season and was limited to 24 starts with a triceps injury; when he returned, Lackey reclaimed his position as the most reliable pitcher the Angels have with a 12-5 record and a 3.75 ERA. Lackey can always be counted on to throw strikes and go deeply into games; he had a contract option exercised and is singing for his supper as he looks for a long-term contract. Lackey is 30-years-old and with the market the way it is, it's hard to imagine anyone outbidding the Angels to keep him. I'd expect a long-term extension sometime soon.

Ervin Santana's name was bandied about as trade bait for a bat as late as spring training in 2008. He had a terrible season in 2007 and the Angels were discussing sending him to the White Sox for Paul Konerko. This was a case of sometimes the best deals are the ones you never make. In the absence of Lackey and Kelvim Escobar, the Angels needed their young pitchers Santana and Joe Saunders to step into the breach and they did. Santana regained his form from 2006, had a blazing hot start and went 16-7, logged 219 innings, struck out 214 and pounded the strike zone. He's still only 26 and should front the Angels rotation for a long time.

Joe Saunders is a strike-throwing lefty who relies on his defense to get him through games. Saunders went 17-7 with a 3.31 ERA and pitched 198 innings in 31 starts. Saunders is about to turn 28 and even though he doesn't have the pure stuff of Santana, he's still an integral part of the rotation as a solid, Tom Glavine-like pitcher.

Jered Weaver is a former first-round draft pick who was relegated to back-of-the-rotation status with the emergence of Santana and Saunders and the acquisition of Jon Garland before last season. Weaver started 30 games and posted an 11-10 record with a high 4.33 ERA. Weaver's motion is long and has the potential to cause shoulder problems, but he throws strikes and if he's healthy, should provide at least the innings that Garland did and have better overall results because Weaver's stuff is far better than Garland's. Weaver isn't a guy who'll explode into 18 wins, but he can be counted on to win 13-15.

Nick Adenhart is a top prospect who got a chance to pitch a few big league games last season and struggled. Adenhart looked nervous and out-of-whack in his brief time with the big club, but he has a great curveball and needs to improve his control if he's going to stick in the big leagues. He may need more minor league seasoning because he's still only 22 and didn't pitch all that well in Triple A last season either.

Kelvim Escobar had finally fulfilled his great potential in 2007 with 18 wins, but shoulder problems shelved him for the entire 2008 season. Escobar is working toward a return, but there's no way of knowing what he's going to be able to provide. Worst case scenario, he can help out of the bullpen since he was a successful reliever earlier in his career with the Blue Jays; although he prefers starting, possibly that role would be an easier way to get something out of him.

BULLPEN:

Brian Fuentes replaces K-Rod as the Angels closer. Fuentes was in heavy demand because he was going to be cheaper than K-Rod and his numbers are considered, in certain circles, to be better. It must be remembered though that as recently as 2007, Fuentes had struggled so mightily for the Rockies that he lost his closer's job to a rookie and it was that rookie, Manny Corpas, who was the Rockies closer as they advanced to the World Series.

Fuentes also has a funky, across-his-body, stiff-legged, slingshot motion that might eventually lead to arm trouble. That motion also accounted for the massive strikeout numbers that Fuentes accumulated last season (82 in 63 innings). Fuentes joined the Angels on an inexpensive, 2-year contract and he'll make things easier for the club to ease young Jose Arredondo into the closer's role rather than throwing him into it before he's ready. K-Rod took advantage of having the best set-up man in baseball, Scot Shields, do the heavy lifting as he racked up a record number of saves, Fuentes should enjoy a similar advantage closing for the Angels.

Scot Shields, as mentioned, is the best set-up man in baseball. He pitches multiple-innings; he throws strikes; he generally doesn't give up many homers and he's durable. Shields has never gotten the credit he's deserved for his contribution to what the Angels do, but his teammates and manager appreciate him and the rest of the league knows how good and valuable Shields is.

Jose Arredondo just turned 25 and was dominating last season in a set-up role. He's the future closer of the Angels; he throws strikes, posted a 1.62 ERA in 52 games and helps the club shorten the game to six innings as he combines with Shields and the closer. Arredondo is a star in the making.

Veteran righty Justin Speier struggled with a 2-8 record and a high 5.03 ERA in 62 games. Speier has been up-and-down in his career, and he allowed 15 homers out of the bullpen last season, which is ridiculous. Performances of veteran relievers seem to fluctuate from one year to the next, but Speier is an extra arm in the Angels bullpen anyway who's only going to pitch when they're behind.

Darren Oliver is the Angels long man and he's been essential to their bullpen since changing his mind about possible retirement after the 2006 season. Oliver pitches multiple innings, throws strikes and isn't bothered by pressure. He was excellent last season with a 7-1 record in relief and a 2.88 ERA.

Righty Kevin Jepson put up excellent numbers in Triple A last season and pitched reasonably well enough with the Angels in nine games to make him a candidate for a bullpen role this season. He strikes out nearly a batter per inning.

LINEUP:

Mike Napoli and Jeff Mathis share the catching duties. Scioscia, having been a defensive-minded catcher himself prefers to have his catchers worry about defense and handling the pitching staff before anything else; both do that well, but what isn't noticed is how productive they are offensively. Mathis was atrocious at the plate with a .194 batting average, but he did hit nine homers. Napoli was very good at the plate with a .273 average and 20 homers in 78 games along with a .374 OBP and he hit a couple of big homers in the playoffs. The two will presumably share the catching duties again and many teams can do worse than having a couple of guys who can play defense behind the plate; call a game; and deliver 29 homers and over 90 RBI.

Kendry Morales is going to be given a chance to win the first base job and replace Teixeira. Morales has put up excellent numbers in the minors but has never produced all that much in his opportunities to play in the big leagues. I'm not convinced that Morales is the answer and there should be some viable replacements available during the season like Lyle Overbay, possibly Carlos Delgado or Dan Uggla. Morales is about to turn 26, so if he's going to make the most of his opportunity, it'd better be now.

Howie Kendrick has hit at every level and he missed time due to injury last season. When he was healthy, Kendrick batted .306 with 31 extra base hits in 340 official at bats. He's got star potential at second base.

Chone Figgins also missed time due to injury; for some reason, Figgins seems younger than he is, but he's 31-years-old. He has great speed and is a feisty, determined player.

Erick Aybar got the majority of the at bats at shortstop last season as he split time with Maicer Izturis. Aybar batted .277 with 26 extra base hits in 98 games. He also made 18 errors at shortstop. The Angels would love for young prospect Brandon Wood to stake his claim at the position and win the job outright so Aybar and Izturis can move back to their utility status.

Bobby Abreu has put up massive, under-the-radar offensive numbers in his career and the financial collapse relegated him from getting the amount of money he was expecting when he entered free agency. Logically, with some of the contracts that far lesser players have gotten in past years (Vernon Wells for example), Abreu had reason to expect $15 million annually. With the lack of interest and few teams willing to spend money, Abreu had to settle for a 1-year, $5 million base with incentives that can push the deal up to $8 million. Abreu will drive in his 100 runs; score his 100 runs; have an OBP of near .400 or higher; and hit his 20 homers. The Angels appear to be preparing to have Abreu play left field, but he's only played left field in 16 games in his entire career; but he's not a good outfielder anyway, so what's the difference? As a replacement for the departed Garret Anderson, Abreu is a giant step up from the declining Anderson. What I would do if I were the Angels is alternate Abreu and Vladimir Guerrero between right field and DH and, if Gary Matthews Jr. hits enough, let him play left because that defense with Matthews and Torii Hunter would be fantastic. Abreu's a great value for that money.

Torii Hunter has never been a prototypical superstar player, but his numbers go up consistently every season along with his Gold Glove defense. Hunter isn't a lineup protector for Guerrero, but even as he's about to turn 34, Hunter will hit his 20+ homers and drive in around 80 runs; plus he's a good guy in the clubhouse.

Vladimir Guerrero is starting his decline from the superstar he was for the past decade-plus, but he's still a dangerous hitter. The hacking Guerrero batted .303 with 27 homers and 91 RBI last season and with Abreu on base in front of him Guerrero should increase his RBI total because of Abreu's skills. Even at age 33, Guerrero shouldn't be counted out as having one more MVP-quality season.

Juan Rivera is listed as the probable DH and he can hit his 15 or so homers if he gets 400+ at bats, but I believe the Angels are going to mix and match with Matthews, Rivera, Guerrero and Abreu sharing time in the outfield and at DH.

BENCH:

Gary Matthews Jr. hasn't lived up to the expectations when he signed that stunningly lucrative free agent contract after a career-year with the Rangers. Matthews is still a Gold Glove caliber outfielder; he hit 8 homers last season in nearly 500 plate appearances. As stated before, Matthews will get his share of playing time because of his defense and he shouldn't be expected to hit anymore than he has in the past couple of disappointing years with the Angels.

Maicer Izturis is more of a utility player than a regular shortstop. Izturis batted .269 in 79 games and saw time all around the infield.

Brandon Wood has seen his stock as a top prospect drop slightly because he's struggled in his rare opportunities in the big leagues and got released from his winter league club in the Dominican Republic after getting off to a terrible start. Frankly, I don't see what the ridicule was all about with the problems in winter ball; it was better that he leave winter ball rather than get into a series of bad habits and perhaps get hurt; my feeling is that the Angels were better off to get him out of there and let him get his head together for the 2009 season with the Angels than save face with analysts, many of whom don't know what they're talking about anyway. Wood is only 24 and has put up numbers in the minors that indicate he's eventually going to be able to hit in the big leagues and it may happen like lightning as soon as this year.

Reggie Willits is a speedy backup outfielder who had an awful year at the plate last season, batting .194.

Robb Quinlan is a veteran backup first baseman; he batted .262 in 68 games and has no power whatsoever, but showed some skills playing part-time in 2006.

Freddy Sandoval is an infielder who put up excellent numbers in the minors last season. He hit 15 homers; drove in 88; batted .335 with a .389 OBP and 62 of his 175 hits were for extra bases. Sandoval played third base most of the season in the minors and he could see regular time in the big leagues this season. He's not some kid at age 26, but his numbers show some promise.

PREDICTION:

The Angels aren't going to win 100 games again, that much is clear.

Their pitching isn't as deep as it was unless Adenhart develops very quickly and Escobar returns healthy; the lineup is going to be similar as it was last season with the acquisition of Abreu and the bullpen should be about as good as it's been with Fuentes smoothly replacing K-Rod even if he doesn't put up the gaudy stats his predecessor did. If there was another team in the division that was a legitimate threat, the Angels might miss the playoffs, but the Athletics haven't improved enough to overtake them; the Rangers are probably a year or two away from contention and the Mariners are retooling under new management. Winning a division with 100 games or 88 games isn't relevant as long as they win the division. The Angels have the pitching from top-to-bottom and enough offense to hold off the improved A's and win the AL West again. Perhaps as less of a favorite and an under-the-radar playoff participant (and if they manage to avoid the Red Sox), the Angels can squeak past the first round and make another championship run. At the very least, they'll win the division again.

PREDICTED RECORD: 87-75

Oakland Athletics
2008 Record: 75-86; Third Place, American League West

2008 Recap:

The A's got off to a surprisingly solid start especially after another off-season housecleaning of big salaries by baseball's mad scientist, Billy Beane. Beane had dealt pitcher Dan Haren and outfielder Nick Swisher for a stack of prospects and were expected to fall to the bottom of the division. Instead, they played quite well into the summer and were thought to be a team that was going to take a shot with some big names at the trading deadline and try to win. Beane saw this as unrealistic and made some more housecleaning maneuvers in trading Rich Harden to the Cubs and Joe Blanton to the Phillies.

Some players the A's had been counting on like Eric Chavez and Daric Barton were injured and unproductive; and they also discovered an unknown gem in new closer, the submariner Brad Ziegler. Other young pitchers and players like Greg Smith, Sean Gallagher, Dana Eveland and Joey Devine showed potential and gained experience to increase their trade value or get ready for the future.

2009 ADDITIONS: OF Matt Holliday was acquired from the Colorado Rockies.
1B/DH Jason Giambi signed a 1-year contract with club option.
INF Joe Dillon was claimed off waivers from the Milwaukee Brewers.
RHP Michael Wuertz was acquired from the Chicago Cubs.
RHP Russ Springer signed a 1-year contract.
INF Yung Chi Chen was claimed off waivers from the Seattle Mariners.
OF Ben Copeland was selected in the Rule 5 draft from the San Francisco Giants.

INF Corey Wimberly was acquired from the Colorado Rockies.

RHP Edgar G. Gonzalez signed a minor league contract.

RHP Chris Schroder signed a 1-year contract.

RHP Kevin Cameron signed a minor league contract.

2009 SUBTRACTIONS: LHP Alan Embree was not re-signed.

DH Frank Thomas was not re-signed.

RHP Huston Street was traded to the Colorado Rockies.

LHP Greg Smith was traded to the Colorado Rockies.

OF Carlos Gonzalez was traded to the Colorado Rockies.

OF Matt Murton was traded to the Colorado Rockies.

OF Richie Robnett was traded to the Chicago Cubs.

INF Justin Sellers was traded to the Chicago Cubs.

2009 PROJECTED LINEUP: C-Kurt Suzuki; 1B-Jason Giambi; 2B-Mark Ellis; 3B-Eric Chavez; SS-Bobby Crosby; LF-Matt Holliday; CF-Ryan Sweeney; RF-Travis Buck; DH-Jack Cust

2009 PROJECTED STARTING ROTATION: Justin Duchscherer; Sean Gallagher; Dana Eveland; Dallas Braden; Gio Gonzalez; Josh Outman

2009 PROJECTED BULLPEN: Brad Ziegler; Joey Devine; Russ Springer; Michael Wuertz; Chris Schroder; Santiago Casilla; Kevin Cameron

2009 BENCH: 1B-Daric Barton; INF-Joe Dillon; INF-Yung Chi Chen; INF-Eric Patterson; 3B-Jack Hannahan; OF-Aaron Cunningham; OF-Rajai Davis; OF-Chris Denorfia; C-Landon Powell; C-Rob Bowen

2009 EXTRA PITCHERS/PROSPECTS: Jerry Blevins; Brad Kilby; Trevor Cahill; Andrew Carignan Jr.; Vin Mazzaro; Mike Benacka; Henry Rodriguez

2009 EVERYDAY PROSPECTS: Danny Putnam; Tommy Everidge; Jesus Guzman; Chris Carter; Sean Doolittle; Jason Christian

ASSESSMENTS:
MANAGEMENT:

I used to be among the crowd that thought Billy Beane was a genius because he was smart, fearless and did everything he could to gain advantages for his club while not spending the tons and tons of money other clubs did for worse results. I'm not a *Moneyball* advocate because the theory as presented in the book simply doesn't work and it's failed in practice in so many places that it should be clear by now how twisted Michael Lewis's narrative really was. After seeing Beane operate for all these years, I've come to the conclusion that he's a mad scientist who tries different things to see if they work. He followed the stat-based system for years; then he's subtly adjusted his theory to sign Latin American prospects like Michael Inoa, something that never would've happened had he followed Lewis's version of what he does. Beane, in recent years has also done the unhinkable in the draft: he's drafted the dreaded *high schoolers*, including the anathema to the concept, *high school pitchers*.

Beane had a team in moderate contention last season, but they were unlikely to be able to maintain that level for the entire season especially with one team in his division getting ready to run away and hide and three teams in the AL East vying for two playoff spots; so Beane started clearing out veterans. After an off-season in which he traded Dan Haren and Nick Swisher, Beane dealt Joe Blanton and Rich Harden a mid-season and managed to get somewhere close to market value for the oft-injured Harden. Then after the season, he changed course again by dealing some of his organizational depth accumulated from previous trades (including closer Huston Street) for star outfielder Matt Holliday. Beane also had interest in signing Rafael Furcal, which was said to end the Athletics career of Bobby Crosby; I happen to think he wanted Furcal to play third because he doesn't know what he's going to get out of rehabbing third baseman Eric Chavez. Then Beane dipped into the Athletics past by signing former star Jason Giambi.

No matter what happens, Beane is proving two things: 1) he's not embedded into any theory despite the force and insistence with which it's presented; and 2) he's always ready to do the exact opposite of what anyone thinks he's going to do, and many times, he's right.

It's hard to know what Bob Geren does or doesn't have to do with the way the club is run. Everyone is clear on the delegation of authority with the A's; the difference between what Beane does and what every other club who treats their manager as a middle-manager and strips any authority he may have is that Beane will get rid of anyone who gets out of line. Geren appears well-liked by his players, has done a good job handling the young players and has extensive minor league experience and success as a manager.

STARTING PITCHING:

Justin Duchscherer had blossomed into an All Star in 2007, but injuries hindered him in his continued success as he was in the middle of a brilliant season. Duchscherer had a 10-8 record with a 2.54 ERA in 22 starts and an excellent hits/innings pitched ratio of 107/142. If the A's are going to contend (as they seem to have designs on doing) they're going to need a healthy Duchscherer.

Sean Gallagher was acquired from the Cubs in the Harden trade and has shown excellent stuff and minor league success while never really getting a chance to pitch in the big leagues with the Cubs. Gallagher struggled in 11 starts after coming to the A's. He could be an innings-eating winner if he's given the chance.

Dana Eveland is a lefty that was acquired in the trade of Dan Haren to the Diamondbacks. Eveland's stats were average with a 9-9 record in 29 starts, but there were many positives in his performance. He allowed 172 hits in 168 innings, but on the positive side, he only gave up 10 homers.

Dallas Braden pitched very well in Triple A and was mediocre in 19 big league appearances, including 10 starts with a 5-4 record overall.

Gio Gonzalez is a hard throwing lefty who showed great promise in Triple A and struggled mightily in his chance to pitch in the majors. He's only 23-years old.

Josh Outman is a lefty acquired from the Phillies in the Blanton trade. He has the perfect name for a pitcher and spent much of the year as a reliever in Double A with the Phillies before the trade to the A's organization and beginning the conversion into a starter. He strikes out nearly a batter an inning.

BULLPEN:

Brad Ziegler came out of nowhere last season to start a streak out of the bullpen of 39 consecutive scoreless innings. After the trade of Street, the submarining Ziegler became the closer and saved 11 games with a 1.06 ERA. Ziegler is a contact pitcher and it's hard to imagine him repeating last season's performance. Lefties batted .280 against him so that's going to be a vulnerability for him as a closer.

Joey Devine has a motion similar to that of David Cone and great stuff that he finally began to translate into a positive big league performance. The Braves are one day going to rue the day they traded Devine in the Mark Kotsay trade and that day may be coming soon. Devine posted a 0.59 ERA in 42 games with 49 strikeouts in 46 innings with—and this is imperative—no homers allowed. Devine may end up being the closer before long because he can get out both lefties and righties, something Ziegler may not be counted on to do.

Successful veteran Russ Springer was signed to a 1-year contract. Springer has been a useful part of many solid bullpens over the years and he posted a 2.32 ERA in 70 games for the Cardinals last season.

Michael Wuertz was a valuable part of the Cubs bullpen that they're going to regret trading unless the two youngsters they received become useful everyday players. Wuertz has a history of being durable; throwing strikes; and performing as a valuable, unappreciated reliever.

Former Nationals reliever Chris Schroder was signed to a 1-year contract. He spent much of last season in the minors and pitched well averaging over 10 strikeouts per nine innings.

Former Padres reliever Kevin Cameron pitched well in Triple A and with the big club in that hopeless and hapless cause.

Santiago Casilla posted a 3.93 ERA in 51 games with 43 strikeouts in 50 innings.

LINEUP:

Kurt Suzuki batted .279 with 7 homers and 42 RBI with a .346 OBP in his first season as the A's starting catcher. Suzuki's main job is handling the young pitching staff.

Jason Giambi takes over at first base returning to the site of his glory years as the leader of the teams that made Billy Beane's reputation as a genius. Giambi can't really move at first base and would be better off as the DH, but Jack Cust is such a hideous outfielder that he's too much of a danger to be on the field for more than a handful of games. Giambi's injuries have piled up over the year, but when he's in the lineup he'll still hit the ball out of the park and rack up a high on base percentage because of his great eye even at 38-years-old.

Mark Ellis is a solid defensive second baseman who hit 12 homers in 117 games; 35 of his 103 hits were for extra bases.

Will Eric Chavez be able to play this year? His injuries have mounted year-after-year and the Athletics can't expect much of anything out of him and be happy if he can play at all. Chavez was one of the members of the

Giambi-led A's of the early part of the decade that Beane kept with a long-term contract, but he's done very little since then. He's got $11.5 million this year and $12.5 million next year coming to him. The A's have been linked with Orlando Cabrera, who's still a free agent as of this writing. Other than that, Jack Hannahan will have to play regularly, and he's not an everyday player. Another option is Daric Barton who played some third base in the minors (poorly), but he can hit and his way to play is blocked at first base by Giambi this year.

Bobby Crosby is a good defensive shortstop who may or may not have been available had the A's been able to bring in Furcal or any of the other available shortstops. Crosby has some occasional pop and doesn't get on base or hit for average, but he's the best the A's have at the moment.

Matt Holliday is going to get the chance to prove that he's not a creature of Coors Field as he heads into his free agent year. Holliday missed a chunk of time due to injury last season, but he's been a consistent power/average hitter who gets on base at a great clip. I think Holliday will be an excellent player wherever he is; he's a leader in the clubhouse who plays hard and he's going to get a lot of money after the season. He does everything anyone could want a player to do: he hits for power and average; he plays good defense; he can run (28 stolen bases in 30 attempts last season); and he's a winner.

Ryan Sweeney was acquired from the White Sox before last season in the Swisher trade. Sweeney has good potential and batted .286 in 115 games. With Carlos Gonzalez traded, Sweeney is going to get a chance to play every day in center field.

Travis Buck wound up back in the minors last season due to his struggles, but he's going to get another chance to win the right field job this season.

Jack Cust is the crème de la crème of Billy Beane's reclamation projects. Cust had so many chances with so many different organizations he could easily have become another Russ Morman as a guy who murdered Triple A pitching but either never really got a chance to play in the big leagues or failed when he *did* get a chance. Cust is a hideous defensive player, but he hit 33 homers and posted a .375 OBP. I've always thought that Beane should trade Cust at his highest value, but he's hung onto him so far. He still might be trade bait if Beane wants to get Barton into the lineup and chooses to DH Giambi.

BENCH:

The aforementioned Daric Barton has been an on base machine in the minors and he, not Dan Haren, was the key to the trade that sent Mark Mulder to the Cardinals. Barton had a bad year on and off the field last season. He got his chance to play and didn't hit; he also could've paralyzed himself or worse by jumping into a friend's pool and bashing his head on the bottom. Barton's only 23, has played some third base before and should get a chance to play that position if Chavez isn't back; it's better to try Barton than to play Hannahan regularly. I think Beane likes Barton and he'll get another chance to play somewhere whether it's in the outfield, third base or first base.

Jack Hannahan is a backup who was forced to play relatively regularly due to injuries. Hannahan batted .218 in 436 at bats with weak across-the-board stats.

Eric Patterson was acquired in the Harden trade and put up excellent numbers at the plate in the minors for both the Cubs and A's. If he's able to win a spot on the big league club, he might get a chance to play over Ellis.

Outfielder Aaron Cunningham put up big power/on-base numbers in Double and Triple A and could get a chance to make the big club out of spring training. Cunningham's 23-years-old and has star potential.

Rajai Davis showed good potential with the Giants before coming over to the A's; he's got great speed and has been more of a defensive replacement than a regular player.

Rob Bowen and Landon Powell will vie to be the backup to Suzuki. Bowen batted .176 in 91 at bats; Powell has shown some pop and on-base ability in the minors.

PREDICTION:

The A's have become a trendy pick to challenge the Angels for the division title with their organizational depth in their pitching staff and the acquisitions of Holliday and Giambi. Their bullpen could be iffy with Ziegler having almost no chance of being as good as he was last year and Devine still young; they've got some veteran depth out there with Springer and Wuertz. The starting rotation is very young and Duchscherer is coming off of that hip injury; there's no way of knowing what he's going to be able to provide and for how long. Gallagher is going to be a good pitcher as are Eveland and Gonzalez, but are they good enough right now to account for the holes in the A's offense? The team is better and will probably be over .500 this year, but even if the Angels fall back from their 100-wins last season, are the A's going to be able to overtake them as they're currently constituted? I can't see it. They may stick close to the Angels for much of the season, but they're not going to realistically contend for a playoff spot unless Beane pulls off another blockbuster trade for a veteran starter and another bat.

PREDICTED RECORD: 84-78

Texas Rangers
2008 Record: 79-83; Second Place, American League West

2008 Recap:

The Rangers got an amazing, inspirational season from Josh Hamilton as the former drug addict blossomed into a star with massive offensive numbers. The Rangers offense was productive as usual, but the pitching from top-to-bottom sabotaged any hope the Rangers might've had to contend. They got off to an atrocious start that put manager Ron Washington's job in such jeopardy that his firing was said to be hours away. In what can only be seen as a tribute to Washington, the team fought back from that start, got over .500 and back onto the periphery of contention. Washington was spared and the club wound up with a 79-83 record, which considering how terrible they were after the first month, wasn't that bad.

2009 ADDITIONS: OF Greg Golson was acquired from the Philadelphia Phillies.
RHP Guillermo Moscoso was acquired from the Detroit Tigers.
RHP Carlos Melo was acquired from the Detroit Tigers.
RHP Beau Vaughn was acquired from the Boston Red Sox.
SS Omar Vizquel signed a minor league contract.
OF Andruw Jones signed a minor league contract.
C Adam Melhuse signed a minor league contract.
RHP Derrick Turnbow signed a minor league contract.
RHP Casey Daigle signed a minor league contract.
RHP Elizardo Ramirez signed a minor league contract.
RHP Brendan Donnelly signed a minor league contract.

2009 SUBTRACTIONS: OF/DH Milton Bradley was not re-signed.
C Gerald Laird was traded to the Detroit Tigers.

OF John Mayberry was traded to the Philadelphia Phillies.
RHP Kameron Loe was released.
INF Ramon Vazquez was not re-signed.

2009 PROJECTED LINEUP: C-Jarrod Saltalamacchia; 1B-Chris Davis; 2B-Ian Kinsler; 3B-Michael Young; SS-Elvis Andrus; LF-David Murphy; CF-Nelson Cruz; RF-Josh Hamilton; DH-Hank Blalock

2009 PROJECTED STARTING ROTATION: Vicente Padilla; Kevin Millwood; Matt Harrison; Brandon McCarthy; Scott Feldman; Kason Gabbard

2009 PROJECTED BULLPEN: Frank Francsico; C.J. Wilson; Derrick Turnbow; Warner Madrigal; Josh Rupe; Doug Mathis; Joaquin Benoit

2009 BENCH: C-Taylor Teagarden; INF/OF-Frank Catalanotto; SS-Omar Vizquel; OF-Marlon Byrd; OF-Brandon Boggs; 2B-Joaquin Arias; OF-Andruw Jones; C-Max Ramirez

2009 EXTRA PITCHERS/PROSPECTS: Eddie Guardado; Casey Daigle; Elizardo Ramirez; Brendan Donnelly; Dustin Nippert; Luis Mendoza; Brian Gordon; Willie Eyre; John Rheinecker; J.B. Diaz; Neftali Felix; Derek Holland; Blake Beavan; Michael Main

2009 EVERYDAY PROSPECTS: Ben Harrison; Mitch Moreland

ASSESSMENTS:
MANAGEMENT:

Who's running things in Texas?
GM Jon Daniels has done many positive things in recent years after a rough start in which he made some deals that were borderline clueless. The Rangers have a well-stocked farm system loaded with young arms that are coming close to being ready for the big leagues; he's made some smart moves to stockpile bats as well as he did in the trades that brought players like David Murphy from the Red Sox and Jarrod Saltalamacchia from the Braves. The Josh Hamilton acquisition cost a very good young starter with All Star potential in Edinson Volquez, but Hamilton put up huge offensive numbers. They got Milton Bradley as a low-cost free agent and got great production.

Daniels has also botched some aspect of being a big league GM with heavyhanded treatment of the players that required more finesse than Daniels displayed. The position shift of Michael Young to third base may be the right move for the franchise, but the way Daniels went to Young and told him that the move was being made in favor of 20-year-old prospect Elvis Andrus was offensive to a team-oriented player in Young and should've been handled better. Another aspect of Daniels that deserves praise is his honesty in saying that he doesn't think the Rangers are going to be ready to turn the corner until the second half of the season; it's an accurate assessment, but probably not the smartest thing for the team's GM to be saying to the press.

I've wondered when team president Nolan Ryan was going to make his presence felt and he finally came out and made a statement about the personnel early in 2009 when he stated his desire for Josh Hamilton to move to right field. Hamilton is a big guy, he had a long year with all the mentally and physically draining emotionality of his comeback from drug abuse to become a phenomenon. Moving him to right field will reduce the amount of ground he has to cover and save some of his energy; but for Ryan to come out and say this instead of Daniels puts into question who's running things. Is it Daniels? Is it Ryan? Is it owner Tom Hicks? Ryan's coming out party will bring this situation to a head sooner rather than later, but it has to be settled for the organization to be able to move forward.

Manager Ron Washington was almost fired early last season, but the team was able to come out of their tailspin and save Washington's job. Washington makes some strange decisions as manager and the team would be better able to take the next step into contention with a manager who holds his players to a harder line; that being said, it's a positive that the players knew that Washington was about to be fired and they continued playing hard, turned things around and saved his job. If they wanted him out, that could easily have come to pass had they mailed it in when his position was at its most precarious. I have mixed feelings about Washington; I don't think he's a very good manager, but the players never quit and sometimes that's more important than strategic acumen.

STARTING ROTATION:

Vicente Padilla's up-and-down career was up in 2008. Padilla had a fine season with a 14-8 record and in 29 starts; he had a relatively high 4.74 ERA, but considering that he pitches in a hitter's paradise at Rangers Ballpark at Arlington, that ERA isn't all that bad. Padilla has this one year guaranteed remaining on his contract and is an enigma; no one knows what they're going to get out of the flighty Padilla from one start to the next; but when he's on, he's tough and he's mean. I'd expect Padilla to be trade bait for a contender this season unless the Rangers surprise and contend.

Kevin Millwood is another veteran who's struggled with injuries over the past couple of years. Millwood also made 29 starts and had a 9-10 record; he gave up a lot of hits with 220 in 169 innings. Millwood's contract is up after next season if he doesn't pitch 180 innings this year, which could be a sticky situation; he could be traded to a contender during the season.

Matt Harrison is 23-years-old and went 9-3 in 15 starts last season. He had a high ERA of 5.49 and gave up a lot of hits and home runs. He's a contact pitcher and that could be a problem playing his home games in Texas.

Brandon McCarthy has had his career derailed by injuries since joining the Rangers in a trade with the White Sox. The 25-year-old McCarthy looked good at the start of last season, but had to be shut down after five starts because of injuries. There's no way to know what McCarthy's going to provide, if anything.

Scott Feldman pitched reasonably well in 25 starts last season with a 6-8 record and a decent hits/innings pitched ratio of 161/151. Feldman's another contact pitcher who allowed 22 homers last season.

Kason Gabbard is a soft-tossing lefty who was acquired in the 2007 trade of Eric Gagne to the Red Sox. Gabbard got off to a fast start with the Rangers then and was mediocre and injured last season, making only 12 starts.

Veteran Jason Jennings is trying to return from numerous injuries; it's hard to see him returning to the form that made him such a solid and unappreciated starter with the Rockies years ago.

BULLPEN:

Frank Francisco took over as the closer last season and took to the role. He saved five games and racked up the strikeouts with 83 in 63 innings. Francisco can't be any worse as the closer than C.J. Wilson was for much of the season.

C.J. Wilson angered teammates with his blogging and analysis of what was going on with the Rangers; leaders in the clubhouse like Michael Young let Wilson know that his opinions would be better shared with the team or kept to himself entirely. I think the lefty Wilson has great stuff and potential to be a solid pitcher, but there's no defending his numbers last season because he was hideous.

Former Brewers closer Derrick Turnbow was signed to a minor league contract. Turnbow was dumped last season because he pitched so poorly and that's a sad state of affairs considering how weak the Brewers bullpen was, but Turnbow has had big league success before and has a power fastball; perhaps there's something salvageable there.

Warner Madrigal is a converted infielder who throws very hard and could be a very good reliever. Madrigal appeared in 31 games and showed some ability especially for someone who hasn't been pitching for that long.

Josh Rupe appeared in 46 games and posted a 5.14 ERA with 93 hits allowed in 89 innings.

Veteran Joaquin Benoit posted respectable numbers with a 3-2 record and a 5.00 ERA in 44 games; he was wild and had a solid number of strikeouts with 35 walks and 43 strikeouts in 45 innings.

LINEUP:

The Rangers have two catchers considered big league ready. Jarrod Saltalamacchia was acquired from the Braves in the Mark Teixeira trade and batted .253 in 61 games with the big club last season; a switch-hitter, Saltalamacchia batted .158 against lefties with little power and a .353 OBP. Taylor Teagarden had a horrible offensive year in the minors and his saving grace was a burst of power when he joined the Rangers. Teagarden hit 6 homers in 47 at bats. Looking at their numbers, the Rangers are going to have to make a decision on which catcher is the better long term option. Saltalamacchia's a year and a half younger, but is a bit flaky. They should give both a chance to play and boost the value of both players, then trade one for some pitching.

Young Chris Davis hit 17 homers in 80 games and is going to play first base. 42 of Davis's 84 hits were for extra bases.

Ian Kinsler was well on his way to being an MVP candidate before getting injured. Kinsler hit 18 homers, drove in 71 and batted .319 in 121 games. He also stole 26 bases and had an OBP of .375. His numbers, like most of the entire Rangers lineup's numbers, were far higher at home than they were on the road.

Michael Young is moving to third base to accommodate young Elvis Andrus. Young's pricey contract is precluding him from being traded unless the Rangers take a bad contract in return. (Interestingly, Young is close friends with another expensive player in Vernon Wells; the Rangers could use a center fielder and if they *really* would like to get out from under Young's contract which runs until 2014, perhaps they and the Blue Jays could come to an agreement of dealing bad contracts and Young could move back to shortstop.) As of right now, Young is a Ranger; he's playing third base and he's still the defacto captain of the team and respected in the clubhouse. Young's a solid player even though he's criticized by the stat geeks; it's not his fault the Rangers offered him that contract; he didn't deserve to be treated the way Daniels did when he unilaterally decided Young was changing positions and disrespected him by telling him that he was changing positions for a 20-year-old kid who may or may not be ready for the majors.

Elvis Andrus will get the chance to play shortstop in the big leagues. Andrus spent last season in Double A; he stole 54 bases (and got caught 16 times); he only had four homers, but presumably as he matures and hits in the hitter's paradise in Texas, his power numbers should improve. There's no way to know if he's ready for the majors; he's never played at a higher level than Double A and he's under scrutiny because of the position change made by a well-liked veteran to accommodate him. That's not Andrus's fault. He'll either explode out of the box once the season starts and be a Rookie of the Year candidate or he'll fall on his face and have to go back to Triple A for more seasoning.

David Murphy has been an impressive hitter since joining the Rangers from the Red Sox in the Gagne trade. Murphy batted .275 in 108 games, but hit 15 homers and drove in 74 and had 46 extra base hits. He deserves a chance to play every day.

If the Rangers are serious about moving Josh Hamilton to right field, they've spoken about giving longtime failed prospect Nelson Cruz the job in center field. Whether or not Cruz can play center field is a great question. Cruz destroyed Triple A pitching last season and looked good playing regularly over the last month of the season for the Rangers, but he's received opportunities to play in the big leagues before and failed miserably. Judging a player on how he does in September for a non-contender is a bad idea. It's going to be enough pressure on Cruz to get off to a good start with the big club; sticking him in center field is not a good idea if he's never played the position.

Josh Hamilton benefited from the friendly confines of Rangers Ballpark and became a heartwarming story about overcoming drug abuse. He was feted as a hero and an inspiration far too soon in my opinion. Hamilton tired toward the end of the season and his blazing hot numbers from the All Star break dwindled down as he ended with 32 homers and 130 RBI, but most of that was accrued in the first half of the season. I wouldn't sign Hamilton to a long-term contract, nor would I put too much pressure on him.

Hank Blalock has become the DH and could be on the trade block. Blalock has value at third base, a position that is becoming notoriously hard to fill; he has a power lefty bat that could help a number of teams. Blalock has endured numerous injuries over the past two seasons, but hit 12 homers in 65 games last season.

BENCH:

Marlon Byrd was mentioned as a possible center fielder if Hamilton is moved to right and Cruz can hack it out there. Byrd is a backup who's useful for his solid all-around play, but it doesn't make much sense for him to be a regular player with all the other prospects the Rangers have.

Frank Catalanotto is a veteran utility player who hits righties well and can play just about any position if necessary.

Brandon Boggs is a switch-hitting outfielder who showed some ability in 101 games; he batted .226 with eight homers.

Veteran Omar Vizquel was signed to a minor league contract as insurance in case Andrus isn't ready for the big leagues and will prevent the Rangers from having to make the embarrassing decision to move Young back to shortstop. Vizquel couldn't hit at all for the Giants last season, but who knows? Perhaps if he has to play for the Rangers, their ballpark will rejuvenate his bat.

Andruw Jones was signed to a minor league contract after he came to a buyout agreement with the Dodgers. I have trouble believing that Jones is finished at age 32, but his performance last season was embarrassing. He's worth a shot as long as no one expects much; maybe they'll hit the jackpot if Jones comes back motivated.

Joaquin Arias is a young second baseman who batted .291 in 110 at bats with the Rangers and put up solid across the board numbers with some speed in Triple A.

PREDICTION:

The Rangers have to come to a conclusion as to who's running things; right now, one day it seems as if Daniels is adhering to a plan (that kind of looks like it's on solid ground considering the young pitching the organization nearing big league readiness); the next day, Ryan comes out and makes a statement that implies he's making the decisions. Ryan isn't going to be taking marching orders from Jon Daniels, so if there's a power struggle, Nolan Ryan isn't going to lose. It all depends on who Tom Hicks trusts more and feels is going to derive more support from the fan base; if that's the criteria, Daniels may be on the way out.

It's very hard for a team like the Rangers to contend playing half of their games in a ballpark which is impossible to pitch in; they don't have very much starting pitching and their bullpen has some talent. If Padilla and Millwood prove that they're healthy, they should both be put on the block. Padilla is such an enigma, he's either going to get hurt again, win 16 games, or lose 16 games. Millwood is on the downside of his career in Texas and might regain his form with a change of scenery.

The Rangers are going to score plenty of runs; the Rangers are going to allow plenty of runs. I doubt that Washington is going to survive another bad start, but the Rangers are unlikely to have the pitching to *avoid* a bad start. I think the Rangers are on the right track, but Washington's going to get fired early in the season and the club will struggle as the young players grow acclimated to the big leagues. They'll play well after the All Star break to have respectable record (still under .500 and close to their record from last season), but improvement is coming in Texas slowly.

PREDICTED RECORD: 78-84

Seattle Mariners
2008 Record: 61-101; Fourth Place, American League West

2008 Recap:

There are teams that are terrible, 100-loss clubs; and then there are teams whose rosters indicate that they shouldn't under any circumstances be that bad, but are caught in a situation where everything goes wrong at once in a matter of symbiotic misery. The Mariners are in that class.

Their manager, John McLaren, was unable to handle a big league clubhouse and was in over his head from the start (some guys are simply better off as bench coaches than bosses); injuries robbed the club of their closer, J.J. Putz, early in the season; free agent import Carlos Silva was disenchanted by the selfish attitude and disinterest in winning among certain players and let it affect his pitching, then he allowed himself to get out of shape; Les Miserables Erik Bedard was a aloof with teammates and the media (as I predicted) and got hurt (as I predicted also); Richie Sexson continues his slide out of the big leagues; Kenji Johjima was signed to a long-term contract and had a terrible season; Miguel Batista was atrocious; the GM Bill Bavasi and manager McLaren were both fired; and the interim GM Lee Pelekoudas had the opportunity to get the club out from under the absudly expensive contract of Jarrod Washburn and let the opportunity pass.

The team had no chance to compete with all of these factors in place and it wasn't entirely the fault of the GM and manager although they took the blame. The Mariners were bad, but they weren't 100-loss bad.

2009 ADDITIONS: GM Jack Zduriencik was hired.
Manager Don Wakamatsu was hired.
OF Ken Griffey Jr. signed a 1-year contract.
INF Russell Branyan signed a 1-year contract.
1B Chris Shelton signed a minor league contract.
RHP Aaron Heilman was acquired from the New York Mets.

OF Endy Chavez was acquired from the New York Mets.

1B Mike Carp was acquired from the New York Mets.

LHP Jason Vargas was acquired from the New York Mets.

OF Ezequiel Carrera was acquired from the New York Mets.

RHP Maikel Cleto was acquired from the New York Mets.

OF Franklin Gutierrez was acquired from the Cleveland Indians.

LHP Tyler Johnson signed a minor league contract.

RHP Tyler Walker signed a 1-year contract.

RHP David Aardsma was acquired from the Boston Red Sox.

INF Ronny Cedeno was acquired from the Chicago Cubs.

LHP Garrett Olson was acquired from the Chicago Cubs.

1B/DH Mike Sweeney signed a minor league contract.

2009 SUBTRACTIONS: INF Willie Bloomquist was not re-signed.

RHP Aaron Heilman was traded to the Chicago Cubs.

RHP J.J. Putz was traded to the New York Mets.

OF Jeremy Reed was traded to the New York Mets.

RHP Sean Green was traded to the New York Mets.

RHP R.A. Dickey was not re-signed.

INF Luis Valbuena was traded to the Cleveland Indians.

LHP Fabian Williamson was traded to the Boston Red Sox.

2009 PROJECTED LINEUP: C-Kenji Johjima; 1B-Russell Branyan; 2B-Jose Lopez; 3B-Adrian Beltre; SS-Yuniesky Betancourt; LF-Endy Chavez; CF-Franklin Gutierrez; RF-Ichiro Suzuki; DH-Ken Griffey, Jr.

2009 PROJECTED STARTING ROTATION: Felix Hernandez; Erik Bedard; Carlos Silva; Jarrod Washburn; Brandon Morrow; Ryan-Rowland Smith

2009 PROJECTED BULLPEN: Miguel Batista; Tyler Walker; Sean White; David Aardsma; Mark Lowe; Roy Corcoran; Cesar Jimenez; Randy Messenger; Garrett Olson

2009 BENCH: C/1B-Jeff Clement; C-Jamie Burke; INF-Ronny Cedeno; OF-Wladimir Balentien; 1B-Chris Shelton; OF-Mike Morse

2009 EXTRA PITCHERS/PROSPECTS: Jose Lugo; Eric Hull; Jason Vargas; Tracy Thorpe; Justin Thomas; Tyler Johnson; Chris Seddon; Rich Dorman

2009 EVERYDAY PROSPECTS: Matt Tuiasosopo; Marshall Hubbard; Adam Moore; Michael Wilson; Mike Carp

ASSESSMENTS:
MANAGEMENT:

Jack Zduriencik was one of the architects of the productive Milwaukee Brewers farm system. A longtime and respected scout, Zduriencik took on the task of rebuilding the Mariners. Aggressive and using every tool at his disposal—classic scouting techniques and numbers—Zduriencik has made some intriguing moves since joining the Mariners. He's building some depth in the organization with the trades of closer J.J. Putz and one of the pitchers he got for Putz, Aaron Heilman; and once the season starts, he's unlikely to stand pat. The Mariners have other veterans and impending free agents for whom Zduriencik could get value. Erik Bedard was a nightmare with the Mariners last season and if he proves he's healthy, he's going to get moved; Jarrod Washburn has aroused interest (don't ask me why) and he'll go as well; Adrian Beltre, Kenji Johjima, it's hard to picture anyone on the Mariners roster aside from Felix Hernandez and Brandon Morrow who aren't up for debate and Zduriencik has the scouting skills to make some smart trades to ramp up the Mariners return to respectability.

Don Wakamatsu is a longtime minor league manager and big league bench coach who's finally getting his chance to manage. Wakamatsu was said to have been the choice of Rangers GM Jon Daniels to replace Buck Showalter, but was overruled by owner Tom Hicks who hired Ron Washington. The Mariners aren't expected to do much at least in the next couple of years, so Wakamatsu will be able to grow into the job if and when the Mariners are ready to contend.

STARTING ROTATION:

Felix Hernandez is eventually going to be a Cy Young contender and 18-20 game winner. Hernandez has also shown a flair for the dramatic with his near no-hitter when he was facing Daisuke Matsuzaka in his first start for the Red Sox in 2007; and he hit a grand slam off of Johan Santana pitching against the Mets at Shea Stadium. Hernandez is still only 23; has excellent control; throws a fastball in the mid-to-high 90s; has a great curve and improving changeup.

Erik Bedard is a free agent at the end of the season, was injured for much of his first season with the Mariners and was an aloof, self-centered presence in the clubhouse. His numbers for the 15 games he started are actually in line with the way he's usually pitched in his big league career. He's got great stuff, is difficult to hit because of his sneaky fastball and that he hides the ball well in his motion, but he's always hurt and is unpopular in the clubhouse because of his belligerent personality. Bedard is recovering from his shoulder injury and with his impending free agency, I expect Zduriencik to trade him if and when Bedard shows himself to be healthy. Other teams will know about the Bedard package when trading for him, but as long as he's pitching well, someone will absolutely take a chance on him to try and bridle that ability and Zduriencik will know how to extract good talent for him.

Carlos Silva had come from a stable and professionally run organization with the Twins and was stunned by the disinterest in winning and losing and the dysfunctionality in the Mariners clubhouse. That's no excuse for a pitcher who signed a contract worth $48 million to go 4-15 with a 6.46 ERA and numbers that I could've put up right now at age 37 with my damaged right elbow and 70 mph fastball. Silva's not going anywhere because no one's taking the contract, so the Mariners might as well try and return Silva to the innings-eater who was, at the very least, a .500 pitcher for the Twins. Silva has to do his part by showing up in shape and staying that way.

Brandon Morrow has to live with the aspect of having been drafted before Washington native and 2008 NL Cy Young Award winner Tim Lincecum. Morrow had been a reliever for the Mariners up until the middle of last season when they began the process of converting him into a starter. Morrow has great potential as a starter and might have a better long-term prognosis than Lincecum; he's much bigger and has a clean motion. In the draft, if I had to choose between the two, I would've taken Morrow. With the Mariners in retooling mode, Morrow can develop as a starter without the pressure as Joba Chamberlain is dealing with under the microscope in New York.

Jarrod Washburn had a mini-hot streak last season that allowed the Mariners an opportunity to get out from under Washburn's $10 million annual contract. They placed him on waivers and he was claimed by the Twins; the Twins were not only willing to take Washburn, but they offered a good young arm in Boof Bonser…and the Mariners said that wasn't enough and pulled Washburn back. The Cardinals were also said to be interested, but nothing came about. Getting Washburn's salary off the books would've been enough for me, but the Mariners stupidly held onto the lefty. Naturally, he got hurt and ended his season poorly with a 5-14 record. Zduriencik would undoubtedly love to get rid of Washburn.

Ryan-Rowland Smith was also converted into a starter last season and showed great promise. I'd keep him in the rotation.

BULLPEN:

Miguel Batista had a terrible year as a starter after winning 16 games in 2007 and is listed on the Mariners depth chart as their closer. Batista has closed before with the Blue Jays, pitched reasonably well and has never been afraid of pressure. Since the Mariners don't really have anyone else who can do the job, they may as well use Batista for most of this season and see if one of their younger pitchers can develop and do the job. Batista's marketability will also be enhanced if he does well out of the bullpen since he can start as well.

Veteran Tyler Walker has had some closing experience and was signed to a 1-year contract. In a pinch, he could do the job if necessary since he throws hard and puts up solid strikeout numbers.

Righty Mark Lowe pitched in 57 games and got knocked around with a 1-5 record and a high 5.37 ERA.

Roy Corcoran had an excellent season with a 6-2 record in 50 games. His across the board numbers were very good; he's a contact pitcher who walks as many as he strikes out.

Cesar Jimenez is a lefty who pitched well in 31 games last season. He struck out 26 in 34 innings and has shown the makings of a solid reliever in the minors.

Randy Messenger is a big righty who throws hard. He doesn't strike out many batters, but he could make it as a cog in the Mariners rebuilding bullpen.

David Aardsma is bouncing around baseball because someone always thinks they're going to be the ones to harness his ability and make him into a useful pitcher. Aardsma has great stuff, but has failed in just about every opportunity he's gotten. Perhaps he could be a set-up man or closer for the Mariners.

LINEUP:

Kenji Johjima looked promising in his first couple of years in the big leagues with power, but after signing a long-term contract extension, he was awful. Johjima batted .227 in 379 at bats with a .277 OBP. Johjima might've been just another solid player who got caught up in the Mariners terrible season, but those numbers are inexcusable. The Mariners have a young catcher in Jeff Clement whose way is blocked by the contract Johjima was given. On the bright side, like many of the Mariners, Johjima can't possibly be any worse than he was last season.

Veteran Russell Branyan was signed to a one-year deal. Branyan's a journeyman who hits the ball out of the park, but for the Mariners, it makes little sense to be playing him regularly when they have young bats like Clement needing a chance to play. Branyan will hit the ball out of the park and draw a lot of walks if he's given a chance to play; he also strikes out a lot.

Jose Lopez is eventually going to be an All Star second baseman. He can hit, hit for power, run and play solid defense. Lopez is still only 25 and needs to be a bit more patient at the plate.

Adrian Beltre is due for free agency at the end of the season and therefore might be trade bait. Beltre receives criticism because he cashed in on his career year with the Dodgers in which he hit 48 homers and then left for the Mariners; he's never approached those numbers again, but he hit 25 homers last season and can be counted on for somewhere in that vicinity of power production. He is a good fielder and is respected in the clubhouse, so if he's playing well and a contending team needs a bat, he could bring back a prospect or two in a trade.

Yuniesky Betancourt could form a long-term double play combination with Lopez. He also needs to work on his patience at the plate, but he's got some pop with 46 extra base hits in 153 games; he's a solid fielder as well.

Endy Chavez is listed as the Mariners starting left fielder, but he's more of a defensive replacement and twice a week starter. Chavez is quite possibly the best defensive outfielder in baseball and is a better hitter than he's given credit for; he also plays the game correctly and will be a good influence on the Mariners younger players.

Franklin Gutierrez was acquired from the Indians in the blockbuster three-way trade with the Mets and Indians that sent J.J. Putz to New York.

Gutierrez has great all-around ability to hit and hit for power, but he's never been given a chance to play every day.

Ichiro Suzuki is given far too much power in the Mariners organization for a player who appears to be as selfish as he is. As the Mariners have struggled, Ichiro has looked like he's more interested in raising his hit total than helping the team get better and win. He was said to be one of the main reasons that former manager Mike Hargrove retired and, as great a fielder as Ichiro is; as fast as he is; and as talented as he is, he's nothing more than a glorified singles hitter who doesn't produce all that much. If I were Zduriencik, I'd trade Ichiro. Perhaps the Cubs, who need a center fielder and have a player they no longer want in Kosuke Fukudome, would be a landing spot to reunite Ichiro with former Mariners manager Lou Piniella.

The Mariners have a group of players who can DH. Ken Griffey Jr. will get a chunk of the at bats in his return to Seattle and he can still hit despite what his critics say. He's not the player he once was, but he's a good pickup as a draw for the fans as he ends his career where it began is an example of a player who did a service to the game and himself by not acquiescing to the pressure of steroid usage and put up his numbers naturally, Griffey's reputation is beyond reproach despite some diva like behavior in his career. He can still hit his 20-25 homers if he gets 400 at bats.

BENCH:

Jeff Clement was a top draft pick who was briefly given a chance to play regularly. Clement tore apart Triple A last season and batted .227 in 66 games for the Mariners. They may give him a chance to catch more regularly despite Johjima's contract and Clement deserves to get his 350 at bats to see what he can do at age 25.

Wladimir Balentien is a power prospect who also hit well in Triple A, but not in the big leagues. He did have 7 homers in 71 games and is 24, so he could develop if allowed to play.

Veteran journeyman Chris Shelton was signed to a minor league contract. Shelton has a habit of getting off to fast starts in the power department and then falling off the cliff as the season moves along. A smart club will take advantage of this attribute, play Shelton a lot early in the season, then dwindle his playing time as he begins to slump. He'll probably end up as Triple A filler.

Backup catcher Jamie Burke is a veteran who can't really hit and won't play much if he makes the team out of spring training.

Veteran backup infielder Ronny Cedeno was acquired from the

Chicago Cubs for Aaron Heilman; Cedeno is a solid player who can play any infield position and the outfield if necessary. He batted .269 in 216 at bats for the Cubs last season.

PREDICTION:

No matter what, the Mariners aren't going to lose 100 games again. Everything that could've gone wrong for them last year, did go wrong. Zduriencik knows talent and looks like he's going to be aggressive in making trades. Many of the veterans are either on, or are going to be on the trading block. They've taken steps to clear out some veterans already and replenishing the organization's weak farm system. The days of making stupid decisions like keeping a mediocre pitcher like Washburn when they could've gotten out from under his contract are over. The younger prospects like Clement are going to receive an opportunity to play and it will determine whether they're actually prospects that will be part of a Mariners turnaround. Their starting pitching should be solid enough with the young pitchers Hernandez and Morrow. They'll finish in last place, but as long as Zduriencik clears out some salary and continues the current road he's on, the Mariners will be back among the living in the next few years.

PREDICTED RECORD: 73-89

AMERICAN LEAGUE PLAYOFF PREDICTIONS:

ALDS:

New York Yankees vs Los Angeles Angels

Yankees in Four

ALDS:

Boston Red Sox vs Cleveland Indians

Red Sox in Five

ALCS:

New York Yankees vs Boston Red Sox

Yankees in Six

AMERICAN LEAGUE CHAMPIONS: NEW YORK YANKEES

AMERICAN LEAGUE AWARDS:

MOST VALUABLE PLAYER: Alex Rodriguez, New York Yankees

CY YOUNG AWARD: C.C. Sabathia, New York Yankees

ROOKIE OF THE YEAR: Elvis Andrus, Texas Rangers

MANAGER OF THE YEAR: Joe Girardi, New York Yankees

National League East
1. Florida Marlins
2. Philadelphia Phillies*
3. New York Mets
4. Atlanta Braves
5. Washington Nationals

*Denotes predicted Wild Card winner

Florida Marlins
2008 Record: 84-77; Third Place, National League East

2008 Recap:

While *Moneyball* anointed their practicioners "geniuses" for using stats and maximizing every single dollar at their disposal, one team has taken that extreme to a successful conclusion using scouting techniques, brilliant trades and annual scrapheap pickups to be even smarter and more financially prudent than any stat-geek-run team with their crop of Ivy League educated experts could ever be.

The Florida Marlins won 84 games last year with a payroll of slightly over $20 million. To put that into context, Carl Pavano made around $10 million last season. The Marlins rely on their young players in Hanley Ramirez; players acquired from the junkpile for nothing in Jorge Cantu, Cody Ross and Wes Helms; and players they found through other teams not appreciating what they had in Dan Uggla and Matt Lindstrom. They have a young lineup and starting rotation and a bullpen filled with retreads for whom Florida is likely their last stop. In an era when people like Paul DePodesta are still considered smart baseball men despite their ineptitude, the true smartest guys in baseball are in Florida and running the Marlins.

2009 ADDITIONS: RHP Leo Nunez was acquired from the Kansas City Royals.
LHP Dan Meyer was claimed off waivers from the Oakland Athletics.
INF Emilio Bonifacio was acquired from the Washington Nationals.
RHP P.J. Dean was acquired from the Washington Nationals.
INF Jake Smolinski was acquired from the Washington Nationals.
RHP Jose Ceda was acquired from the Chicago Cubs.
INF Andy Gonzalez signed a minor league contract.

LHP Zachary Kroenke was selected in the Rule 5 draft from the New York Yankees.
RHP Scott Proctor signed a 1-year contract.
OF Jay Gibbons signed a minor league contract.
LHP John Koronka signed a minor league contract.
LHP Willie Collazo signed a minor league contract.
RHP Mike Wood signed a minor league contract.

2009 SUBTRACTIONS: 1B Mike Jacobs was traded to the Kansas City Royals.
LHP Scott Olsen was traded to the Washington Nationals.
OF Josh Willingham was traded to the Washington Nationals.
RHP Kevin Gregg was traded to the Chicago Cubs.
C Matt Treanor was released.
RHP Joe Nelson was non-tendered.
RHP Doug Waechter was not re-signed.
OF Luis Gonzalez was not re-signed.
LHP Mark Hendrickson was not re-signed.
RHP Justin Miller was not re-signed.

2009 PROJECTED LINEUP: C-John Baker; 1B-Gaby Sanchez; 2B-Dan Uggla; 3B-Jorge Cantu; SS-Hanley Ramirez; LF-Cody Ross; CF-Cameron Maybin; RF-Jeremy Hermida

2009 PROJECTED STARTING ROTATION: Josh Johnson; Ricky Nolasco; Chris Volstad; Andrew Miller; Anibal Sanchez; Rick Vanden Hurk

2009 PROJECTED BULLPEN: Matt Lindstrom; Jose Ceda; Leo Nunez; Renyel Pinto; Scott Proctor; Logan Kensing; Willie Collazo; Mike Wood; Zachary Kroenke

2009 BENCH: C-Mike Rabelo; 1B/3B-Wes Helms; OF-Alfredo Amezaga; INF-Emilio Bonifacio; OF-Alejandro De Aza; SS-Robert Andino; 3B/1B-Dallas McPherson

2009 EXTRA PITCHERS/PROSPECTS: Carlos Martinez; Eulogio De La Cruz; Jesus Delgado; Harvey Garcia; Burke Badenhop; Ryan Tucker; Willie Glen; Jay Buente; A.J. Battisto; Corey Madden

2009 EVERYDAY PROSPECTS: Jai Miller; Chris Coghlan; John Raynor; Logan Morrison; Bryan Peterson; Miguel Fermin; Ernesto Manzanillo

ASSESSMENTS:
MANAGEMENT:

The Marlins are ridiculed because they don't spend any money, but why should they? Their front office led by Larry Beinfest finds players anywhere and everywhere; they're always aggressive and ready to make a move; they try and keep their superstar players and if they can't, they trade them. They signed Hanley Ramirez to a long term deal, but were still willing to at least discuss trading him to the Red Sox before the steep asking price was too much to consummate a deal. The Marlins make a mockery of the idea that teams that don't spend a lot of money can't compete. They draft smartly and find players in Latin America; they have a nonpareil eye for talent and when it comes time for a player to make an amount of money the Marlins don't want to pay, they trade them for more young talent. If anyone wants to look at a system to copy, forget Billy Beane and the A's; watch the Marlins and do what they do because they're the true geniuses in baseball.

Fredi Gonzalez led the young Marlins onto the outskirts of contention and they won 84 games with that minimalist payroll. It's interesting to note that Joe Girardi had won Manager of the Year in 2006 as he won 78 games with a different group of young players, and when Gonzalez and Girardi were managing different teams at the same time, it was *Gonzalez* who turned out to be the more successful of the two as Girardi missed the playoff with the $200 million Yankees and Gonzalez led the Marlins into respectability and more. He's a solid manager who, for the most part, has control of his young players; they play the game the right way and aren't afraid to make mistakes; that comes from the manager and is an important and unappreciated attribute to being successful.

STARTING PITCHING:

Josh Johnson returned from Tommy John surgery for 14 starts; he went 7-1, posted a 3.61 ERA. The 25-year-old Johnson is a star in the making and will contend for the Cy Young Award as he fronts the young Marlins rotation.

Ricky Nolasco went 15-8 in 32 starts; his hits/innings pitched ratio was an excellent 192/212 with 186 strikeouts and great control.

6'8" Chris Volstad was excellent in 14 starts with a 6-4 record and a fantastic 2.88 ERA. He showed great poise and control for a 22-year-old.

Andrew Miller was compared with a young Randy Johnson when he was acquired in the trade that sent Miguel Cabrera and Dontrelle Willis to the Tigers. Just as Johnson did when he was young, Miller had trouble with his control and struggled with his results. Miller went 6-10 and needs to work on his control, but he has all the equipment and showed flashes of being a future star.

Anibal Sanchez is injured too often to be able to count on, but despite a 2-5 record in 10 starts last season, he didn't pitch all that badly. Sanchez has the potential to be a solid starter if he can ever stay healthy.

The tall righty from the Netherlands Rick Vanden Hurk has also shown flickers of being able to dominate. He got knocked around in four big league starts, but he could find himself in the Marlins rotation sometime this season.

BULLPEN:

Matt Lindstrom was stolen from the Mets in a trade for Jason Vargas a couple of years ago and took over as the closer for Kevin Gregg last season. Lindstrom's fastball reaches 100 mph. He doesn't strike out many hitters considering how hard he throws, but what's important for Lindstrom is that he only gave up one home run in 66 appearances. He should make a fine closer and one that's much better than the wild and shaky Gregg ever was.

Leo Nunez was acquired from the Kansas City Royals for Mike Jacobs. Nunez had a fine year with the Royals with a 2.98 ERA in 45 games; he's a strike thrower and a contact pitcher who should do well with the Marlins.

Jose Ceda is a big, hard-throwing righty acquired from the Cubs in the trade that sent the aforementioned Gregg away. The Cubs are going to rue the day they made that move. Ceda is a strikeout pitcher who's going to be a force in the Marlins bullpen.

Renyel Pinto appeared in 67 games and had an up-and-down season with a 2-5 record, a high 4.45 ERA, but only 52 hits allowed in 65 innings pitched. He can be more than a lefty specialist out of the bullpen.

Logan Kensing is a hard-throwing righty who struck out 55 in 55 innings last season.

Dan Meyer was once a top prospect for the Braves and Athletics, but his progress has been hampered by injuries; he's just the type of pitcher that the Marlins pick up, rehabilitate and gets great value out of him inexpensively. He can start or relieve.

Veteran righty Scott Proctor was signed to a 1-year contract. It should be strange for Proctor to be away from his manager with the Yankees and Dodgers, Joe Torre. Proctor's arm will probably appreciate it as well since he was Torre's designated abused reliever. If Proctor's healthy, he throws hard and has had success in the past.

Willie Collazo is a former Met who's shown some ability to be a lefy specialist out of the pen.

LINEUP:

John Baker is a catcher who took over as the starter late last season and batted .299 with a .392 OBP in 61 games. 19 of his 59 hits were for extra bases and his main attribute is his batting eye.

Gaby Sanchez is a power hitting first base prospect who's going to get a chance to win the everyday job. Sanchez hit 17 homers and drove in 92 with a .314 batting average and a .404 OBP. He should be a contender for Rookie of the Year.

Dan Uggla may be on the trading block since he won in arbitration, is starting to make a little too much money to suit the frugal tastes of the Marlins and had an awful second half of the season last year. Uggla would probably benefit from a position change and the Marlins acquired a possible replacement in the off-season in Emilio Bonifacio; but for now, Uggla's the second baseman and he's a pure slugger who hits his 30 homers and drives in 90 runs. He had a strangely poor season against lefties batting only .191.

Jorge Cantu was a scrap heap pickup who regained the power he'd shown earlier in his career with the Devil Rays. Cantu had a great offensive year with 29 homers, 95 RBI and 70 extra base hits. Cantu seems like he's been around for awhile, but he's still only 27.

Hanley Ramirez is one of the best players in baseball. His fielding leaves something to be desired suggesting he may eventually be moved to first base, third base or the outfield, but for now he's still at shortstop. Ramirez is an offensive machine who can do everything at the plate. He hit .301 with 33 homers, 81 extra base hits and 35 stolen bases; he also had an on base percentage of .400. He's a one man gang and could win the MVP.

Cody Ross has become a feisty power hitter who can be counted on to hit his 20+ homers. Ross had 56 extra base hits last season.

Cameron Maybin was acquired in the Cabrera/Willis trade and spent most of last season in Double A for another year of seasoning. Maybin will get his chance to play every day this season and if he continues his progression, he should be a force in the lineup. He batted .277 with improving power and speed and as he matures, he'll hit his 20 homers and steal his 25+ bases.

Jeremy Hermida struggled a bit with a .249 average and a .323 OBP with 17 homers. He's only 25 and has the ability to be an above average outfielder with good power and solid outfield defense.

BENCH:

Mike Rabelo will be the backup catcher. He's a switch hitter who probably won't get to play all that often.

Wes Helms is the backup first baseman/third baseman with occasional pop.

Emilio Bonifacio was acquired in the trade with the Nationals that sent Scott Olsen and Josh Willingham to Washington. Bonifacio has put up big batting averages in his pro career, but has no power. He has great speed and could get a chance to play depending on what they do with Uggla.

Robert Andino is the backup shortstop who played in 44 games with the Marlins as a defensive replacement. He hit pretty well in Triple A last season, but he's not going to get much of a chance to play in the big leagues considering who he has in front of him.

Dallas McPherson's numbers at Triple A Albuequerque are obscenely good. He hit 42 homers with 98 RBI in 127 games. McPherson's gotten his chances in the big leagues with the Angels, but never did much of anything notable. If Sanchez struggles, McPherson could see some time at first base for the big club.

Alfredo Amezaga is a 31-year-old outfielder who batted .264 in 311 at bats last season. He's got some speed.

An interesting signing made by the Marlins was an admitted steroid user Jay Gibbons. Gibbons probably won't even make the team and might be released from the organization rather than waste a spot with him in the minors, but it'll be interesting to see how he does if he's playing clean.

PREDICTION:

The Marlins have enough young starting pitching to be able to vault into contention despite that low payroll. They always score plenty of runs and find dispatched pitchers to fill out the relief corps very well. Owner Jeffrey Loria spent some money to improve the club when they had a chance to win in 2003 and I expect the Marlins to be around a playoff spot late in the season and for Loria to do something similar. The NL East isn't as tough as it once was with the Phillies possibly experiencing a championship hangover and the Mets still trying to find themselves.

The Marlins are going to win a stunning division title in a close race over the Phillies with two of their young stars—Josh Johnson and Hanley Ramirez—contending for the Cy Young Award and MVP, respectively. Maybe someone will take the initiative and write a book about a team that really deserves it, the Florida Marlins; and instead of copying the Athletics with no result but abject failure, other teams will copy the Marlins and find some success; but the Marlins aren't built through numbers, they're built through recognition of talent and that's not something for which any formula can be created and adhered to.

PREDICTED RECORD: 90-72

Philadelphia Phillies
2008 Record: 92-70; First Place, National League East
Defeated Milwaukee Brewers in NLDS 3 games to 1
Defeated Los Angeles Dodgers in NLCS 4 games to 1
Defeated Tampa Bay Rays in World Series 4 games to 1

2008 Recap:

The Phillies rode a deep top-to-bottom pitching staff and clutch power hitting lineup to win the World Series. With Brad Lidge having a Cy Young/MVP-quality comeback season, the Phillies finally had the last piece to their championship puzzle. Their homegrown stars Cole Hamels, Ryan Howard, Chase Utley, Jimmy Rollins and Pat Burrell all grew up together, learning how to win. Their experienced veterans like Jamie Moyer led the club on the field and manager Charlie Manuel pushed all the right buttons. With the aggressive maneueverings of GM Pat Gillick to acquire important mid-season additions in Joe Blanton, Matt Stairs and Scott Eyre, the Phillies got blazing hot to end the regular season and kept winning, winning and winning all the way through to a their first World Series title since 1980.

2009 ADDITIONS: OF Raul Ibanez signed a 3-year contract.
RHP Scott Nestor was claimed off waivers from the Florida Marlins.
OF John Mayberry was acquired from the Texas Rangers.
C Ronny Paulino was acquired from the Pittsburgh Pirates.
RHP Chan Ho Park signed a 1-year contract.
RHP Robert Mosebach was claimed in the Rule 5 Draft from the Los Angeles Angels.
INF Kyle Haines was claimed in the minor league phase of the Rule 5 Draft from the San Francisco Giants.

OF Javis Diaz was claimed in the minor league phase of the Rule 5 Draft from the San Diego Padres.
C Paul Hoover signed a minor league contract.
OF Jason Ellison signed a minor league contract.
RHP Gary Majewski signed a minor league contract.
RHP Yorman Bazardo signed a minor league contract.
INF Jorge Velandia signed a minor league contract.
INF Pablo Ozuna signed a minor league contract.
LHP Jake Woods signed a minor league contract.
2B Marcus Giles signed a minor league contract.

2009 SUBTRACTIONS: RHP Tom Gordon was not re-signed.
OF Pat Burrell was not re-signed.
OF So Taguchi was released.
C Jason Jaramillo was traded to the Pittsburgh Pirates.
2B Tad Iguchi was not re-signed.
RHP Adam Eaton was released.

2009 PROJECTED LINEUP: C-Carlos Ruiz; 1B-Ryan Howard; 2B-Chase Utley; 3B-Pedro Feliz; SS-Jimmy Rollins; LF-Raul Ibanez; CF-Shane Victorino; RF-Jayson Werth

2009 PROJECTED STARTING ROTATION: Cole Hamels; Brett Myers; Jamie Moyer; Joe Blanton; Kyle Kendrick; J.A. Happ

2009 PROJECTED BULLPEN: Brad Lidge; Ryan Madson; J.C. Romero; Scott Eyre; Chad Durbin; Clay Condrey; Chan Ho Park

2009 BENCH: C-Ronny Paulino; C-Chris Coste; OF-Geoff Jenkins; 3B/OF-Greg Dobbs; OF/1B-Matt Stairs; INF/OF-Eric Bruntlett

2009 EXTRA PITCHERS/PROSPECTS: Carlos Carasco; Dave Borkowski; Robert Mosebach; Scott Nestor; Mike Koplove; Jake Woods; Mike Zagurski; Yorman Bazardo; Sergio Escalona; Antonio Bastardo; Matt German; Tyson Brummett; Chance Chapman; Drew Naylor

2009 EVERYDAY PROSPECTS: Jason Donald; Lou Marson; Clay Harris; Jay Miller; Michael Taylor; Travis D'Arnaud

ASSESSMENTS:
MANAGEMENT:

New GM Ruben Amaro Jr. has some Hall of Fame caliber shoes to fill with the retirement of GM Pat Gillick. Amaro is well-respected, but there's a difference between being the assistant to the GM and being the man making the decisions. Everything that Gillick did last season worked and it's going to be hard to replace the experience and skills that Gillick had accrued over his long and storied career as an executive.

Amaro made some aggressive decisions like not even making anything more than a cursory attempt to keep Pat Burrell and acting quickly to replace him with the veteran Raul Ibanez. He also shored up the backup catching position with Ronny Paulino and added a bullpen/spot-starter with Chan Ho Park. More importantly, Amaro locked up the core of the Phillies championship team with multi-year contracts. Ryan Howard, Jayson Werth and Ryan Madson were all signed to keep them away from arbitration and free agency and he kept Jamie Moyer. One thing that has to be a concern is that Amaro has never been a GM and experience counts for something. Will Amaro be able to make the bold moves that Gillick made over the past few years to improve the club on the fly without giving up too much? Plus Gillick was in a position where he had little to lose in gutting a chunk of the Phillies farm system trying to win immediately because once the fallout from those decisions becomes reality, it won't be Gillick taking the blame for it and having to dig the team out of the hole; that'll fall to his replacement, Amaro.

Charlie Manuel is still feisty as he gets kicked out of games regularly and cusses a blue streak in the dugout; he disciplines his players—veterans or youngsters—and he's liked and respected in the clubhouse. Manuel managed during the post-season after his mother passed away and did an amazing job of keeping his focus and guiding his team to the championship. Manuel makes some strange strategic decisions, but he looked like John McGraw compared to the inexcusable screw-ups by Joe Maddon of the Rays in the World Series in which he managed circles around his counterpart. He also out-managed Joe Torre in the NLCS.

STARTING PITCHING:

Cole Hamels was brilliant last season when it counted. He was the unquestioned ace of the Phillies in the playoffs and helped carry the team to the championship. Hamels signed a long-term contract in the off-season, but one thing that has to be a concern is the number of innings he pitched in 2008. With over 250 innings at his age, there's every possibility that he'll be affected in 2009. He's had arm trouble before and he's only 25, so he'll have to be watched throughout the season.

Brett Myers was so awful in the first half that he wound up having to go back to the minors to straighten himself out. Part of that was due to the sudden change in 2007 from starting to closing; mentally and physically, it's a totally different ballgame and Myers looked like he'd grown to prefer pitching out of the bullpen. When he finally accepted that he was a starter again, he began pitching better and his overall numbers weren't all that bad despite a 10-13 record. He allowed 197 hits in 190 innings, gave up a lot of homers (29) and had excellent control. Myers has the potential to be an 18 game winner, but he's been so inconsistent in his career, a 13 or 14 win season is a more reasonable expectation.

Jamie Moyer signed another 2-year contract to continue pitching. Moyer is an artist with his control and ability to change speeds and get by with a fastball that barely breaks 80 mph. One concern I'd have with Moyer, even though he won 16 games last season and pitched remarkably well, is that he is eventually going to hit a wall and not be able to perform anymore. He's 46-years-old, so the Phillies should go into this contract knowing that Moyer may eventually, finally run out of gas; and with veteran pitchers, it happens suddenly, before anyone realizes that it *is* happening.

Joe Blanton is the perfect pitcher for Philadelphia; he pounds the strike zone and looks like he'd be more comfortable playing softball in a beer league than as a big leaguer. Blanton was having a terrible year with the A's before he was traded to the Phillies and went 4-0 in 13 starts and pitched well in the post season.

Kyle Kendrick is the type of pitcher who finds ways to win games. He doesn't strike out many; he gives up a lot of hits and runs out of gas late in the season. The Phillies should use him and his positives to their advantage, get what they can out of him and then shift him to the bullpen as the long man late in the season.

I've seen J.A. Happ pitch several times and like his stuff. He's a lefty who throws strikes, changes speeds and has the ability to strike guys out. The Phillies would probably be a better club with Happ as their fifth starter than Kendrick. I think Happ could be a 13-16 game winner eventually.

BULLPEN:

As great as Brad Lidge was last season, there's no possible way for him to repeat his perfect 41 for 41 in save opportunities. Lidge regained his form in a very difficult town in which to pitch; had he gotten off to a bad start, the Philadelphia fans would not have had the patience to let him get straightened out. Luckily for him and the Phillies, that wasn't an issue. Had the Phillies not had such a perfect season from Lidge, there's every possibility that they wouldn't have made the playoffs. Lidge is a good closer, but last season was his career year and he's due for a slight downgrade in his numbers. I'd even expect him to blow a few games early in the season.

Ryan Madson found his groove as the set-up man for Lidge. His velocity rose to the upper 90s late in the regular season and in the playoffs. After the season, Madson signed a contract extension to forego free agency at the end of 2009. He's had arm trouble in the past and his motion is herky-jerky, so just like with Hamels, he has to be kept an eye on due to his heavy workload.

Chad Durbin was a reclamation project who'd never had any legitimate big league success and suddenly became a dominant set-up man. Durbin had a 2.87 ERA in 71 games with 88 innings pitched. Durbin has never pitched that many games and he too should be watched. I'd be stunned if Durbin's able to repeat last season's success.

J.C. Romero failed a drug test for an over-the-counter supplement and will be suspended for the first 50 games of the season. In the long run, this may be a blessing in disguise. Romero will be rested and ready for the last two-thirds of the season to help the Phillies in the stretch run. As long as the other lefty in the bullpen, Scott Eyre and possibly the returning from injury Mike Zagurski are able to pick up for Romero, his loss won't be that much of an issue.

Scott Eyre emerged from the doghouse of Lou Piniella in Chicago when he was traded to the Phillies. Eyre pitched brilliantly not just against lefties, but against righties as well. Eyre's been a solid reliever for most of his career and racked up the strikeouts. He's also 37-years-old, so counting on him as a fulltime replacement for Romero may be a bit much at this stage of his career.

Clay Condrey was a useful long reliever who appeared in 56 games with a 3.26 ERA. He doesn't strike out many hitters and was raked around for a .302 batting average last season.

Chan Ho Park was signed to a 1-year contract and may get an opportunity to make the starting rotation. Park's career has been inconsistent over the past few years, but he did very well for the Dodgers last season pitching mostly in relief. He's better off pitching out of the bullpen at this point in his career.

LINEUP:

Carlos Ruiz is listed as the starting catcher but Ronny Paulino is a better hitter than Ruiz is; if Ruiz hits as poorly as he did last season (his good work in the playoff notwithstanding), he's going to find himself sharing time with Paulino. Ruiz is a solid defensive catcher, but his bat is very poor and I think Paulino's a better all-around player.

Ryan Howard puts up the power numbers annually. He's finally signed to a long-term contract and doesn't have to worry about arbitration for the next three years. Howard is very streaky and racks up 200 strikeouts a year; he's an atrocious defensive player, but has the gift of being able to hit the ball out of any ballpark. If Chase Utley is out for any substantial amount of time after hip surgery, that will affect Howard's RBI opportunities.

Chase Utley's hip may or may not keep him out until June. The latest coming from Philadelphia is that Utley *might* be ready to start the season. He keeps himself in great shape and plays very hard, so it wouldn't be stunning to see him ready earlier than expected. I think Utley is the best all-around hitter in baseball and a future MVP. He's invaluable to the Phillies lineup and they're going to struggle if he's out for the first couple of months.

Pedro Feliz had some big hits in the playoffs and has pop. Feliz has never been selective at the plate, but he's a good fielder and hits the ball out of the park.

Jimmy Rollins's numbers may be on the decline. He missed time due to an injured ankle (and I believe that affected his performance), but he's small and aging (he's 30). Rollins's numbers were never as great as they were in 2007, so if he continues to play similarly as he did last season, it could be reasonable to think that that's the player he actually is and not the player who won the MVP. He's never been all that selective either and as he becomes less of a threat, pitchers are going to be less concerned about dealing with him and his numbers will decline even further. I think Rollins is beginning the downside of his career.

Raul Ibanez replaces Pat Burrell in left field. Ibanez is a good player, hits both lefties and righties well and will hit his 25 homers and drive in runs for the Phillies; the predominately lefty lineup could be a problem during the season. As streaky as Burrell was, he was still a guy who made the opposing hitter hesitate from bringing in a lefty reliever; there's no hesitation now. The Phillies also paid a lot of money for Ibanez with a 3-year, $30 million contract. Had they known how the market was going to crash for the likes of Adam Dunn and Bobby Abreu, they might not have paid the amount of money they paid for Ibanez; in fact, they might have really waited things out and taken a shot at Manny Ramirez.

Shane Victorino became a star in the post-season. Victorino can run like the wind; has some pop and plays excellent defense.

Jayson Werth was injury-prone before the last two seasons and now he's become an indispensable part of the Phillies offense and defense. Werth walks a lot; hits homers; steals bases; gets clutch hits and plays excellent defense in the outfield. That injury history should be a concern because players who have that history can have a couple of injury-free seasons and then the bug could jump up and bite them again.

BENCH:

Ronny Paulino has been a solid player in the past but rarely played last season for the Pirates. If he's healthy, he's a better catcher than Carlos Ruiz.

Chris Coste's storybook career took another turn when he got himself a championship ring. Coste has some pop in his bat, but it's hard to see where he's going to get his at bats if Paulino and Ruiz are sharing catching duties.

Greg Dobbs was briefly bandied about as a replacement for Burrell in left field, but Dobbs is one of those players who's supposed to be a part-timer and only get his 250 at bats. He has great power from the left side of the plate and a flair for the dramatic, but he's rotten defensively. He'll get his at bats at third base and in the outfield, but any more than the 250 at bats or so will expose Dobbs for the limited player he is.

Matt Stairs is still around and his acquistion was justified by his massive homer against the Dodgers in the NLCS. Stairs is one of those guys who'll still be able to hit when he's 50 (and conveniently, he *looks* like he's 50). He's not going to get that many at bats with the Phillies this year because he has a stone glove, but as a lefty power bat off the bench, Stairs is a useful asset.

Geoff Jenkins was supposed to be part of the platoon in right field with Werth, but he's been a disappointment. Jenkins didn't hit all that much last season and is probably not going to play regularly even as a platoon player.

Eric Bruntlett was the daily defensive replacement for Burrell in left field, but now he'll probably be doing that sporadically for Ibanez. Bruntlett can play all the infield positions, but he probably won't be the second baseman if Utley's unable to start the season.

Young Jason Donald was playing shortstop in Double A last season and might be given a chance to play in place of Utley. Donald bashed the ball with speed and power in the minors last season.

PREDICTION:

Things aren't going to go as smoothly for the Phillies this season as they did in 2008. They've done many good things in locking up their young stars to long term contracts, but the absence of Gillick is going to be felt as the season moves along. Doing the "right" things doesn't always tranlsate into play on the field. Hamels is going to feel the effects of last season; Lidge won't be as good as he was last season; Romero's going to miss the first two months of the season due to his suspension; and who knows with Utley? The Phillies might take a step back if one of the other teams in the NL East plays better than expected, but unless that happens, the Phillies are lucky in that there isn't a team in the Central or West that can compete with them for a playoff spot even if it's the Wild Card they're fighting for. If, as I expect, the Marlins emerge from the East, it's again going to come down to the Phillies and Mets for the Wild Card; given how the Phillies have exerted their will on the Mets in 2007 and 2008, and that the Mets haven't improved enough to pass the Phillies, there's no reason to believe that 2009 is going to be any different. The Wild Card will be down to the Phillies and Mets late in the season with the Phillies winning it and making the playoffs for the third straight season. The hangover from 2008 will prevent them from going very far, but it's better than missing the playoffs entirely.

PREDICTED RECORD: 88-74

New York Mets
2008 Record: 89-73; Second Place, National League East

2008 Recap:

The Mets got off to a mediocre start under manager Willie Randolph; after the 2007 collapse, the Mets were vacillating on what to do with Randolph. In June, with the club playing as if they were sleepwalking and under .500, Randolph and pitching coach Rick Peterson were fired. New manager Jerry Manuel turned the club around and they had a comfortable lead in the division by mid-September, but injuries and slumping bats sabotaged another playoff spot. The loss of closer Billy Wagner and the struggles of the entire bullpen cost the Mets numerous games and their inability to hit in the clutch allowed the Phillies to pass them; the Brewers had a slump of their own, but were able to steer out of it in time to win the games they had to win and make the playoffs, something the Mets have been unable to do in the past two seasons.

2009 ADDITIONS: RHP Francisco (K-Rod) Rodriguez signed a 3-year contract.
RHP J.J. Putz was acquired from the Seattle Mariners.
OF Jeremy Reed was acquired from the Seattle Mariners.
RHP Sean Green was acquired from the Seattle Mariners.
INF Alex Cora signed a 1-year contract.
RHP Tim Redding signed a 1-year contract.
RHP Freddy Garcia signed a minor league contract.
RHP Connor Robertson was acquired from the Arizona Diamondbacks.
RHP Rocky Cherry was claimed in the Rule 5 Draft from the Baltimore Orioles.
RHP Darren O'Day was claimed in the Rule 5 Draft from the Los Angeles Angels.

OF Cory Sullivan signed a minor league contract.
RHP Livan Hernandez signed a minor league contract.
LHP Tom Martin signed a minor league contract.
LHP Casey Fossum signed a minor league contract.
C Omir Santos signed a minor league contract.
OF Rob Mackowiak signed a minor league contract.
LHP Jon Switzer signed a minor league contract.
RHP Kyle Snyder signed a minor league contract.
RHP Elmer Dessens signed a minor league contract.
LHP Valerio De Los Santos signed a minor league contract.
OF Bobby Kielty signed a minor league contract.
RHP Matt DeSalvo signed a minor league contract.

2009 SUBTRACTIONS: RHP Pedro Martinez was not re-signed.
OF Moises Alou was not re-signed.
RHP Orlando Hernandez was not re-signed.
OF Trot Nixon was not re-signed.
OF Endy Chavez was traded to the Seattle Mariners.
RHP Aaron Heilman was traded to the Seattle Mariners.
1B Mike Carp was traded to the Seattle Mariners.
OF Ezequiel Carrera was traded to the Seattle Mariners.
RHP Maikel Cleto was traded to the Seattle Mariners.
LHP Jason Vargas was traded to the Seattle Mariners.
RHP Joe Smith was traded to the Cleveland Indians.
LHP Scott Schoeneweis was traded to the Arizona Diamondbacks.
RHP Luis Ayala was not re-signed.
RHP Ambiorix Burgos was non-tendered.
INF Damion Easley was not re-signed.

2009 PROJECTED LINEUP: C-Brian Schneider; 1B-Carlos Delgado; 2B-Luis Castillo; 3B-David Wright; SS-Jose Reyes; LF-Daniel Murphy/Fernando Tatis; CF-Carlos Beltran; RF-Ryan Church

2009 PROJECTED STARTING ROTATION: Johan Santana; Oliver Perez; John Maine; Mike Pelfrey; Freddy Garcia; Tim Redding

2009 PROJECTED BULLPEN: Francisco Rodriguez; J.J. Putz; Pedro Feliciano; Duaner Sanchez; Sean Green; Brian Stokes; Connor Robertson; Bobby Parnell; Rocky Cherry; Valerio De Los Santos

2009 BENCH: C-Ramon Castro; INF/OF Marlon Anderson; INF-Alex Cora; OF/1B-Nick Evans; OF-Jeremy Reed; OF-Cory Sullivan; OF-Angel Pagan

2009 EXTRA PITCHERS/PROSPECTS: Billy Wagner; Jon Niese; Livan Hernandez; Casey Fossum; Tom Martin; Kyle Snyder; Elmer Dessens; Nelson Figueroa; Darren O'Day; Jon Switzer; Mike Antonini; Emary Frederick; German Marte; Dylan Owen; Tobi Stoner; Steven Cheney; Nick Waechter

2009 EVERYDAY PROSPECTS: Fernando Martinez; Caleb Stewart; Josh Thole

ASSESSMENTS:
MANAGEMENT:

GM Omar Minaya's main problem in 2008 was his reluctance to fire manager Willie Randolph. The vacillation had little to do with any decisionmaking problem, but that Minaya didn't want to lay all the blame for the team's struggles on Randolph. Once the guillotine that had been hanging over Randolph's head since the 2007 collapse was put to use, the Mets began to play a better, more relaxed style of baseball under Jerry Manuel. No team can function with the daily questions about the manager's status and their perormance reflected that under Manuel.

Minaya is aggressive and smart and a fine judge of talent. He made some mistakes with relying too heavily on oft-injured veterans Orlando Hernandez and Moises Alou; he was right not to give up on Carlos Delgado and resisted the nonsensical calls to trade franchise cornerstones David Wright and Jose Reyes. He's again rolling the dice with a left field of Daniel Murphy and Fernando Tatis, but with the way the economy is, he's likely going to have his choice of power hitters available as the season moves along, so his judgment may again prove to have been right. He addressed the dual bullpen needs of getting rid of most of the failures from 2007 and

2008 and acquired two successful, fearless closers to pitch the eighth and ninth innings in J.J. Putz and Francisco Rodriguez.

Manager Jerry Manuel stabilized the club with his charm and strategic skills, which are superior to those of Randolph. He steered the Mets back into contention and on the brink of a playoff spot and did the best he could with a tattered and mentally fried bullpen. The pitchers flourished under Manuel and new pitching coach Dan Warthen and the press took to Manuel's infectious personality in comparison to the paranoid Randolph. Manuel's fiery temper was also a welcome change from Randolph's reluctance to ever explode to a point where he got himself ejected even if the situation warranted it. Manuel learned from his mistakes in his first job with the White Sox and is a solid manager on and off the field.

STARTING PITCHING:

Johan Santana continued his trend of feeling his way through the first half of the season and dominating in the second half. He was heroic late in the season as he tried to singehandedly carry the Mets into the playoff and almost did, all the while pitching on a knee that needed off-season surgery. Santana was everything the Mets expected when they acquired him from the Twins and paid all that money to sign him to a contract extension. Now that he's got a year under his belt, he should return to his 20-win form and contend for the Cy Young Award.

Oliver Perez was a free agent who wasn't expected to return to the Mets, but the economy dashed his hopes to get a long term contract for the $50-60 million he and agent Scott Boras were expecting. After a long negotiation, Perez returned to the Mets for 3-years and $36 million. Perez is still only 27 and has ace-potential. He pitched better when Rick Peterson was fired as pitching coach and Dan Warthen's more hands-off approach appeared to be preferred by the Mets pitching staff. (Peterson was always in everyone's—especially Perez's—face, so a semi-trained monkey would've been a welcome relief.) Perez is durable and can be counted on to pitch some games that make him look like a Cy Young contender; and other games that make him look like he should be released. One of these years he's going to put together an 18 win season, but your guess is as good as mine for when that's going to be.

John Maine required surgery on his shoulder and the injury which sabotaged his 2008 season. Maine throws a lot of pitches and (like Perez) taxes the bullpen. Also like Perez, Maine has the potential to win 18 games.

If he's healthy, he should rebound and probably repeat his 15-win season from 2007.

Mike Pelfrey finally rewarded Minaya's faith in him by pounding the strike zone with his heavy sinker and became one of the Mets most important pitchers from the early part of the summer on. Pelfrey is big and should be durable; he pitched just over 200 innings last season and only allowed 12 homers; that should be an indicator at the effectiveness of his sinker.

The fifth spot in the rotation will come down to who wins the spring battle between veterans Tim Redding, Freddy Garcia, Livan Hernandez and young Jon Niese. Redding had a decent enough season with the Nationals last season; he's durable and throws strikes, but he's a journeyman who has a guaranteed contract. If Garcia's healthy, Redding will probably end up as a spot starter/long reliever.

Freddy Garcia was a consistent, innings-gobbling winner before injuries began hindering him and he hasn't pitched much since 2006. Garcia was serviceable in a late season audtion with the Tigers last year and pitched in the Venezualen Winter League before more shoulder woes forced him to shut it down. A healthy Garcia is a strike-throwing winner, but I'd be hesitant to expect Garcia to suddenly regain his durability.

Young lefty Jon Niese showed some potential late in the season and will probably start the season in the minors.

BULLPEN:

Francisco (K-Rod) Rodriguez joins the Mets after setting the record for saves with 62 pitching for the Los Angeles Angels last season. K-Rod has a stressful, over-the-top, all out motion, but he's maintained his health up to now despite a consistently heavy workload. He benefited from having baseball's best set-up man Scot Shields doing the heavy lifting for most of his time in Anaheim and he's got another solid guy in front of him with J.J. Putz. K-Rod can be wild and gives up some homers, but he won't be afraid of pitching in New York and the Mets got a young closer at a relatively cheap rate on a short-term deal for someone of his caliber and resume.

J.J. Putz's injury was one of the main reasons that everything fell apart for the Mariners last season. Putz is very big and throws very hard; as a former closer, he has to readjust to being a set-up man, but he's still young enough (32) that he'll be able to get a closer's job elsewhere when free agency arrives. Getting two closers for short money and moderate prospects was a great piece of work by Minaya.

Pedro Feliciano will again be the lefty specialist out of the pen. Feliciano gives up the occasional homer, but he's always willing to take the ball and he's been a historically reliable lefty out of the bullpen.

Sean Green was also acquired in the Putz deal and he reminds me of the former Athletics reliever Jim Mecir with his motion and stuff. Green appeared in 72 games last season, throws strikes and should benefit from the move to the National League.

Brian Stokes throws very, very hard and appeared to find a home in the bullpen for the Mets. He did give up five homers last season, but for the most part he was reliable and threw strikes.

Veteran reliever Rocky Cherry was selected in the Rule 5 Draft from the Orioles. Cherry throws hard and has been given a shot at closer a couple of times in his career with little success. He could have some value.

The Mets have brought in a bunch of veterans on minor league deals. Casey Fossum, Jon Switzer, Kyle Snyder and Valerio De Los Santos will get a look in spring training. I think Snyder's probably the most likely to make the team. They also have young Bobby Parnell, who's been a starter in the minors, but might make the club pitching out of the bullpen to get him acclimated to the big leagues.

Billy Wagner is recovering from Tommy John surgery and he could be a factor late in the season. If he's able to return anywhere close to form, the Mets could have a devastating late inning combination of Wagner, Putz and K-Rod, but that's too far into the future to be able to accurately speculate one way or the other.

LINEUP:

Catcher Brian Schneider's name was bandied about in trade rumors, but he's still there. Schneider showed some pop at the plate late in the season and handled the pitching staff well. His specialty is defense, but the Mets could use him to hit 12 homers or so with extra base power he's shown in the past.

Carlos Delgado had people advocating his release as he slumped from the beginning of the season until early summer. Almost coinciding directly with Randolph's firing (the two never got along), Delgado suddenly started hitting the ball out of the park and carried the team from the summer onward. Delgado ended with 38 homers and 115 RBI and became a legitimate MVP candidate. He's a free agent at the end of the season and if he wants another lucrative contract as perhaps a DH in the American League, he'll be motivated to have a productive season.

Luis Castillo practically begged for another chance to redeem himself and the contract he signed after 2007 to remain with the Mets. The Mets were looking for a replacement, but are going to give Castillo an opportunity to earn his money. Castillo has always been able to get on base and they are paying him $6 million a year, so if he's that determined to return in shape and play well, I'd give him that chance. He'll probably get the first month of the season to prove himself before being benched or dumped.

David Wright has become one of the best players in the National League and will be an annual MVP candidate. Wright hits the ball out of the park, gets on base and drives in runs; his defense still has to improve although he's become the designated NL Gold Glove winner at third base.

Jose Reyes is also a star at shortstop. His stolen base numbers dropped in 2008 seemingly by design to keep him from beating himself up during the season. Manuel has mentioned moving Reyes to third in the batting order; a good idea. Reyes is eventually going to win a Gold Glove and he too had trouble getting along with Randolph. Manuel laid down the law with Reyes the night he took over as manager as Reyes balked at being removed after tweaking a muscle. Reyes still has to mature, but he's going to be a superstar.

Daniel Murphy and Fernando Tatis are slated to share time in left field. Murphy opened eyes with his hustling, clutch play and brilliant patience at the plate. Giving him the job as part of a platoon is a risk, but worst case scenario, he'll be able to get on base. Tatis had a comeback season after bouncing around baseball and even left the game for a couple of years. Tatis was an inspiration in the clubhouse and had many big hits; whether or not he'll be able to repeat those feats or will again become the player who couldn't stick in the big leagues the five previous years will be a question that has to be answered.

Carlos Beltran puts up the offensive numbers every year and wins the Gold Glove. Beltran is beginning to try to take more of an active leadership role and can be coutned on to post the numbers that are on the stat sheet year-after-year.

Ryan Church was on his way to a great season when he got his second concussion of the year trying to break up a double play in Atlanta. Church was terrible in the second half of the season after his return, but that may have been due to the injury. There was also talk that Church didn't really like playing in New York and I'm sure the Mets would be willing to trade him if the right deal came along.

BENCH:

Vereran Alex Cora was signed to be a backup infielder and is more suited to the role than Damion Easley was. Cora is a solid all-around player and may find himself in the regular lineup if Castillo can't return to form.

Nick Evans is a young outfielder/first baseman with some pop in his bat. He was a counterpart to Murphy in the outfield and has a solid future.

Ramon Castro is the backup catcher to Schneider. Castro has some good power when he's healthy, but every time he gets a chance to play more than once or twice a week, he gets hurt. The Mets were discussing dealing him, but he's making a lot of money. I'd trade him if the chance arises.

Marlon Anderson is a veteran utility player who had a terrible season in 2008. In his career, he's been a solid, clutch hitter off the bench, but he might get traded if the Mets find a taker.

Jeremy Reed was acquired in the Putz deal and hits righties well. He's solid defensively and has doubles power.

With the Mets corner outfielders not being fully established or reliable, there's a chance that they're expecting their top young outfield prospect Fernando Martinez to be ready sometime this season. If either Tatis or Church aren't producing, there's a chance they might give Martinez an opportunity. Minaya loves Martinez and he's been off limits in all trade talks. He's had a rash of injuries throughout his minor league career, but Reyes had injury problems as a youngster as well. It may be time to see what Martinez, at age 20, can do.

PREDICTION:

The Mets offense is centered too heavily around the foursome of Wright, Reyes, Beltran and Delgado. If their starting pitching behind Santana is as inconsistent as it's been in the past couple of years, it won't matter how improved the bullpen is. If any of the four star bats are slumping, the entire offense is compromised. The bullpen will be much better if only because the arsonists they've used in the last few years are gone. The Mets will almost definitely in the market for a bat early in the season because I can't believe that either Church or Tatis are going to produce enough to do the job. Some names that might be available are Jermaine Dye and Magglio Ordonez, who I'm sure Minaya would love to get his hands on. As the team is currently constructed, the Mets aren't only behind the Phillies, but they're behind the Marlins too. They're going to have to improve on the fly to become a title contender, because as of right now, they're not.

PREDICTED RECORD: 86-76

Atlanta Braves
2008 Record: 72-90; Fourth Place, National League East

2008 Recap:

Everything that could've gone wrong for the Braves in 2008 did go wrong. The reuniting of John Smoltz and Tom Glavine to form important cogs in their rotation resulted in both veterans spending almost the entire season on the disabled list. Ace Tim Hudson required Tommy John surgery and will be out until mid-2009 at the earliest. The bullpen was horrific; their offense unproductive and overtly weak. The team was out of contention early enough to necessitate the trade of impending free agent Mark Teixeira; young players they relied on took several steps back in their development (Jeff Francoeur), and failed tests for PEDs (Jordan Schafer); and the Braves finished 20 games behind the division champion Phillies. The saving graces for the Braves season were the continued brilliance of Chipper Jones and the improvement of catcher Brian McCann and young starter Jair Jurrjens.

2009 ADDITIONS: RHP Javier Vazquez was acquired from the Chicago White Sox.
RHP Derek Lowe signed a 4-year contract.
LHP Boone Logan was acquired from the Chicago White Sox.
LHP Eric O'Flaherty was claimed on waivers from the Seattle Mariners.
RHP Jairo Cuevas was claimed on waivers from the Kansas City Royals.
C David Ross signed a 2-year contract.
RHP Kenshin Kawakami signed a 3-year contract (Japan).
OF Garret Anderson signed a 1-year contract.

2009 SUBTRACTIONS: RHP John Smoltz was not re-signed.
C Corky Miller was non-tendered.

C Tyler Flowers was traded to the Chicago White Sox.

INF Jon Gilmore was traded to the Chicago White Sox.

INF Brent Lillibridge was traded to the Chicago White Sox.

LHP Santos Rodriguez was traded to the Chicago White Sox.

LHP Chuck James was non-tendered.

LHP Will Ohman was not re-signed.

2009 PROJECTED LINEUP: C-Brian McCann; 1B-Casey Kotchman; 2B-Kelly Johnson; 3B-Chipper Jones; SS-Yunel Escobar; LF-Garret Anderson/Matt Diaz; CF-Gregor Blanco; RF-Jeff Francoeur

2009 PROJECTED STARTING ROTATION: Derek Lowe; Jair Jurrjens; Javier Vazquez; Kenshin Kawakami; Jorge Campillo; Jo-Jo Reyes; Tom Glavine

2009 PROJECTED BULLPEN: Mike Gonzalez; Rafael Soriano; Manny Acosta; Blaine Boyer; Boone Logan; Jeff Bennett; Buddy Carlyle; Eric O'Flaherty

2009 BENCH: C-David Ross; 1B/OF-Greg Norton; INF-Martin Prado; INF-Omar Infante; OF-Josh Anderson; OF Brandon Jones; C-Clint Sammons

2009 EXTRA PITCHERS/PROSPECTS: Anthony Lerew; Peter Moylan; Tim Hudson; Emiliano Fruto; Phil Stockman; Juan Perez; Stephen Marek; Jeff Ridgway; Charlie Morton; James Parr; Tommy Hanson; Kris Medlen; Scott Diamond; Bryan Dumesnil; Cory Gearrin; Michael Mehlich

2009 EVERYDAY PROSPECTS: Barbaro Canizares; Kala Ka'aihue; Willie Cabrera; Eric Campbell; Brandon Hicks; Travis Jones; Freddie Freeman; Cody Johnson

ASSESSMENTS:
MANAGEMENT:

Team president John Schuerholz didn't do GM Frank Wren any favors by kicking himself upstairs at the time he did. Wren was left with an aging and undisciplined lineup; overrated pitchers; and a shoddy bullpen. Their prospects were dealt away in desperation trades for the likes of Mark Teixeira, who they were unable to sign and had to trade away themselves. The continued attempts to win and develop on the fly were based on the Braves unprecedented run of success from 1991-2005; as the years pass, it's becoming clearer and clearer that the success those Braves teams had was based on having three Hall of Fame starting pitchers gobbling innings year-after-year. In 2008, the Braves tried to repeat some of that magic with John Smoltz and a returning Tom Glavine; it didn't work.

Wren spent the off season trying to upgrade the pitching staff. They tried to trade for Jake Peavy from the Padres, but the Padres demands were too steep and their indecision frustrating; they tried to sign A.J. Burnett, but the Yankees swooped in and offered more money (luckily for the Braves); they also tried to sign their former shortstop Rafael Furcal, but there were accusations of dishonesty between the Braves and Furcal's agent Paul Kinzer as to what was actually agreed to. To add to the misery, the Braves fell asleep at the switch under the impression that John Smoltz would return for whatever the Braves offered as he tried to make a comeback from shoulder surgery. The Red Sox swooped in and signed Smoltz, further embarrassing the organization. Wren was having a bad time.

In actuality, the Braves did quite well in upgrading their starting pitching considering these embarrassing episodes. Instead of Burnett, the Braves spent their money on Derek Lowe; they acquired Javier Vazquez from the White Sox; and they signed a Japanese pitcher Kenshin Kawakami. Wren hasn't done much else and he still has a flawed team that needs a bit more work than what he's done so far, and not all of it is his fault, but he's replacing a future Hall of Famer in Schuerholz, so Wren's going to get the blame, deserved or not.

Bobby Cox's reputation is also taking a beating. As respected, well-liked and successful as Cox has been, the way the Braves have struggled in the past few years hammers home the point that it's the players who win games. A manager can only do so much. Cox is a fine manager, but the Braves really need to start a rebuilding project and Cox's presence is making that very difficult; at his age, he's not going to want to hang around as the team rebuilds, so the Braves are treading water and trying to repeat the strategy from the 90s that's no longer working because they don't have the pitching they once had. It's not going to happen, but a parting of the ways might be positive for both sides if they're going to move forward.

STARTING PITCHING:

Derek Lowe was the Braves third choice and they signed him out of desperation. That being said, Lowe was the best option of the pitchers they'd targeted. Peavy's motion is so stressful that he's eventually going to get hurt; Burnett's record of not pitching unless he has a load of money on the line is well-known and documented. Lowe goes out there every fifth day, he throws strikes and wins games. The best thing about Lowe is, despite his age (35), he's historically durable and by the third or fourth year of the contract, he could conceivably move back to the bullpen where he spent his early career with the Red Sox. He's also a good influence on the young pitchers and pitches well in the clutch.

Javier Vazquez has also been historically durable. He doesn't pitch well under pressure, but he'll gobble innings and win his 13-15 games (and lose 13-15 games). He throws strikes and Vazquez has the type of personality that will appreciate the laid back approach of Bobby Cox.

Kenshin Kawakami was signed from Japan. Japanese pitchers are always a gamble because there's no way to know whether they're going to be able to translate to the West.

Jair Jurrjens has the makings of an All Star. He was stolen from the Braves for Edgar Renteria before last season and was a contender for Rookie of the Year. He went 13-10 in 31 starts and had excellent across the board stats; he threw strikes for the most part and only allowed 11 homers in 188 innings.

Jorge Campillo is a righty from Mexico who posted solid numbers in 25 starts and 14 relief apperances. He's a soft-tosser and looked like he tired down the stretch, but should be useful as a swing starter and a long reliever.

Jo-Jo Reyes got pounded for much of 2008. Reyes went 3-11; gave up a load of hits and home runs and didn't have very good control. He's a soft-tossing lefty with a questionable future. He may forge a career as a lefty-specialist out of the bullpen.

Tom Glavine is returning to the Braves for another season after his injured elbow ended his 2008 season. The Braves have no reason to bring Glavine back other than nonsensical sentimentality. Smoltz is gone, Greg Maddux is retired and Glavine has very little left in the tank. The Braves should move on and if he looks bad in the spring, they should tell him he's not going to make the team and allow him to bow out gracefully.

BULLPEN:

Mike Gonzalez took over as the closer and rode a power fastball and wicked slider into a very good late season surge. He angered opponents with his swinging and swaying as he looked in for the catcher's sign and he's had a long history of injuries. I'd be prepared for Rafael Soriano or Manny Acosta to take over as closer if Gonzalez struggles or gets hurt.

Rafael Soriano has closer stuff, but may not have the mentality for the job. He's had injury problems and gives up a lot of homers and only appeared in 14 games last season. If he proves himself to be healthy, the Braves might be well-served to trade him.

Manny Acosta throws very hard and could emerge as the closer if Gonzalez and Soriano falter. Acosta's wild and he gives up too many homers, but he has good stuff otherwise and he's young enough to grow into the job.

Jeff Bennett also throws very hard. Bennett pitched well in 72 games last season and allowed 86 hits in 97 innings with 3 saves.

Eric O'Flaherty was claimed from the Seattle Mariners and had a terrible year for the Mariners, winding up back in the minors. He could find a home with the Braves as a lefty specialist.

Buddy Carlyle is a veteran utility-pitcher who can do anything the manager asks him to do. Carlyle is better than Cox seems to think he is and throws strikes.

Lefty Boone Logan was acquired in the Vazquez deal and throws hard. Logan is far better pitching to lefties than righties.

Blaine Boyer is a workhorse righty who appeared in 76 games last season.

LINEUP:

Brian McCann is emerging as the best catcher in the National League. McCann has power, gets on base and as a left-handed bat, hits both lefties and righties.

Casey Kotchman was acquired in the trade of Mark Teixeira to the Angels. Kotchman doesn't hit for much power and wasn't all that productive in his time with the Braves. He may deserve a brief pass for that because he was such a longtime member of the Angels organization (his father still works there). Kotchman had 12 homers when he was traded, but he's not much of a power hitter. I'm not a big fan of Kotchman as an everyday player.

Kelly Johnson was rumored to be heading for the outfield and he still might be. He's a rotten defensive second baseman and might be better off playing left field. He's a good hitter with power.

Chipper Jones has cemented his place as a future Hall of Famer. Last season his numbers were absurdly good with a .364 batting average winning the batting title; a .470 OBP; 22 homers and 75 RBI. Jones is 37 and the Braves and Jones would be better off if they sent him to the American League where he could DH, but until they realize and accept that they're not contenders, that's not going to happen.

Yunel Escobar was involved in trade discussions for Peavy and the Braves tried to sign Furcal, possibly to play shortstop. Escobar has star potential and I haven't heard of an issues that would make the Braves want to trade him other than a bit of a temper when he does poorly. He's got a great arm and the Braves are lucky they still have him.

Garret Anderson was signed to a 1-year contract when Ken Griffey Jr. became the latest free agent to spurn the Braves. Anderson can still hit, but he's gotten very streaky as he's aged; he's a good hitter, but not a difference-maker and is a stopgap; he's going to be 37 at mid-season.

Matt Diaz received his chance to play every day and failed before getting hurt. The Braves have other outfielders who deserve to play regularly. I'd put Gregor Blanco in left every day and play one of their youngsters in center field and use Diaz exclusively against lefties and as a pinch hitter because that's what he's best suited for.

Blanco may get a chance to play center field. He's fast and fearless—he has a habit of bunting to try and break up no hitters which is perfectly legal, but unhealthy; if he does it to the wrong guy, he's eventually going to get hit in the head. I think Blanco's going to be a very good, disliked, pesky player.

Jeff Francoeur's great progress in 2007 took about three steps back in 2008. His plate discipline, which had improved from his hacking at anything and everything, diminished to the point where he wound up back in the minor leagues. Francoeur's only 25 and still has star potential offensively and defensively. His aggressiveness has to be bridled and he's probably available in a trade and going to another organization might be the best thing for Francoeur's career.

BENCH:

David Ross was signed to a 2-year contract to be a backup to McCann. Why he received anything more than a 1-year deal is beyond me. Ross has shown some pop in the past, but with McCann entrenched, Ross is probably never going to play.

Greg Norton is a veteran outfielder/first baseman who has some pop off the bench.

Omar Infante is a useful utility player who batted .293 in 96 games playing all over the field.

Josh Anderson is a center fielder who put up good numbers in the Astros system before being traded to the Braves. Anderson had an excellent season in Triple A Richmond with the Braves batting .314 with some pop and 42 stolen bases.

Jordan Schafer was a top Braves prospect before failing a drug test. He hasn't really taken responsibility for the failure saying that he was hanging around with the wrong people, whatever that means. He had a bad year when he played in Double A and his future in the big leagues is in doubt.

PREDICTION:

The Braves are reluctant to accept their current predicament and until they do that, they won't be able to move forward. They're not a good team and they continue to make attempts to patch their glaring flaws with duct tape and by clinging to the past. They were lucky that they missed out on Burnett and Peavy, but Lowe doesn't solve the problems in the bullpen or lineup. No one in power in the organziation is accepting that they need to rebuild, and considering the young talent they currently have, if they started a project now, they could reasonably expect to be contending in two years. Cox is too old to be willing to partake in that, but there are veteran teams who'd love to have Bobby Cox managing their teams. The departure of Smoltz may have been one of the best things to happen to the Braves if they take it as a signal to make the necessary changes without Glavine and the other heroes from the 90s. Unfortunately, they're not seeing reality and they're not going to get much better until reality does set in, *if* it does before they fall to last place and lose 95 games.

PREDICTED RECORD: 75-87

Washington Nationals
2008 Record: 59-102; Fifth Place, National League East

2008 Recap:

The Nationals had no pitching, no hitting, a bad bullpen and an unproductive farm system. They were a halfway house for troubled players whose crap wouldn't be accepted in 99% of the other teams in baseball and for journeymen who can't find work or an opportunity to play elsewhere. Their bright spot Ryan Zimmerman sat alone as the one big time performer who played and knew how to behave as a professional. They were a clueless and hideously run organization with no discipline and little hope.

2009 ADDITIONS: LHP Scott Olsen was acquired from the Florida Marlins.
OF Josh Willingham was acquired from the Florida Marlins.
1B/OF Adam Dunn signed a 2-year contract.
RHP Daniel Cabrera signed a 1-year contract.
RHP Terrell Young was claimed in the Rule 5 Draft from the Cincinnati Reds.
INF Freddy Bynum signed a minor league contract.
1B Brad Eldred signed a minor league contract.
INF Joel Guzman signed a minor league contract.
RHP Josh Towers signed a minor league contract.
LHP Wil Ledezma signed a minor league contract.
C Javier Valentin signed a minor league contract.
INF Alex Cintron signed a minor league contract.
RHP Jorge Sosa signed a minor league contract.

2009 SUBTRACTIONS: RHP Chad Cordero refused an assigment to the minor leagues and elected free agency.
INF Emilio Bonifacio was traded to the Florida Marlins.

RHP P.J. Dean was traded to the Flordia Marlins.
INF Jake Smolinski was traded to the Florida Marlins.
RHP Tim Redding was non-tendered.
1B/3B Aaron Boone was not re-signed.
LHP Odalis Perez was released.

2009 PROJECTED LINEUP: C-Jesus Flores; 1B-Adam Dunn; 2B-Ronnie Belliard; 3B-Ryan Zimmerman; SS-Cristian Guzman; LF-Josh Willingham; CF-Lastings Milledge; RF-Elijah Dukes

2009 PROJECTED STARTING ROTATION: Scott Olsen; Daniel Cabrera; John Lannan; Shairon Martis; Shawn Hill

2009 PROJECTED BULLPEN: Joel Hanrahan; Saul Rivera; Jesus Colome; Jason Bergmann; Garrett Mock; Jorge Sosa; Wil Ledezma; Steven Shell; Terrell Young

2009 BENCH: 1B-Nick Johnson; C-Wil Nieves; OF-Austin Kearns; OF-Corey Patterson; INF-Anderson Hernandez; OF-Willie Harris; OF-Wily Mo Pena; INF-Alex Cintron

2009 EXTRA PITCHERS/PROSPECTS: Mike O'Connor; Jordan Zimmerman; Josh Towers; Collin Balester; Tyler Clippard; Michael Hinckley; Bobby Brownlie; Gustavo Chacin; Brian Sanches; Yunior Novoa; Craig Stammen; Adrian Alaniz; Luis Atilano

2009 EVERYDAY PROSPECTS: Roger Bernadina; Leonard Davis; Dan Lyons

ASSESSMENTS:
MANAGEMENT:

On March 1st, Jim Bowden resigned as GM of the Washington Nationals amid a bonus skimming investigation by the FBI; a prospect whose age was inaccurate; and having done an overall bad job in his time running the organization.

Manager Manny Acta is in a very difficult situation. The behavior of a chunk of his clubhouse requires an immense amount of attention to keep them from getting arrested and then he has to try to navigate through that roster. Acta is an excellent strategic manager in an impossible situation.

If another GM is hired, he should seriously consider keeping Acta; and if Bowden is allowed to fire Acta, the manager won't be out of work very long because any other situation will seem like paradise compared to what's going on in Washington.

STARTING PITCHING:

Scott Olsen was acquired in a trade with the Florida Marlins. Olsen has been in trouble with the law and has gotten into numerous confrontations with teammates due to his immature attitude. Olsen has great ability and he needs the discipline instilled in him by former Marlins manager Joe Girardi during Olsen's rookie year. The Nationals, with the other troublemakers that are already present, isn't the place for Olsen. Olsen went 8-11 last season with a high ERA and gave up a lot of homers; but his hits/innings pitched ratio was quite good at 195/202. He has incredible potential and the only thing holding him back is how he behaves; I'd expect that to be a problem sometime this year due to the Nationals atmosphere.

Daniel Cabrera has unlimited potential with a high 90s fastball and the ability to dominate. Cabrera was released by the Baltimore Orioles in a very odd move. Cabrera should've been tradeable for at least a couple of minor leaguers. Cabrera has a temper and a meanness that's necessary on the mound. Again, the Nationals is a bad situation for any pitcher who needs discipline; talentwise, Cabrera's a step up from what the Nats had before, but his results aren't going to be much better there than they were in Baltimore.

John Lannan was the Nationals best pitcher last season with a 9-15 record in 31 starts. Despite the poor won/lost record, Lannan had a very solid ERA of 3.91 and very solid across the board numbers. He's only 24-years-old.

Shairon Martis showed some great potential in 4 late season starts. He has a good fastball and changeup and is only 22. He struck out over a batter per inning in his brief tour in the majors.

Shawn Hill was one of the Nats better pitchers in previous years, but he got shelled last season in 12 starts.

BULLPEN:

Joel Hanrahan throws very hard and has the stuff to be a dominating closer. He saved 9 games after previous closer Jon Rauch was traded to the Diamondbacks. Hanrahan struck out 94 in 83 innings and allowed 5 homers, but once he grows accustomed to the job, he's going to be nasty.

Saul Rivera is a historically good reliever and workhorse who appeared in 76 games last season. He posted a 3.96 ERA and only allowed 3 homers.

Jesus Colome throws very hard and posted a 4.31 ERA in 61 games.

Steven Shell had a fine season pitching in 31 games in relief. He had an excellent hits/innings pitched ratio of 34/50 and a 2.16 ERA, and he struck out 41 in 39 innings.

Jason Bergmann got pounded in 22 starts with a 2-11 record. I've always thought Bergmann had great stuff, but it didn't translate into success on the mound. Perhaps if he's used out of the bullpen as a set-up man, he'll find more success.

Garrett Mock struck out 46 in 41 innings and posted a 4.17 ERA in 26 games, all but three in relief.

Veteran Wil Ledezma was signed to a minor league contract and he's a lefty who's got a good fastball. He's had moderate success over the years, but he could be a useful pickup for the Nats.

LINEUP:

Jesus Flores is a young catcher who won overtook veterans Paul Lo Duca and Johnny Estrada to start the majority of the time. Flores didn't hit all that much with a .256 average and a .296 OBP. He did have some pop with 18 doubles and 8 homers in 301 at bats.

Adam Dunn was signed to a 2-year, $20 million contract. In years past, Dunn would probably have gotten at least quadruple what he ended up settling for with the Nationals. Dunn is a player who is either beloved for his attributes of power and patience, or scoffed at because of his penchant for striking out and seeming lack of passion for the game. At the very least, Dunn is the model of consistency and the Nationals can write in ink what he's going to provide. He'll hit his 40 homers; he'll walk a *lot*; he'll strike out even more; and he'll only drive in slightly over 100 runs because of his failures with runners on base. Unlike many of the Nationals players, he's not a troublemaker and is well-liked in the clubhouse.

Ronnie Belliard had a very good statistical year in limited play. The Nationals might be able to get some value for him if they truly intend to give young Anderson Hernandez a chance to win the everyday job. (I've seen enough of Hernandez with the Mets to let Bowden and co. know that he's not going to make it as an everyday player.) Belliard batted .287 with a .372 OBP and 11 homers in 96 games. He'll be the everyday second baseman by May if Hernandez is given the job out of spring training.

Ryan Zimmerman is the best all-around player the Nationals have. He's a good fielder and a power hitter. Zimmerman missed time with a shoulder problem and hit 14 homers in 106 games. He was the guy that the opponents said wasn't going to beat them last season and with the improved lineup, he should see better pitches to hit and put up bigger numbers.

Cristian Guzman was an All Star with a .316 batting average and 183 hits; he had some pop with 9 homers and played solid defense. Guzman has been injury prone in his career and his numbers have been up and down; he signed a long-term extension to stay with the Nationals when Bowden should've maximized his value by trading him as he should've with Dmitri Young and Belliard.

I've always liked Josh Willingham as a hitter. He's a pure slugger who hits the ball out of the park in big situations. Willingham's had some back problems in the past, but he'll put up his 20+ homers and drive in 80+ runs for the Nats.

Lastings Milledge finally got his chance to play regularly and did a reasonably good job for such a young player in a hopeless situation. Milledge hit 14 homers and drove in 61 runs in 138 games. I believe Milledge has the ability to be a very solid player; probably never a "star", but someone who'll hit 20 homers, play solid defense and show some speed. He behaved himself relatively well last season after some disciplinary issues with the Mets.

Elijah Dukes has the potential to be an MVP. Elijah Dukes also has the potential to kill someone in a rage-fueled temper tantrum. He's been in trouble with the law for various offenses from threatening to kill his estranged wife to assaulting teammates in the minors for the Rays. Last season, his anger was evident several times on the field, but he did play pretty well when his focus was on playing baseball. He also showed some evidence of maturity when he apologized for overreacting after he thought the Mets' Mike Pelfrey was throwing at him. There's hope for Dukes, but I wouldn't put up with anything from him and I'd let him know that Washington is probably his last stop before he's out of baseball since no one else is going to put up with the potential for violence because he can hit a baseball 500 feet.

BENCH:

Journeyman Wil Nieves got far too many at bats for a catcher of his caliber. Nieves is a decent defensive catcher who can't hit.

Austin Kearns had a truly awful season in 2009 batting .217 in over 300 at bats. With the number of outfielders on the Nats roster, he could be traded if anyone will take his contract.

Willie Harris is a good defensive outfielder with speed and some pop. He had 13 homers in 367 at bats last season.

Nick Johnson may be trade bait if he ever shows he can stay healthy. He's always had some pop in his bat and a gift for getting on base, but he's also very unlucky in that he's always hurt. There are many teams that could use Johnson if he's ready to play.

As mentioned before, Anderson Hernandez will be given a chance to win the everyday second base job. Hernandez doesn't hit enough to be an everyday player.

Wily Mo Pena has great potential but doesn't look like a player who's ever going to put it all together. He's another player who could be an odd man out in the Nats outfield.

PREDICTION:

The Nationals are never going to truly turn things around until they bring in a GM who's going to change the entire culture of the organization. Bowden needs to be replaced by someone who has the patience to build the club from the bottom up. That person needs to be a young talent evaluator who's not going to be concerned about trying to rehabilitate the true talents like Dukes and Milledge, but also institutes a zero-tolerance policy that will be followed. (I'll listen to a job offer; I'd love to work in Washington.) Their farm system needs to be repaired and some discipline and a code of conduct implemented. Until that happens, the team is never going to be any better than they are now.

The pitchers they've brought in should ensure that the team won't lose 100 games again, but what's the difference between losing 100 or losing 90? They're not contenders one way or the other. Why Bowden brought in all those outfielders is a mystery to me and it's a question what he's going to do with his surplus. They'll score more runs with the additions of Dunn and Willingham and they're going to be better, but it's going to be hard to notice with the disciplinary concerns and no matter what, they'll still be in last place.

PREDICTED RECORD: 70-92

National League Central
1. Chicago Cubs
2. Cincinnati Reds
3. St. Louis Cardinals
4. Milwaukee Brewers
5. Houston Astros
6. Pittsburgh Pirates

Chicago Cubs
2008 Record: 97-65; First Place, National League Central
Lost to Los Angeles Dodgers in NLDS 3 game to 0

2008 Recap:

The Cubs were expected to be a World Series participant as they easily won their division; had a deep starting rotation and bullpen, a powerful lineup and a successful and intense manager. Having made several on-the-fly improvements and mid-season deals to get outfielder Jim Edmonds and starting pitcher Rich Harden, the Cubs were favorites to win the National League pennant—then their flaws came to light in the NLDS against the Dodgers. Their number one starter, Ryan Dempster, wasn't a prototypical ace; their overly right-handed lineup couldn't solve the Dodgers pitching staff and they were unable to overcome the blazing hot Manny Ramirez and the Joe Torre-playoff luck. What had been seen as a season in which their long string of losing would end, turned into another disappointment as they were elminated from the playoffs before they even knew what hit them.

2009 ADDITIONS: RHP Kevin Gregg was acquired from the Florida Marlins.
OF Milton Bradley signed a 3-year contract.
OF Joey Gathright signed a 1-year contract.
RHP Luis Vizcaino was acquired from the Colorado Rockies.
C Paul Bako signed a 1-year contract.
INF Aaron Miles signed a 2-year contract.
RHP Aaron Heilman was acquired from the Seattle Mariners.
RHP David Patton was acquired from the Cincinnati Reds.
RHP Jeff Stevens was acquired from the Cleveland Indians.

RHP Chris Archer was acquired from the Cleveland Indians.

LHP John Gaub was acquired from the Cleveland Indians.

LHP Bill White signed a minor league contract.

LHP Matt Smith signed a minor league contract.

OF So Taguchi signed a minor league contract.

LHP Garrett Olson was acquired from the Baltimore Orioles.

RHP Henry Williamson was acquired from the Baltimore Orioles.

LHP Mike Stanton signed a minor league contract.

INF Luis Rivas signed a minor league contract.

2009 SUBTRACTIONS: INF/OF Mark DeRosa was traded to the Cleveland Indians.

RHP Jason Marquis was traded to the Colorado Rockies.

RHP Kerry Wood was not re-signed.

OF Jim Edmonds was not re-signed.

OF Felix Pie was traded to the Baltimore Orioles.

LHP Rich Hill was traded to the Baltimore Orioles.

C Henry Blanco was not re-signed.

LHP Garrett Olson was traded to the Seattle Mariners.

INF Ronny Cedeno was traded to the Seattle Mariners.

3B Casey McGehee was claimed off waivers by the Milwaukee Brewers.

1B Daryle Ward was not re-signed.

RHP Jon Lieber was not re-signed.

RHP Jose Ceda was traded to the Florida Marlins.

RHP Michael Wuertz was traded to the Oakland Athletics.

RHP Bob Howry was not re-signed.

2009 PROJECTED LINEUP: C-Geovany Soto; 1B-Derrek Lee; 2B-Mike Fontenot; 3B-Aramis Ramirez; SS-Ryan Theriot; LF-Alfonso Soriano; CF-Reed Johnson/Kosuke Fukudome; RF-Milton Bradley

2009 PROJECTED STARTING ROTATION: Carlos Zambrano; Ryan Dempster; Ted Lilly; Rich Harden; Sean Marshall; Aaron Heilman

2009 PROJECTED BULLPEN: Carlos Marmol; Jeff Samardzija; Kevin Gregg; Luis Vizcaino; Neal Cotts; Angel Guzman; Mike Stanton; Jose Ascanio; Chad Gaudin; Kevin Hart

2009 BENCH: C-Paul Bako; 1B-Micah Hoffpauir; INF-Aaron Miles; OF-Joey Gathright; OF-So Taguchi; C-Koyie Hill; INF-Luis Rivas

2009 EXTRA PITCHERS/PROSPECTS: Matt Smith; Jeff Stevens; Chad Fox; Randy Wells; Bill White; Marco Carrillo

2009 EVERYDAY PROSPECTS: Jake Fox; Marquez Smith; Josh Harrison; Ryan Keedy; Josh Vitters

ASSESSMENTS:
MANAGEMENT:

GM Jim Hendry is all in for this year. The Cubs have few prospects remaining in their organization after the "go for it now" trades they've made for the likes of Rich Harden and Kevin Gregg; all they have left as far as young players who'd be in demand is former top draft pick Josh Vitters. They were interested in Jake Peavy of the Padres and for awhile, it looked like the Cubs were the only viable landing spot for him, but the Cubs didn't have the prospects the Padres wanted and the deal fell apart several times. Hendry's made some strange trades and desperation moves. Was it really necessary to trade Mark DeRosa for three minor league pitchers? Was Milton Bradley the best fit for a lefty bat to complement the Cubs overtly right-handed hitting lineup? This may be the last chance for Hendry to be the GM of the Cubs as they try to win that elusive championship; if they don't make it to the World Series, it's not manager Lou Piniella who's going to get blamed and on a short term deal, I think it's very possible that Piniella's longtime friend and cohort from the Mariners, Pat Gillick, will come out of retirement one more time to try and win another championship.

Manager Lou Piniella has never been one to keep his emotions to himself and that was never more evident as when he benched a struggling Kosuke Fukudome and said straight out that he wasn't going to play in the playoffs. Piniella has gotten to the Cubs to the playoffs in each of the past two seasons and their record in those two years is 0-6. He made a terrible mistake in starting Ryan Dempster in game one of the playoffs and things snowballed from there as the Cubs were dispatched by the Dodgers in three straight games. Piniella was on the record as not wanting to trade one of his favorite players in Mark DeRosa, but DeRosa was traded anyway in a salary dump/replenishing the farm system move. Piniella will get his teams to the playoffs, but since winning the World Series with the Reds in 1990, he hasn't had much success at all in the post-season. The Cubs are the National League favorites again and he's going to get another chance to win that elusive pennant for the long suffering Cubs fans.

STARTING PITCHING:

Carlos Zambrano is considered one of the best pitchers in baseball when he's on his game, but it's about time for him to start acting like an ace. With Zambrano, it's either he's great or he's terrible. He slumped badly toward the end of last season and was passed over for the game one start in the playoffs in favor of Ryan Dempster. Zambrano is supposed to be the horse carrying the Cubs and he hasn't learned how to handle that responsibility.

Ryan Dempster was an injury prone starter and a shaky closer before the decision was made to move him back into the rotation and he undertook an intense regimen to get into great physical condition. It paid off as he had his career year at 17-6 with a 2.96 ERA and allowed 174 hits in 207 innings. He got shelled in the opening game of the playoffs, opening the floodgates for the Cubs panic and the Dodgers sweep. Dempster was also a free agent at the end of the season and was re-signed to a 4-year, $52 million contract. Dempster's injury history and that he had his career year in 2008 would concern me. There's no way he's going to ever be as good as he was in 2008, but they'll be paying for that season over the next four years.

Ted Lilly won 17 games and didn't get a chance to pitch in the playoffs because Piniella chose Rich Harden to pitch game three instead of Lilly. Lilly has become a durable, gutty innings-eater who pounds the strike zone. He can be counted on to win his 14-16 games and deserves to start one of the first two games of the playoffs over both Dempster and Harden.

Rich Harden was acquired from the Oakland Athletics for a large package of youngsters. Harden has some of the best stuff in baseball, but his injury history makes A.J. Burnett look like Greg Maddux in terms of durability. I don't see any way the Cubs are even going to get 20 starts out of Harden even though his contract is up at the end of the season. It doesn't do much good to have such great ability if that ability is attached to a body that can't stay healthy.

Sean Marshall is a tall lefty who spent most of last season in the bullpen. He's going to get a chance to nail down job as the fifth starter and Piniella seems to like him. He has good control and great ability.

Aaron Heilman will finally get a legitimate chance to be a starting pitcher and not a perfunctory spring training look to humor him with no intention of using him in his preferred role as the Mets used to do with him. Heilman's motion is such that former Mets pitching coach Rick Peterson insisted that it was difficult for him to repeat over and over again, but it was also the type of motion which would cause arm problems if he's asked to pitch too many innings. Heilman doesn't like pitching out of the bullpen and he's 30-years-old now; the Cubs are going to give him his wish of trying to make it as a starting pitcher and if any manager is able to get through to Heilman, it'll be Piniella. I expect him to be a decent back of the rotation starter for the Cubs this season.

BULLPEN:

Carlos Marmol takes over as the closer for the departed Kerry Wood. Marmol throws very hard, has a wicked slider and puts up absurd strikeout numbers out of the bullpen. He did allow 10 homers in 82 innings as a set-up man last season, so that's something to be concerned about, but I think he'll be an absolutely dominating short reliever for the Cubs and far better and more trustworthy than Wood and Dempster ever were.

Kevin Gregg has two characteristics that are going to put him into Piniella's doghouse sooner rather than later: he gives up a lot of home runs and he has trouble thowing strikes. Why the Cubs traded a young power pitcher like Jose Ceda for a shaky journeyman-quality pitcher like Gregg is beyond me and they're going to regret it when Gregg is blowing games in April and Piniella relegates him to mopup duty.

Veteran reliever Luis Vizcaino was acquired from the Rockies for Jason Marquis. Vizcaino tends to get off to slow starts, but as the season moves along he turns into a trustworthy reliever. He'll supplant Gregg as the primary set-up man very early in the season.

Jeff Samardzija is a hard-throwing former promising wide receiver for the University of Notre Dame who chose baseball over football. He throws very, very hard and is also going to get a shot as a starter this season. I think he'll end up back in the bullpen because he did very well as a reliever last season, didn't allow any homers and strikes out a lot of batters.

Chad Gaudin was acquired in the Harden trade and has the ability to start or relieve. He struggled with the Cubs after the trade, but has been a historically solid pitcher.

Neal Cotts was the lefty specialist out of the pen last season and appeared in 50 games with only 36 innings pitched. He throws strikes and struck out over a batter an inning. He also gave up seven homers.

Veteran Mike Stanton was signed to a minor league contract and if I had to guess, Piniella will want to keep him around unless he shows he literally can't pitch at all anymore in the spring. I don't know how much Stanton has left.

Angel Guzman reminded me of Mariano Rivera when I saw him pitch. He has a similarly lively fastball and motion. He's just coming back from injury and was a failed starting pitcher, but I'd keep an eye on him for a prominent bullpen role.

Jose Ascanio was a closer in the minors and allowed an inordinate amount of home runs. He strikes out about a batter an inning.

LINEUP:

Geovany Soto dealt with the twin chores of handling the pitching staff and placating a feisty manager who asks a lot from his catchers. That Soto was up to the task as a rookie says something about his mental toughness. Soto won the Rookie of the Year and showed himself to be an all-around player. He hits the ball out of the park, gets on base and does a solid enough job with the pitchers. He's already a star.

Derrek Lee is a great fielder, a good hitter with power, he's durable and he's a leader in the clubhouse. Lee batted .291 with 20 homers and 90 RBI and can be counted on for at least with those numbers and probably more.

Mike Fontenot will be the everyday second baseman with the departure of Mark DeRosa. Fontenot has some pop (9 homers) and showed a good ability to get on base (.395 OBP) in just under 300 at bats.

Aramis Ramirez is one of the best third baseman in baseball. He hits the ball out of the park and has the ability to be a solid defender as long as his mind doesn't wander in the field. Ramirez drove in 111 runs and gets on base at a good rate.

Ryan Theriot batted .307 as the everyday shortstop last season. He has speed (22 stolen bases); plays solid defense and gets on base (.387 OBP).

There's been talk that Alfonso Soriano may finally be moved out of the leadoff spot in the lineup as I've believed he should've been years ago. Soriano likes hitting leadoff and sulks if he's moved anywhere else, but he strikes out so much; doesn't get on base and goes up to the plate hacking away trying to hit home runs; he should be batting fifth or sixth. Soriano is very, very streaky and when he's on a hot streak, he hits a load of home runs. My guess is if he's asked to bat anywhere but leadoff, he'll go into a self-pitying slump and will get his way before too long and again be batting leadoff.

Kosuke Fukudome got off to a great start with the Cubs last season as he hit a game-tying, three run homer to tie the game on opening day, but his performance for the season was up and down. He's a useful player, but not someone to build around or for the opponents to be concenred about. He and Jim Edmonds were the lone lefty bats in the Cubs lineup and that was one of their main problems last season. His struggles culminated when Piniella benched him for the playoffs. Fukudome is going to share time in center field with veteran Reed Johnson. Johnson was a useful player for the Cubs after coming over from the Blue Jays (for nothing). He has some pop and can play any outfield position.

Milton Bradley put up massive numbers with the Rangers last season and, most importantly, he stayed healthy. Much of that can be attributed to two things: hitting in the friendly home park of Rangers Ballpark in Arlington and that he was primarily a DH. The switch-hitting Bradley signed a 3-year contract with the Cubs to be their left-handed threat; Bradley is always hurt and misses a chunk of every season. When he's in the lineup, he's a fine hitter who gets on base, but he's never able to stay in the lineup. The Cubs are so solid that they can make it to the playoffs with Bradley only playing in 100 or so games, so they should periodically rest him whether he likes it or not and make sure he's ready for the playoffs because that's when he's going to earn his money. Bradley's temper has been a problem for his entire career, but if anyone can handle him and keep him from imploding, it's Piniella.

BENCH:

Veteran utility infielder Aaron Miles signed a contract with the Cubs after the Cardinals let him go. The switch-hitting Miles batted .317 and was one of the players that Cardinals manager Tony La Russa loved. He has some pop in his bat and is willing to do anything to help his team win because he's a winning player.

Longtime minor leaguer Micah Hoffpauir opened some eyes with his late season power display for the Cubs. He hit 8 homers in 33 games for the Cubs after destroying the Pacific Coast League in Triple A Iowa with numbers that were absurd. He batted .362 with 25 homers and 100 RBI in 71 games. He can play the outfield a bit as well and deserves to get some at bats this season.

Koyie Hill and veteran Paul Bako will replace the popular veteran

Henry Blanco who signed with the Padres. Hill has shown some pop in his bat in the minors and Bako is a pitcher's favorite because he's easy to work with. Neither will play very much with Soto in front of them.

Joey Gathright is a speedy, defensive minded outfielder who was signed as a free agent. He's not a very good hitter, but he can run and steal bases.

PREDICTION:

The Cubs are the class of the National League. They're the most complete team with pitching, power, defense and a fine manager. It's gotten to the point that just making the playoffs isn't enough; they've done that in the past two seasons and been knocked out before they even knew what happened. It's up to Zambrano to finally step up and become the star pitcher he has the potential to be and that means doing it in the playoffs. Their bullpen will be better at the back end with Marmol taking over as the closer and Samardzija and Guzman will be the primary set-up men in front of him. Gregg is going to be Piniella's nemesis before April is out.

Bradley, if he's able to stay healthy, will be the powerful left-handed bat the Cubs need, but he has to be healthy for the playoff first and foremost. His injury history leaves that in question. Their starting rotation will carry them even if Dempster takes a few steps back from last season (as he undoubtedly will). The Cubs are finally going to bust through to win the National League pennant and make it to the World Series, where they'll lose to the Yankees.

PREDICTED RECORD: 96-66

Cincinnati Reds
2008 Record: 74-88; Fifth Place, National League Central

2008 Recap:

The Reds had a bit of upheaval early in the season when veteran GM Walt Jocketty replaced Wayne Krivsky and took steps to build for the future by clearing out two of their veteran outfielders when they traded Ken Griffey Jr. and Adam Dunn. Having integrated youngsters Joey Votto and Jay Bruce into the lineup; and Johnny Cueto and Edinson Volquez into the starting rotation, the Reds weren't as bad as their 74-88 record indicated. Had Aaron Harang not gotten hurt and had such a terrible season, the Reds might have hung around on the outskirts of contention and they increased their depth with the trades of the veteran outfielders that they weren't going to keep past 2008 anyway.

2009 ADDITIONS: C Ramon Hernandez was acquired from the Baltimore Orioles.
RHP David Patton was claimed in the Rule 5 Draft from the Colorado Rockies.
OF Willy Taveras signed a 2-year contract.
LHP Arthur Rhodes signed a 2-year contract.
OF Laynce Nix signed a minor league contract.
RHP Jeff Kennard signed a minor league contract.
OF Jonny Gomes signed a minor league contract.
OF Jacque Jones signed a minor league contract.
1B/OF Daryle Ward signed a minor league contract.

2009 SUBTRACTIONS: INF/OF Ryan Freel was traded to the Baltimore Orioles.
LHP Jeremy Affeldt was not re-signed.
INF Andy Phillips refused an assignment to the minor leagues and elected free agency.

INF Brandon Waring was traded to the Baltimore Orioles.

INF Justin Turner was traded to the Baltimore Orioles.

RHP Matt Belisle was non-tendered.

RHP Gary Majewski was non-tendered.

2009 PROJECTED LINEUP: C-Ramon Hernandez; 1B-Joey Votto; 2B-Brandon Phillips; 3B-Edwin Encarnacion; SS-Alex Gonzalez; LF-Jerry Hairston; CF-Willy Taveras; RF-Jay Bruce

2009 PROJECTED STARTING ROTATION: Aaron Harang; Edinson Volquez; Bronson Arroyo; Johnny Cueto; Micah Owings; Homer Bailey

2009 PROJECTED BULLPEN: Francisco Cordero; David Weathers; Arthur Rhodes; Jared Burton; Mike Lincoln; Billy Bray; Nick Masset

2009 BENCH: C-Ryan Hanigan; OF-Chris Dickerson; INF-Danny Richar; INF-Jeff Keppinger; OF-Norris Hopper; OF-Jonny Gomes; 1B/OF-Daryle Ward; INF-Paul Janish

2009 EXTRA PITCHERS/PROSPECTS: Carlos Fisher; Robert Manuel; Aaron Fultz; Adam Pettyjohn; Ron Flores; Danny Herrera; Ramon Ramirez; Josh Roenicke; Ben Jukich; Misael DeJesus; Enerio Del Rosario; Jeremy Horst

2009 EVERYDAY PROSPECTS: Daniel Dorn; Chris Valaika

ASSESSMENTS:
MANAGEMENT:

Walt Jocketty was the longtime GM of the St. Louis Cardinals during their recent run of excellence. He was forced out because of differences between his philosophy and the direction the Cardinals ownership wanted to head. (In short, he wanted to spend some money; they don't.) He was an advisor for the Reds for a short while before he was hired to take over for Wayne Krivsky. Jocketty is a smart, aggressive baseball man who isn't afraid to make mistakes. He knows talent and he knows how to build teams to win quickly. Jocketty likes veteran players, but he's also not afraid to let youngsters play. In his trades of Dunn and Griffey, Jocketty brought in a pretty good haul of youngsters to provide some depth in the organization.

Manager Dusty Baker receives criticism from all sides because of accusations that are either misleading or inaccurate. He has his own way of doing things to be sure; he doesn't subscribe to the theory of forcing his hitters to take a ton of pitches, but there are two sides to that story; if a hitter is just that type of hitter in which he's becoming a detriment to what it is he does, then he shouldn't take pitches just to appease the manager. There's such a thing as aggressiveness within structure and maybe that's a better way to run one's club than insisting that they take pitches they should be hacking at.

Baker has also been criticized for not wanting to give young players a chance to play. Joey Votto, Jay Bruce, Edinson Volquez and Johnny Cueto all played a big part on the Reds last season and all did quite well. It may have been that Baker didn't have very many young players available to him that deserved to play. Looking at the kinds of teams he managed before—the Giants and Cubs—they were veteran-laden teams that were built to win immediately. Now he's proving himself to be able to handle young, talented players as well. Baker has one attribute that is conveniently ignored by those who criticize him: his teams win and eventually, he and Jocketty are going to have the Reds winning too.

STARTING PITCHING:

In addition to picking the Reds (who ended up in fifth place) to win the division last season, I picked Aaron Harang to win the Cy Young Award. It wasn't like I was pulling the opinion out of my butt; Harang had been one of the most underrated and durable pitchers in baseball over the previous three seasons. Last year, he struggled and got hurt and had a truly awful season with a 6-17 record with a ridiculous 35 homers allowed along with terrible stats across the board (except for his control; Harang always throws strikes). Had Harang been able to win his usual 15 games, the Reds would have been hovering around the outskirts of contention. A pitcher as good as Harang has been isn't suddenly going to lose his ability to pitch at age 30. He'll have a solid comeback year and return to the quality pitcher he was in years past. (And no, I'm not picking him to win the Cy Young Award.)

Edinson Volquez was the other part of a truly mutually advantageous trade between the Rangers and the Reds before last season. Volquez was acquired in the deal that sent Josh Hamilton to the Rangers. Volquez was brilliant and the only reason he didn't win the Rookie of the Year is because he technically wasn't a rookie. Volquez was a viable Cy Young candidate as well. With a 17-6 record, 206 strikeouts and 167 hits allowed in 196 innings, and a 3.21 ERA, Volquez was excellent and if he can even approach those results this year, he'll get the recognition as an emerging star that he deserves.

Bronson Arroyo was getting pounded early in the season and was pitching terribly. He was on the trade block but remained in Cincinnati and began pitching better. Arroyo is a case in point that gutty veterans whose stuff has been maintained can be counted on to put up the same numbers year-after-year. After his terrible start, Arroyo ended his season with a 15-11 record, pitched his 200 innings and his 4.77 ERA is quite good considering that there's one game he pitched against the Blue Jays in which he allowed 10 runs in one inning. Other than that, he had a very respectable season and is a useful middle-to-back of the rotation starter who can be trusted to gut his way through, especially in a big game.

Johnny Cueto is a 23-year-old righty whose stuff and motion has been compared to that of a young Pedro Martinez. That may be a bit of a stretch, but Cueto has the chance to be a very good pitcher. He went 9-14 as a rookie and put up pretty good across the board stats with flashes of brilliance (including a flirtation with a no-hitter against the Braves).

Micah Owings was acquired in the Dunn trade and contributed to a couple of Reds wins with his bat, but was injured and unable to pitch for the Reds. There's been talk that Owings is such a good hitter that he should be made into a position player; that may still happen eventually, but I think he's got the stuff to be a 12-15 game winner as a pitcher. Last year he got off to a fast start and began slumping to the point where he was shifted to the bullpen and even went back to the minors for a spell. I wouldn't give up on Owings as a pitcher just yet.

Homer Bailey was a touted prospect who was horrible all season long wherever he pitched. He was atrocious in the minors with a 4-7 record in 19 starts in Triple A; and in the big leagues (why he got called up is a mystery), he went 0-6 and got *rocked*. Bailey has a reputation of not listening to his coaches and I can tell you right now that Reds pitching coach Dick Pole (credited by Greg Maddux for teaching him proper mechanics) is *not* going to put up with that, and neither is Baker; and neither is Jocketty. The Reds were said to be discussing trading Bailey in a possible trade to the White Sox for Jermaine Dye, but there were conflicting reports as to the accuracy of that rumor. Bailey's still there and if he wants to pitch in the big leagues, he'd better start listening to people who are trying to help him.

BULLPEN:

Francisco Cordero was signed to a lucrative contract before the season started and pitched well as the closer saving 34 games. Cordero tends to slump at various times during the season, but he strikes out over a batter an inning, throws very hard and is a good guy in the clubhouse.

David Weathers's stuff isn't what it once was, but the 39-year-old takes the ball whenever he's needed; throws strikes and guts his way through games with good control. He's probably not at his best if he's asked to pitch as often as he once was and his workload needs to be lowered to keep him fresh, but he can still be a useful component in a bullpen as a veteran influence.

Jared Burton emerged as a favorite of Baker as the season moved along and showed the potential to be a good set-up man. He throws hard; he racks up the strikeouts at one per inning; and he throws strikes.

I'm still waiting for Billy Bray to fulfill the abilities I see in him every time he pitches. Bray's numbers were very good as a lefty specialist last season, but I see him as having the stuff to get out righties and lefties. Bray put up a 2.87 ERA and struck out 54 in 47 innings. At worst, he'll do the same job he did last season.

Mike Lincoln appeared in 64 games and pitched better than his numbers. He's a veteran who throws strikes and strikes out close to a batter per inning. He gave up ten homers, which is a lot.

Arthur Rhodes signed a 2-year contract as another veteran lefty in the bullpen. Rhodes has done his job for a long time and has bounced from team-to-team, but he's popular in his clubhouse, always takes the ball, and gets the job done. A 2-year contract may have been a bit much, but Rhodes still showed to have something left in the tank last season.

Nick Masset is a big righty who was acquired in the Griffey trade. Masset can be a bit wild, but could be a useful long man.

LINEUP:

Ramon Hernandez was acquired in a trade with the Orioles to add a bat and decent veteran catcher to handle the pitching staff. Baker likes having a catcher who he can trust to call a solid game and that explains why the light-hitting Paul Bako saw so much time as the Reds catcher last season. Hernandez isn't great defensively; he'll hit his 15-20 homers and drive in a few runs; overall he'll be an upgrade over Bako.

Joey Votto had an excellent rookie season with a .287 batting average; 24 homers; 59 extra base hits; a .368 OBP; and 84 RBI. He's an emerging All Star.

Brandon Phillips could be one of the best hitting second basemen in all of baseball. His numbers were down from 2007, but he did hit 21 homers and drive in 78 runs; he stole 23 bases and played solid defense. I'd expect him to rebound to what he produced in the previous year.

Edwin Encarnacion's main problem seems to be concentration. He'll make a defensive play that one would expect to see from Brooks Robinson or Graig Nettles, then he'll let a ground ball roll through his legs and stare into his glove as if it was the glove's fault. He has power and a flair for the dramatic with his bat; he hit 26 homers last season. Encarnacion could explode into a star or he could find himself benched and then traded because of his attitude. I wouldn't give up on him, but I would understand if the Reds got a good offer and jumped at it.

Alex Gonzalez is set to return from injury and take over at shortstop. Gonzalez is a vacuum cleaner defensively and has enough pop to hit his 15-20 homers. He missed the entire 2008 season and if he can't come back the Reds have a couple of young talented shortstops in their organization in Paul Janish and Chris Valaika.

Jerry Hairston had a solid year as a part-time player. He batted .326 in 80 games and had a .384 OBP. He's more suited to be a rotating utility player, but unless Chris Dickerson proves he's ready to start in left field, Hairston should get the at bats in left until Dickerson's ready.

Willy Taveras signed a 2-year contract with the Reds after being non-tendered by the Rockies. Taveras is a very good defensive outfielder with great speed. He strikes out too much; has no power; bunts a lot and doesn't have a lot of skill at getting on base, but he did steal 68 bases and his faults aren't going to be held against him by Baker; he'll probably be batting leadoff when he should be batting eighth.

Jay Bruce was called up from the minors and exploded onto the scene. He was on fire for the first month of his big league career and proved that the hype surrounding him was legit. Bruce only batted .254 and was horrible against lefties with a .190 batting average. He hit 21 homers in 108 games and at age 22, he has nowhere to go but up; he hit lefties well in the minors and will learn to do the same in the majors.

BENCH:

Chris Dickerson hit well in a brief trial late in the season and his numbers in the minors indicate he can be a solid player with some pop. He's not young at 26, so if he gets the opportunity to play, he'd better take advantage of it.

Ryan Hanigan will be the backup catcher to Hernandez and has shown he can hit in the minors. He'll see negligible time in the lineup unless Hernandez gets hurt.

Jeff Keppinger was forced into regular duty at shortstop when he's more suited to be a utility player. Keppinger is a decent enough little hitter with doubles power, but he shouldn't get even half the number of at bats (459) he got last season.

Feisty Jonny Gomes was signed to a minor league contract after being non-tendered by the Rays. Gomes was always there to stick up for his teammates with the Rays and has some power. I think Baker will want to keep him on the roster for some power off the bench.

Veteran journeyman Daryle Ward was signed to a minor league contract and he has power and on base ability; I'd expect him to make the team as a backup first baseman.

Paul Janish is a young infielder who was one of the Reds top prospects; he got a chance to play briefly last season and contributed a few big hits.

PREDICTION:

The Reds pitching should keep them competitive especially if Arroyo and Volquez can repeat last season's work; Cueto can continue to improve and mature; and if Harang is the pitcher he was before his disastrous 2008. I also think there's still hope for Owings. Their bullpen is deep and serviceable. It's their offense that's the key to possibly being on the outskirts of contention or finishing under .500. If Bruce, Phillips, Encarnacion and Votto put up the power numbers, scoring runs won't be an issue; if they slump, they're going to have trouble scoring runs and winning. I believe the Reds are going to improve substantially from last season and while not being contenders, they're going to be a tough team to play. They'll hover around the .500 mark and not be considered serious playoff possibilities and end the season well with a solid record and a bright future.

PREDICTED RECORD: 85-77

St. Louis Cardinals
2008 Record: 86-76; Fourth Place, National League Central

2008 Recap:

    Thanks to the strategic wizardry of manager Tony La Russa and the way pitching coach Dave Duncan can mold just about any pitcher into a competent and useful cog in the machine, the Cardinals played so far above their talent level that 2008 probably one of La Russa's best tricks in a long and storied career. Using underachieving journeymen (Kyle Lohse); players who were alleged to have used PEDs and converted from other positions (Troy Glaus and Rick Ankiel); career minor leaguers (Ryan Ludwick); and one historic superstar (Albert Pujols), the Cardinals won a surprising 86 games. They did it with a hideous bullpen and a short-handed starting rotation and lineup. Had the Cardinals acquired some veteran bats and arms, they might have been the team that took the Wild Card instead of the Brewers and La Russa proved in 2006 that all he has to do is make it to the playoffs; after that, anything can happen, but the front office was reluctant to do anything at all and because of that, they faded out at the end and missed the playoffs and in the process justifiably angered the manager and the fan base.

2009 ADDITIONS: SS Khalil Greene was acquired from the San Diego Padres.
LHP Trever Miller signed a 1-year contract.
LHP Royce Ring signed a 1-year contract.
LHP Charlie Manning was claimed off waivers from the Washington Nationals.

2009 SUBTRACTIONS: RHP Russ Springer was not re-signed.
RHP Jason Isringhausen was not re-signed.
LHP Mark Mulder was not re-signed.
2B Adam Kennedy was released.
INF Aaron Miles was non-tendered.

LHP Randy Flores was non-tendered.
OF Juan Encarnacion was not re-signed.
LHP Tyler Johnson was non-tendered.
RHP Mark Worrell was traded to the San Diego Padres.
C Mark Johnson refused an assignment to the minor leagues and elected free agency.
SS Cesar Izturis was not re-signed.
RHP Braden Looper was not re-signed.
INF Felipe Lopez was not re-signed.

2009 PROJECTED LINEUP: C-Yadier Molina; 1B-Albert Pujols; 2B-Brendan Ryan; 3B-Troy Glaus; SS-Khalil Greene; LF-Skip Schumaker; CF-Rick Ankiel; RF-Ryan Ludwick

2009 PROJECTED STARTING ROTATION: Adam Wainwright; Kyle Lohse; Chris Carpenter; Todd Wellemeyer; Mitchell Boggs; Joel Piniero

2009 PROJECTED BULLPEN: Chris Perez; Jason Motte; Ryan Franklin; Josh Kinney; Trever Miller; Royce Ring; Brad Thompson; Kyle McClellan; Jess Todd

2009 BENCH: C-Jason LaRue; INF-Brian Barden; OF-Brian Barton; OF-Colby Rasmus; OF/1B-Chris Duncan; 3B-Davie Freese; INF-Joe Mather

2009 EXTRA PITCHERS/PROSPECTS: Matthew Scherer; Justin Fiske; Luke Gregerson; Richard Castillo; Francisco Samuel; Nicholas Additon; Pete Parise; Eduardo Sanchez

2009 EVERYDAY PROSPECTS: Andrew Brown; Allen Craig; Jon Jay; Mark Shorey; Donovan Solano

ASSESSMENTS:
MANAGEMENT:

GM John Mozeliak is under fire not only for his lack of movement in improving a team that could've made the playoffs with a tweak here and a tweak there, but his attitude and obnoxious reactions to the loyal Cardinals fans legitimate griping at said lack of movement is not only making him look inept at his job, but despised on a personal level.

Mozeliak has a Hall of Fame manager in Tony La Russa who he seems to be doing his best to alienate into leaving at the conclusion of his contract at the end of the 2009 season. In a market flush with closers, he did nothing to fill that gaping hole in the Cardinals bullpen (and one of the main reasons why they stumbled toward the end of the 2008 season). Albert Pujols is still essentially on an island in the Cardinals lineup and the only reason they were able to upgrade with a veteran shortstop in Khalil Greene is because the cost-slashing Padres gave him away for a midline prospect in Mark Worrell. All Mozeliak has done in addition to acquiring Greene was to acquire two journeyman left-handed relievers by signing Trever Miller and Royce Ring. In a division with the Cubs, he can't possibly believe that's enough to contend for a division title; and with the Wild Card likely to be fought out by the Mets, Marlins, Phillies, Dodgers, Giants and Rockies, Mozeliak hasn't done anything to put his club into a position to contend there either.

The farm system is weak; the team has become cheap and their GM is incapable of doing anything other than angering the fan base with his arrogance. When La Russa leaves, this team is going to fall apart completely and the responsibility will land at the feet of Mozeliak, one of the game's worst GMs.

Tony La Russa appears resigned to his fate and that he's going to have to go elsewhere if he wants to work for a team that's going to spend the money and bring in the players he needs to win. La Russa, with his resume and at his age (64) doesn't need to be lied to; he doesn't need to be humored; he doesn't need to publicly ask for reinforcements and be ignored. He's such a great manager that he'll help the Cardinals overachieve again and again, but has really no chance of making the playoffs. After this season, I expect La Russa to look for a new home; one in which he'll be given the respect he's earned and the players he needs to contend for one more title run. I believe Tony La Russa and pitching coach Dave Duncan will join the Baltimore Orioles for the 2010 season.

STARTING PITCHING:

Adam Wainwright missed a chunk of 2008 with injuries, specifically to his finger. His performance in the 2006 playoffs and as a starter in 2007-2008 show a pitcher on the brink of stardom. Wainwright was on his way to 17-20 wins when he got hurt last season and he'll pick up where he left off this season if he's healthy. Wainwright is a contact pitcher who throws strikes and goes deeply into games; he's got a good fastball and a wicked curveball and could be a Cy Young contender this year.

Kyle Lohse priced himself out of a the multi-year deal he wanted before last season and signed with the Cardinals on a 1-year contract in the hopes that La Russa and Duncan could unlock his massive potential and he'd get the money he wanted. Lohse responded with an All Star caliber season and went 15-6 with fine across-the-board stats. Lohse has always had great stuff; a good fastball and a wicked slider, but never put it together for a full season. He signed an extension to stay in St. Louis and while he's been so flighty and inconsistent during his career that it's quite possible that he'll take a step back now that he's not singing for his supper, I think he'll still pitch well enough to win his 13-16 games.

Chris Carpenter's arm woes have kept him out for most of the past two seasons. La Russa had expressed a desire to move Carpenter to the bullpen and try him out as the closer, a good idea; but the front office doesn't want Carpenter to close and he's preparing himself as a starter this season. Who knows if Carpenter, at age 34, will be able to return to his Cy Young Award-winning form? He might be able to pitch effectively, but his durability is going to get worse, not better. I'll be stunned if he returns healthy enough to start more than 20 or so games, if that.

Longtime minor league journeyman Todd Wellemeyer blossomed into a solid starter last season. Wellemeyer went 13-9 in 32 starts with a 3.76 ERA and a very good hits/innings pitched ratio of 178/192.

Mitchell Boggs got knocked around in eight big league apperances last season (including six starts), but the 25-year-old was very good for Triple A Mephis and should get a shot as a fulltime starter this year.

Veteran Joel Piniero missed time with a strained back muscle and pitched shakily when he was healthy enough to pitch. Piniero went 7-7 and gave up a lot of hits and home runs. He's been a successful starter in the past and a comeback to something close to what he was at his best isn't out of the question.

BULLPEN:

Young Chris Perez was given a chance as the closer last season and performed well. Perez was a bit wild, but struck out a batter per inning and saved seven games. He allowed five homers in 42 appearances, which is a concern. La Russa seemed reluctant to go with Perez as his closer, but that concern has fallen on deaf ears in the front office.

Jason Motte is a young reliever who put up massive strikeout numbers in the minors and in a brief time in the big leagues. He has good control and that strikeout ability might make his a better candidate for the closing job than Perez.

Ryan Franklin has found his niche as a reclamation project by La Russa and Duncan. He closed for awhile after Jason Isringhausen asked out of the job and did admirably well, but he's not a closer. Franklin's durable and throws strikes; he's more of a veteran set-up man than he is a closer.

Veteran lefty specialist Trever Miller has been a part of some very good bullpens in his career including the Astros of the middle part of the decade and last year's Rays. Miller can be counted on to do his job and be used in the best possible situations for him to succeed by La Russa.

I've seen enough of Royce Ring to know that he's a journeyman lefty who isn't very good. Maybe La Russa and Duncan can work their magic with him as they've done with some other heretofore bad relievers.

Josh Kinney missed 2007 and most of 2008 after Tommy John surgery; he was a useful righty reliever before that and there's no reason to believe he won't be that again.

Brad Thompson is a righty contact pitcher who was something of a jack-of-all-trades for La Russa; he started six games last year and relieved in 20 others. He gave up 72 hits in 65 innings last season and allowed five homers.

Young Jess Todd put up excellent numbers in Double and Triple A as a starter and, at age 23, he may go the route some other young pitchers have for La Russa and get his big league career going out of the bullpen.

Righty Todd McClellan appeared in 68 games in relief last season. He allowed 79 hits in 76 innings and has good control.

LINEUP:

Yadier Molina's offense has finally begun to catch up with his defense and it all started with his excellent post-season in 2006. It's easy to forget that Molina is still only 26; last season he batted .304 with 7 homers and 56 RBI in 124 games. He's pretty much the best defensive catcher in baseball who handles the pitching staff very well.

What is there to say about Albert Pujols that hasn't already been said. He's quite simply the best hitter of his generation and his pure numbers don't do him justice. Not only did he win the MVP with a .357 average; 37 homers; 81 extra base hits; a .462 OBP; and 116 RBI; but he walked 104 times with no lineup protection and only struck out 54 times. It's hard to imagine what kind of numbers Pujols would put up if he were in the lineup of the Yankees or Phillies; and he's a Gold Glove first baseman as well. Pujols must be getting frustrated with what's going on with the Cardinals; he said in the winter that he'd like the Cardinals to pursue Manny Ramirez and Mozeliak's response was condescending and insulting to the team's star player. If La Russa leaves and the Cardinals continue to pinch pennies, I wouldn't be stunned to see Pujols start rattling his cage and possibly ask out of St. Louis unless they start making a more concerted effort to win.

Veteran Adam Kennedy was released in February, thereby swallowing his $3 million salary, which made little sense; they couldn't have gotten something for him by eating some of his salary? Aaron Miles was not tendered a contract, so the Cardinals are left with Brendan Ryan or Brian Barton to play the position. Ryan his .261 in 80 games last season and has no power, but some speed.

Troy Glaus is scheduled to miss a chunk of the first half of the season with shoulder surgery. Glaus was one of the only bats that could protect Pujols just a little bit; Glaus was a step-up from Scott Rolen after the two were traded for one another before last season. Glaus's contract is up at the end of the season, so when he returns, he'll be motivated to do well. Young David Freese has shown power in the minors and presumably he'll get a chance to be the everyday third baseman while Glaus is out. Freese strikes out a lot and gets on base.

The Cardinals got Khalil Greene for almost nothing because the Padres wanted to slash every big salary they had before they reached agreement to sell the club. Greene was atrocious last season batting .213 with 10 homers and grew so frustrated with his play that he broke his hand slamming it in anger. Greene is a free agent at the end of the year, has been a good fielder in his career and, while not being an on base guy, does hit the ball out of the park. He's the type of player that La Russa will be able to get a career-year from.

Skip Schumaker batted .302 in 153 games. He has speed, a little pop, gets on base at a reasonable clip and is a good defensive outfielder.

Rick Ankiel was supposedly discussed in trade possibilities and given his history, I'd trade him if a good offer was presented. (The Yankees were said to be interested and one thing I would *not* do is put Ankiel in the Yankees fishbowl.) Ankiel hit 25 homers and drove in 71 runs in 120 games. If he repeats those numbers, the Cardinals should be very happy.

Ryan Ludwick exploded with a massive year of 37 homers; 113 RBI; .375 OBP and a .299 batting average. Ludwick is 31-years-old and was a journeyman before last season, so 2008 could've been his season of a lifetime. I can't imagine him repeating those numbers.

BENCH:

Backup catcher Jason LaRue's power numbers earlier in his career with the Reds are a bit dubious. LaRue can't hit and won't play if Molina's healthy for the whole season. He handles the pitchers well and is reasonably good defensively.

Chris Duncan is trying to return after a career-threatening herniated cervical disc in his neck. Whether he'll be able to is an open question; it's a shame.

Brian Barden will get some time at second base and he hit well in Triple A and has some pop in his bat.

Young Colby Rasmus is one of the Cardinals top hitting prospects. He's got good power and some speed and might make the big league club as an outfielder.

Joe Mather is a backup outfielder who put up big on base and power numbers in Triple A. He's 26-years-old, so he's a bit old to be considered a prospect, but has some useful skills.

I haven't checked, but I'll assume that Jarret Hoffpauir is related to Micah from the Cubs; I can't imagine there'd be two people in pro baseball with the name Hoffpauir. He's a 25-year-old second baseman who might actually get a chance to play in the big leagues if no one else claims the job. Hoffpauir has doubles power and gets on base at a reasonably good clip (.352 at Triple A).

PREDICTION:

If the Cardinals invested some money in their current big league roster—a power bat for the outfield or second base, a veteran starter and some legit bullpen help—they'd be able to challenge the Cubs for the Central Division title and would be the favorites for the Wild Card; but they haven't and won't. Again the front office is going to rely on Pujols's greatness and La Russa's brilliance and it's not going to work any better than it did last season. The Cubs are going to run away with the division; the Cardinals may stay within striking distance of the Wild Card for the duration of the season, but they're not real contenders. La Russa's contract is up at the end of the season and I can't imagine any circumstances under which he'll return. The Cardinals are going to finish above .500 because of the talent they currently have, but until they decide to make some moves to improve, they're not going to contend and it's the fault of the front office and GM John Mozeliak. Their fans had better enjoy their manager and their club while they can because after this season, they're going to go down the road of the Padres and after 2009, their results will be similar and that's going to be an embarrassment for one of the proudest and most admired franchises in baseball history.

PREDICTED RECORD: 85-77

Milwaukee Brewers
2008 Record: 90-72; Second Place, National League Central; Wild Card winner
Lost to Philadelphia Phillies 3 games to 1 in NLDS

2008 Recap:

With a crop of homegrown talent and an oft-injured ace whose contract was up at the end of the season, the Brewers went for it all in 2008. First they made a series of aggressive moves, one of which brought C.C. Sabathia to Milwaukee. Sabathia picked the club on his back after his arrival and almost singlehandedly brought them to the playoffs with a display of heroics I haven't seen since Orel Hershiser in 1988. The Brewers looked like they couldn't be stopped from making the playoffs when for the second straight year, they collapsed. Once September hit, all the Brewers did was lose, lose and lose some more. It got to the point that owner Mark Attanasio and GM Doug Melvin couldn't afford to let the season go down the tubes and took the unprecedented step of firing manager Ned Yost with three weeks left in the season. The team regained it's footing under new manager Dale Sveum and, assisted by the Mets (who also collapsed for the second straight year), made the playoffs as the Wild Card. They were eliminated in four games by the Phillies.

2009 ADDITIONS: Manager Ken Macha was hired.
RHP Trevor Hoffman signed a 1-year contract.
RHP Braden Looper signed a 1-year contract.
3B Casey McGehee was claimed off waivers from the Chicago Cubs.
1B Scott Thorman signed a minor league contract.
RHP Jorge Julio signed a 1-year contract.
RHP Eduardo Morlan was claimed in the Rule 5 Draft from the Tampa Bay Rays.
OF Trot Nixon signed a minor league contract.

LHP Chase Wright was acquired from the New York Yankees.

RHP Nick Green was claimed off waivers from the Los Angeles Angels.

2009 SUBTRACTIONS: LHP C.C. Sabathia was not re-signed.
RHP Ben Sheets was not re-signed.
RHP Salomon Torres retired.
OF Gabe Kapler was not re-signed.
INF Joe Dillon was claimed off waivers by the Oakland Athletics.
2B/OF Ray Durham was not re-signed.
OF/C Eric Freyer was traded to the New York Yankees.
RHP Guillermo Mota was not re-signed.
LHP Brian Shouse was not re-signed.
RHP Derrick Turnbow was released.
INF/OF Russell Branyan was not re-signed.

2009 PROJECTED LINEUP: C-Jason Kendall; 1B-Prince Fielder; 2B-Rickie Weeks; 3B-Bill Hall; SS-J.J. Hardy; LF-Ryan Braun; CF-Mike Cameron; RF-Corey Hart

2009 PROJECTED STARTING ROTATION: Yovani Gallardo; Jeff Suppan; Braden Looper; Manny Parra; Dave Bush; Chris Capuano

2009 PROJECTED BULLPEN: Trevor Hoffman; David Riske; Jorge Julio; Seth McClung; Mitch Stetter; Eduardo Morlan; Nick Green; Todd Coffey; Eric Gagne

2009 BENCH: INF-Craig Counsell; INF-Mike Lamb; OF-Tony Gwynn, Jr.; SS-Alcides Escobar; OF-Trot Nixon; C-Mike Rivera; 1B-Brad Nelson; 1B-Scott Thorman

2009 EXTRA PITCHERS/PROSPECTS: Mark DiFelice; Tim Dillard; R.J. Swindle; Chris Narveson; Joe Bateman; Lindsay Gulin; Omar Aguilar; Steve Hammond; Dave Johnson; Bobby Bramhall; Corey Freichs

2009 EVERYDAY PROSPECTS: Mat Gamel; Cole Gillespie; Angel Salome; Taylor Greene; Jonathan Lucroy; Caleb Gindl; Steffan Wilson

ASSESSMENTS:
MANAGEMENT:

GM Doug Melvin is a solid all-around baseball executive. The Brewers organization is loaded with prospects and he used some of that surplus to go for it all in 2008 when the opportunity presented itself; Melvin gave up a haul of prospects for C.C. Sabathia and Sabathia was masterful from the time he put on the Brewers uniform. It took courage to fire the manager with the team spiraling in September, but had they not done it, the Brewers would not have made the playoffs. Melvin made a good faith effort to re-sign Sabathia, but there was never much of a chance of the big lefty returning to Milwaukee with the money the Yankees were throwing at him. Now, the Brewers find themselves in a position where they'll be willing to sell instead of looking to buy. Melvin's top talent evaluator, Jack Zduriencik (who was said to be a major reason the organization is so prospect-heavy) left to take over as the Mariners GM. Melvin knows how to run a team and he'll be able to make smart deals and keep his team relatively competitive despite payroll constraints.

Ken Macha was hired as the new manager after interim manager Dale Sveum wasn't retained as manager (he stayed as the hitting coach) Macha had an excellent record working under Billy Beane with the Athletics, but so did Art Howe who was blamed for the entire disaster that the New York Mets were when he became their manager. Macha is in the exact same position now with the Brewers. Like the Mets under Howe, there are some good young players in Milwaukee; like the Mets under Howe, they're undermanned to be able to compete; unlike Howe, Macha's not walking into Milwaukee under relentless scorn and ridicule. To me, Macha has more to prove than Howe did because at least Howe had some success as manager of the Astros before going to the A's; Macha was a minor league manager and a bench coach for the A's and was seen as having stabbed Howe in the back to get the A's job to begin with. Macha made some odd strategic decisions with the A's and if he fails, he'll be another in the line of managers who worked under Beane and failed as soon as they left that safe, secure place.

STARTING PITCHING:

Yovani Gallardo missed most of last season with a knee injury, but returned late in the season to pitch well over the last two weeks and in the playoffs. Gallardo is only 23 and has Cy Young caliber stuff. If he's healthy, he'll be the Brewers ace for a long time.

Jeff Suppan has become a very expensive and less-than-mediocre pitcher. His reputation had been as a money pitcher in big spots, but he was terrible down the stretch and in the playoffs last season. Suppan doesn't have the stuff to get out good major league hitters anymore; his fastball is not major league caliber; his breaking stuff is weak. He gives up a lot of hits; a lot of home runs and he's at best a back of the rotation starter with very little left.

Braden Looper has turned into a solid big league starter after spending years in the bullpen as a set-up man and closer. Looper pitched better than his 12-14 record last season and much better than his 12-12 record the season before. He gives up a lot of home runs, but as a middle of the rotation starter, Looper has proven himself to be a surprisingly durable and effective starting pitcher.

Manny Parra's claim to fame last season was getting shoved around the dugout like a crash test dummy in a confrontation with Prince Fielder. Parra went 10-8 last season and slumped toward the end; his control is decent enough and he could be a 10-12 game winner in the future.

Dave Bush went 9-10 with a very solid hits/innings pitched ratio of 163/185. Bush is a contact pitcher whose record is around .500 every single year.

Chris Capuano is trying to come back after missing all of last season with arm problems. He was a useful pitcher before his injury.

BULLPEN:

Veteran Trevor Hoffman wanted desperately to stay with the Padres and finish his career; Hoffman was a victim of the arrogance and disregard for people that is a hallmark of soon-to-be former Padres CEO Sandy Alderson's management style. Hoffman signed with the Brewers to take over as their closer on a 1-year deal and while he doesn't have much left in his tank, he'll still be better than the crew the Brewers were using last season. For the most part, Hoffman will convert his save opportunities; he gives up too many homers, his fastball doesn't hit more than 83 mph, and his control leaves something to be desired; but perhaps the change of scenery will help him regain some of his former glory. He's still a smart pitcher with a great changeup.

David Riske was signed as a free agent before last season and had injury problems and struggled. He walked as many people as he struck out and gave up too many homers. Riske's been a solid and durable reliever for most of his career and it's reasonable to believe he can rebound into the pitcher the Brewers thought they were getting.

Jorge Julio is a hard-throwing journeyman who's got some experience closing. Julio rejuvenated his career to a certain degree with the Indians last season. He can get wild and panic in important games, but he should have some use for the Brewers and he can't be any worse than what they were using last season in Eric Gagne, Guillermo Mota and Salomon Torres.

Seth McClung is a big hard thrower who could get a chance as a starter, but I believe will end up in the bullpen. McClung had a very good hits/innings pitched ratio and could be a solid reliever.

Mitch Stetter is a lefty who, I think, has the stuff to be a very good reliever. He throws hard; racks up the strikeouts; and has had enough success against righties that he should be given a chance to be more than a lefty specialist.

Eduardo Morlan was claimed in the Rule 5 Draft from the Rays. Morlan pitched in Double A last season and put up very good numbers with impressive strikeout totals.

Nick Green was claimed off waivers from the Angels; he was a starter in Triple A last season and got knocked around in 28 starts.

Todd Coffey is the former occasional closer for the Reds and pitched well in nine games for the Brewers after being traded. Coffey throws hard and puts up the strikeouts.

Eric Gagne found no takers on the free agent market and signed a minor league contract to try and make the Brewers again; he's up and down and may have some use as a set-up man.

LINEUP:

Jason Kendall didn't get along with manager Ken Macha when the two were together in Oakland and whether or not their relationship will be better in Milwaukee remains to be seen. The Brewers have a young, talented catcher named Angel Salome in the minors who's near big league ready, so Macha-Kendall is something to watch. Kendall has no power and can't really hit; he calls a solid game behind the plate.

Prince Fielder was rumored to be discussed in trades before signing a 2-year contract. Fielder is fat and going to get fatter; the look on his face is that of a miserable human being; and he failed in the post-season. I'd absolutely look to trade Fielder sooner rather than later because I think he's a divisive clubhouse presence and is going to have trouble getting along with Macha; it's going to be up to new bench coach Willie Randolph to be a buffer between the two. Fielder's numbers also took a dive from his 50 homer 2007, to 34 in 2008.

Rickie Weeks is so streaky that he loses his job for weeks at a time and warrants a demotion to the minors, then gets back into the lineup and murders the ball. Weeks batted .234 last season with 14 homers and 19 stolen bases; it's time for him to show some consistency as a big league player.

Bill Hall tore a muscle in his calf and will miss the first month of the season. Hall batted .225 last season with 15 homers and an atrocious .295 OBP. It's possible that Ryan Braun could be asked to move back to third base until Hall comes back; or perhaps veteran Mike Lamb could play the position. They could also shift either Alcides Escobar or J.J. Hardy over there, in which case Hall might be relegated to a utility role when he returns. He's more suited to that anyway.

J.J. Hardy is a power hitting shortstop who hit 24 homers last season and had 59 extra base hits. Hardy was said to be a target of the Angels for their hole at shortstop in exchange for some pitching, but he's still with the Brewers and it doesn't look like they're going to deal him.

Ryan Braun was a MVP candidate because of his leadership and clutch play as the Brewers fought for their playoff spot down the stretch. Braun batted .285 with 37 homers and 107 RBI; he stole 14 bases and played surprisingly solid defense in left field.

Mike Cameron had his $10 million option exercised in an attempt by the Brewers to lure his close friend C.C. Sabathia to come back to the Brewers. Cameron is trade bait personified. The dearth of center fielders available will make Cameron a target for teams like the Yankees whose center fielder is still a question mark. His pending free agency and game flaws (he's very streaky and strikes out too much) will diminish his value as he's put on the block, but Melvin should be able to get a prospect or two for him at the trading deadline or sooner.

Corey Hart batted .268 with a Jeff Francoeur-like .300 OBP. He hit 20 homers and stole 23 bases and played solid defense.

BENCH:

The aforementioned veteran Mike Lamb may have to play third base if the Brewers don't move one of their youngsters over there in the absence of Hall. Lamb had some pop in his bat with the Astros, but was so bad for the Twins last season that they swallowed his contract and released him. He didn't hit for the Brewers either.

Alcides Escobar is a highly touted shortstop prospect who batted .328 with 34 stolen bases in 131 games in Double A. He made 20 errors at shortstop and moving him to third base may not be that bad of an idea.

Mike Rivera is a veteran backup catcher who batted .306 in 21 games.

Craig Counsell is a useful infielder who can play any position; bunts; gets on base; runs the bases well; is a good guy in the clubhouse and plays the game correctly.

Tony Gwynn Jr. could finally get a chance to play if Cameron is traded. Gwynn spent most of last season in Triple A and batted .275. He's a backup outfielder who may have been overrated when he was drafted because of his name.

Beefy, lefty-swinging backup first baseman Brad Nelson hit 18 homers in Triple A with a .380 OBP. He'd be an adequate (and more) replacement for Fielder if they trade him for pitching.

Scott Thorman was given a chance to win the Braves first base job a couple of years ago and doesn't do much other than hit the ball out of the park occasionally. He's Triple A filler at best.

PREDICTION:

The Brewers are in the midst of a retooling. They went for it all last season with Sabathia and Sheets knowing that they were probably not going to be able to keep either. They made the playoffs, but were dispatched in four games by the Phillies; now they have a new manager and a chunk of their lineup could be on the trading block. They still have a load of talent in their organization and players like Braun are guys you build around. Their starting rotation is shaky after Gallardo; they have serviceable parts like Looper, but Suppan is borderline non-competitive at this point. Their bullpen isn't all that great either. They can hit and score runs as currently constituted and should be hovering around .500 because of that. This season will be an opportunity to watch Macha and determine if he's another of the Billy Beane success stories or if he can make it on his own. The Brewers aren't contenders; but they're not going to fall to the bottom of their division either. They'll hover around .500 and finish the season at exactly that level.

PREDICTED RECORD: 81-81

Houston Astros
2008 Record: 86-75; Third Place, National League Central

2008 Recap:

The Astros had built a team heavy on offense and light on pitching which was the opposite of the way they'd built their pennant contending teams with Roger Clemens, Andy Pettitte and Roy Oswalt. Early in the season, they were nowhere near contention and despite calls to start clearing out some veterans—possibly including Oswalt—owner Drayton McLane chose to *add* the mediocre veterans LaTroy Hawkins and Randy Wolf. Suddenly, the Astros became blazing hot and launched themselves back into Wild Card contention before fading out during the last two weeks of the season.

Their offense, which made do without the presence of RBI machine Carlos Lee, was carried by annual MVP candidate Lance Berkman, Hunter Pence and the fiery Ty Wigginton. Had the Astros not been forced to move their series with the Cubs from Houston to Milwaukee due to the hurricane, there's every chance that they would've won the Wild Card.

2009 ADDITIONS: LHP Mike Hampton signed a 1-year contract.
INF Aaron Boone signed a 1-year contract.
OF Jason Michaels signed a 1-year contract.
C Lou Palmisano was acquired from the Baltimore Orioles.
RHP Jeff Fulchino was claimed off waivers from the Kansas City Royals.
LHP Gilbert de la Vara was claimed in the Rule 5 Draft from the Kansas City Royals.
LHP Tyler Lumsden was acquired from the Kansas City Royals.
INF Matt Kata was signed to a minor league contract.
INF Jason Smith signed a minor league contract.
OF John Gall signed a minor league contract.
RHP Clay Hensley signed a minor league contract.

RHP Russ Ortiz signed a minor league contract.
C Toby Hall signed a minor league contract.
RHP Danny Graves signed a minor league contract.
RHP Jose Capellan signed a minor league contract.

2009 SUBTRACTIONS: LHP Randy Wolf was not re-signed.
3B Ty Wigginton was non-tendered.
C Brad Ausmus was not re-signed.
RHP Dave Borkowski refused an assignment to the minor leagues and elected free agency.
INF Jose Castillo refused an assignment to the minor leagues and elected free agency.
INF Mark Loretta was not re-signed.

2009 PROJECTED LINEUP: C-J.R. Towles; 1B-Lance Berkman; 2B-Kaz Matsui; 3B-Geoff Blum; SS-Miguel Tejada; LF-Carlos Lee; CF-Michael Bourn; RF-Hunter Pence

2009 PROJECTED STARTING ROTATION: Roy Oswalt; Wandy Rodriguez; Brian Moehler; Mike Hampton; Brandon Backe; Russ Ortiz

2009 BULLPEN: Jose Valverde; Doug Brocail; LaTroy Hawkins; Geoff Geary; Clay Hensley; Chris Sampson; Tim Byrdak; Wesley Wright; Chad Paronto; Fernando Nieve

2009 BENCH: C-Humberto Quintero; C-Toby Hall; 1B/3B-Aaron Boone; OF-Jason Michaels; OF/1B-Darin Erstad; INF/OF-David Newhan; OF-Reggie Abercrombie

2009 EXTRA PITCHERS/PROSPECTS: Gilbert de la Vara; Danny Graves; Alberto Arias; Tyler Lumsden; Jeff Fulchino; Jose Capellan; Douglas Arguello; Fernando Abad; Jay Pacella; Eduin Ciriaco; Danny Meszaros

2009 EVERYDAY PROSPECTS: Brian Bogusevic; Drew Sutton; Mark Ori; Jordan Parraz; Phil Disher

ASSESSMENTS:
MANAGEMENT:

   GM Ed Wade wasn't particularly well thought of before the incident in which he was physically attacked by pitcher Shawn Chacon in the lunchroom at Minute Maid Park, but in what can only be seen as a bizarre set of circumstances for someone who was physically assaulted, it became clear that Wade shared a major part of the blame for the incident by cursing and being verbally abusive to Chacon; that's not defending Chacon, but cursing at someone is not the way to curry favor with the other players.

Wade doesn't appear to have all that much sway with what goes on in the organization. Owner Drayton McLane ordered the acquisitions of veterans Randy Wolf and LaTroy Hawkins and as bad as the decisions appeared to be when they were made, one can't argue with the results as the Astros got blazing hot right after the deals. This past off-season has been pretty unproductive for the Astros. They non-tendered Ty Wigginton; didn't re-sign Wolf; and the only recognizable name they've added is former Astro Mike Hampton. The team hasn't improved on the 86 win team they were last season and if Wade isn't going to get the credit for last season, he shouldn't get the blame for this season, but he's just sort of there as a figurehead and little else.

Manager Cecil Cooper was also to be a figurehead as the clubhouse was considered to be a case of the inmates running the asylum. I have no idea one way or the other, but as far as game managing went, I thought Cooper was pretty good. He handled the shaky pitching staff well and it always reflects well on the manager if a struggling team doesn't give up. Cooper was an excellent player when he was active and has experience as a manager in the minor leagues. He deserves a legitimate chance to run the team without looking over his shoulder wondering if he's going to get fired.

STARTING ROTATION:

Roy Oswalt rebounded from a slow start, got healthy and again became the dominating ace he's been for much of his career. Oswalt went 17-10 with 199 hits allowed in 209 innings. Oswalt is 31, but he still has the power fastball and wicked curve to anchor a staff.

I may be in the minority, but I think Wandy Rodriguez has the stuff to be a 13-16 game winner in the big leagues. Rodriguez went 9-7 in 25 starts and had a solid strikeout/walk ratio and allowed 136 hits in 137 innings. Rodriguez has to stay healthy and he's going to be 30 this year, so it's about put up or shut up time.

Veteran Brian Moehler went 11-8 appearing in 31 games including 26 starts. Moehler is a contact pitcher whose main attribute last season was that he managed to win 11 games. He's 37-years-old, so expecting him to repeat last season's performance is a bit unrealistic.

Mike Hampton was signed to a 1-year contract to return to the site of his prime years. Hampton has been injured for most of the past six years and the idea that he was going to return to the Astros now and become the pitcher he was with the Astros then is absurd. This was evident when he had to leave camp right after it began for treatment of an irregular heartbeat; he's supposed to recover at full strength, but even though he pitched serviceably for the Braves late last season after returning from his usual vast array of injuries, I wouldn't expect anything from him this year.

Veteran Russ Ortiz was signed to a minor league contract. Ortiz has done nothing since his big year with the Braves in which he won 22 games and then parlayed that into a long-term contract with the Diamondbacks and was horrible. He's bounced around since then and I wouldn't expect anything from him either.

Brandon Backe went 9-14 in 31 starts with rotten numbers across the board. He allowed 202 hits in 167 innings with 36 homers allowed. Backe's actually got pretty good stuff. On the bright side, he has to be better this year because he can't possibly be any worse.

BULLPEN:

Jose Valverde throws very, very hard and had a solid year as the Astros closer. He did allow 10 homers, but he struck out over 10 hitters per nine innings and saved 44 games. Valverde is due for a hefty raise in the coming years and if things go badly for the Astros (badly enough for McLane not to insist on adding instead of subtracting) Valverde could be moved.

Tough veteran Doug Brocail isn't the prototypical set-up man especially at nearly 42-years-old. Brocail pitched well in 72 games with 63 hits allowed in 69 innings with 64 strikeouts.

LaTroy Hawkins was so terrible with the Yankees that they dumped him at mid-season and the Astros picked him up. Hawkins was brilliant with the Astros in 24 games and 21 innings with only 11 hits allowed and 25 strikeouts. I cannot *imagine* Hawkins being even half that good this season given his career history.

Geoff Geary had an excellent season in 55 games with a 2.53 ERA. He allowed 45 hits in 64 innings and 3 homers. Geary has been a serviceable reliever throughout his career, but he won't be as good as he was in 2008.

Wesley Wright showed great ability in 71 games last season. Wright is 24 and struck out a batter per inning.

Big, hard throwing Chad Paronto spent most of the season in Triple

A and pitched well. He should get a chance to make the club out of spring training.

Tim Byrdak was the lefty specialist out of the bullpen and posted a 3.90 ERA in 59 games; he allowed 10 homers and lefties only hit .135 against him.

Journeymen Clay Hensley and Danny Graves were signed to minor league contracts. Hensley might be able to help out of the bullpen for the Astros; Graves is done.

LINEUP:

J.R. Towles got the starting catcher's job out of spring training and was *awful*, batted .137 in 146 at bats and wound up back in the minors. Towles will have to win the job in spring training and since the Astros brought in veteran Toby Hall, there's every chance that Hall will be the Astros catcher this season. Hall's been a regular player in the past and has had some pop.

Lance Berkman is one of the most underrated players in all of baseball. Every single year the numbers go up on the board. The switch hitter hits for average (.312 last season); power (29 homers); drives in runs (106); scores runs (114); gets on base (.420 OBP) and can run (18 stolen bases). He's a leader in the clubhouse and is heading for the Hall of Fame when his career is over.

Kaz Matsui was predictably injured when the season started. When he returned, he played as well as he did with the Rockies in the previous couple of years. Matsui batted .293 with 35 extra base hits in 96 games with 20 stolen bases. It's time to realize he's not the washout he was with the Mets and is a solid player.

Geoff Blum takes over for Ty Wigginton at third base. Blum is more of a utility player, but he has some pop (14 homers) and hits in the clutch.

Miguel Tejada just reached a plea agreement for lying to congressional investigators in the PED scandal; he's not going to do any jail time. Tejada had a bad year last year. Not only did he have the steroid issue hanging over his head, but he was blindsided in an ESPN interview in which they ambushed him with proof that he was lying about his age and was two years older than what was listed. On the field, Tejada got off to a good start and made the All Star team, but ended with 13 homers and 66 RBI with a .283 average. His career is on the decline.

Carlos Lee got hurt last season and the Astros got hot at almost the exact time he left the lineup. It was just a coincidence. Like Berkman, Lee is horribly underrated. He hits the ball out of the park; is an RBI machine;

doesn't strike out; gets on base at a reasonable clip and is well-liked in the clubhouse; he plays very hard and isn't as bad defensively as is implied.

Michael Bourn was awful after coming over as the centerpiece in the trade that sent Brad Lidge to the Phillies. Bourn has hit in the minors comparitavely to Kenny Lofton and I thought he's be able to hit in the big leagues if he was given a chance, but he was horrible. He batted .229 with a .288 OBP and no power. He stole 41 bases in 51 tries, but it doesn't do much good to be a basestealer if a guy can't get on base.

Hunter Pence got off to a slow start and ended with reasonably good stats of 25 homers and 83 RBI; his OBP was a terrible .318 and he batted .269. I still think Pence has star potential and 2008 may have been a sophomore slump rather than the pitchers figuring out how to pitch to him effectively.

BENCH:

Darin Erstad played more than the Astros would've liked with the struggles of Bourn in center field and he didn't hit all that much. Erstad batted .276 with 20 extra base hits. He shouldn't be playing as much as he did last year at this point in his career.

Along with Hall, who was mentioned earlier, Humberto Quintero could also see time behind the plate. He's a veteran who doesn't hit.

Veteran Aaron Boone signed a 1-year contract to back up at first base and third base. Boone didn't hit all that much in 2008 with the Nationals and he may end up sharing time at third base with Blum.

Outfielder Jason Michaels signed a 1-year contract. Michaels has gotten his chances to play regularly before and has never really lived up to his talents. I've always thought that Michaels should be better than he's been on the stat sheet, but he's never lived up to that potential. He could see playing time if Bourn doesn't improve his hitting and Pence is moved to center field. Maybe one day the 32-year-old Michaels can fulfill that potential.

Drew Sutton has put up excellent across-the-board numbers in Double A; he's going to be 26 in early summer, so he's not exactly young, but there's an opportunity at third base for him if Blum and Boone aren't the answer (and they're not).

David Newhan is another utility player for the bench. He can't hit.

PREDICTION:

The Astros have a weak starting rotation and an old bullpen that had too many pitchers performing far over their heads during their hot streak last season. Their lineup has the bats to score runs, but not enough to counteract that pitching staff. In the past few years, the Astros have been a predominately competitive team, but their farm system is gutted and they have players that they should probably trade to start a retooling process. Even with the way they played late last season, they still were a flawed team and they're worse this season. The Astros are going to play close to their on-paper level this year and that means non-contending status. The problem with an owner who demands that a team continue trying to compete when they should start getting younger is that if it works, the owner thinks he's always right. It happened with Peter Angelos of the Orioles in the late 90s and it set the organization back to the point that they've been in shambles for years; the same thing could happen with the Astros and Drayton McLane because they're a mirror image of those Orioles teams. This is going to be a bad year.

PREDICTED RECORD: 75-87

Pittsburgh Pirates
2008 Record: 67-95; Sixth Place, National League Central

2008 Recap:

New regime in Pittsburgh, same old story.

The Pirates were not only bad, but they were in many ways *worse* than they were under overmatched former GM Dave Littlefield. In years past at least Littlefield was working on borrowed time; the new management crew, led by club president Frank Coonelly and GM Neal Huntington, made a series of shaky trades for pennies on the dollar in dealing away three veteran assets in Jason Bay, Xavier Nady and Damaso Marte; they got back far less that what they should've. They compounded their terrible season with Coonelly engaging in a very public pissing contest with the agent Scott Boras over the Pirates top draft pick, third baseman Pedro Alvarez. The situation with whether or not Alvarez's contract was valid is more about Coonelly trying to prove a point with Boras than it is about Alvarez. Coonelly came out of the commissioner's office for MLB and if he's more interested in validating the slotting system in the draft than he is about improving the Pirates, they're in deeper trouble than they were before. At least Littlefield had his ineptitude as a crutch; what does Coonelly have?

2009 ADDITIONS: OF/3B Eric Hinske signed a 1-year contract.
C Jason Jaramillo was acquired from the Philadelphia Phillies.
INF Ramon Vazquez signed a 2-year contract.
INF Andy Phillips signed a minor league contract.
OF Jeff Salazar signed a minor league contract.
INF Anderson Machado signed a minor league contract.
INF Pedro Lopez signed a minor league contract.
OF Craig Monroe signed a minor league contract.
C Erik Kratz signed a minor league contract.

RHP Virgil Vazquez was claimed off waivers from the San Diego Padres.

RHP Chris Bootcheck signed a minor league contract.

2009 SUBTRACTIONS: C Ronny Paulino was traded to the Philadelphia Phillies.

INF Chris Gomez was not re-signed.

INF Doug Mienkiewicz was not re-signed.

2009 PROJECTED LINEUP: C-Ryan Doumit; 1B-Adam LaRoche; 2B-Freddy Sanchez; 3B-Ramon Vazquez; SS-Jack Wilson; LF-Nyjer Morgan; CF-Nate McLouth; RF-Brandon Moss

2009 PROJECTED STARTING ROTATION: Ian Snell; Paul Maholm; Tom Gorzelanny; Zach Duke; Ross Ohlendorf; Phil Dumatrait

2009 PROJECTED BULLPEN: Matt Capps; John Grabow; Craig Hansen; Tyler Yates; Sean Burnett; Daniel McCutcheon; Jeff Karstens; Denny Bautista

2009 BENCH: 3B/OF-Eric Hinske; C-Jason Jaramillo; 3B-Andy LaRoche; OF-Steve Pearce; OF-Jeff Salazar; INF-Andy Phillips; INF-Brian Bixler; OF-Jose Tabata

2009 EXTRA PITCHERS/PROSPECTS: Donald Veal; Juan Mateo; Brian Slocum; Virgil Vasquez; Evan Meek; Romulo Sanchez; Jimmy Barthmaier; Chris Bootcheck; Jason Davis; Eric Krebs; Harrison Bishop; Tim Boleska

2009 EVERYDAY PROSPECTS: Pedro Alvarez; Jonel Pacheco; Jared Keel; Jamie Romak; Miles Durham

ASSESSMENTS:
MANAGEMENT:

Who's running things? Is it team president Frank Coonelly or GM Neal Huntington? Coonelly came out of the commissioner's office and his back-and-forth with Scott Boras makes it look like Coonelly is using his position with the Pirates to put forth the preferred agenda of Major League Baseball. The whole mess with Pedro Alvarez has drawn battle lines between Boras and Coonelly with Alvarez and the Pirates organization in the middle. Coonelly's baby was the pay slots for draftees which some teams followed and others didn't. Of course it's more financially prudent to limit the amount of bonus money paid to an amateur who may or may not make it, but this is America and the draft slots aren't mandated; they're sort of a "suggestion"; and if a team like the Pirates has divergent agendas, they're never going to get any better because for them to be able to have a turnaround, their front office has to be focused on one thing: getting better. Until that's the case, they're going to continue on the treadmill they've been on for almost twenty years of cluelessness.

Neal Huntington worked in one of baseball's best front offices with the Indians before taking the job as the Pirates GM. There's debate as to how much power he has and from the way things are going in Pittsburgh, it looks like he's still an assistant and not the man making the final decisions. The trades that the Pirates made in which they cleared out their in demand talent—Nady, Bay and Marte—brought back an arguable quality return; the consensus is that they didn't get as much as they could have.

Manager John Russell was a journeyman catcher in his playing career and his claim to fame was catching one of Nolan Ryan's no-hitters. Russell showed some strategic promise last season calling for some gutsy, aggressive, classic inside baseball plays like suicide squeezes in surprising situations; he also handled his pitching staff pretty well; but the talent level is so short that it's hard to know how good a manager he's going to be until there's enough talent available to him to win.

STARTING PITCHING:

Ian Snell had a fine year in 2006 and pitched better in 2007, last season, he was bad. Snell went 7-12 with a 5.42 ERA in 31 starts; he gave up a lot of hits and his strikeout numbers were down. Snell is still only 27, but the Pirates might be well-served to explore trade options for him to replenish the organization.

Lefty Paul Maholm went 9-9, but had excellent stats across the board. He has good control and allowed 201 hits in 206 innings.

Tom Gorzelanny was terrible and wound up back in the minors. He went 6-9 with a bloated and evil sounding (in more ways than one) 6.66 ERA; he gave up a lot of home runs (20 in 21 starts) and his control was poor. He did pitch well in Triple A after his demotion.

I was halfway expecting the Pirates to non-tender Zach Duke. After bursting on the scene in 2005, he's been atrocious. Duke's numbers have been consistently hideous since that 2005 season and I see no reason to think that's going to change.

Ross Ohlendorf was acquired in the trade that sent Xavier Nady and Damaso Marte to the Yankees. Ohlendorf was used in relief by the Yankees and pitched poorly. The Pirates are moving him into the starting rotation and I think that's a good idea. (He made five starts late last season and got shelled.) He has a power fastball that shows promise.

Lefty Phil Dumatrait started 11 games and relieved in 10 others last season. His numbers across the board were quite respectable and he could be a solid starter.

Jeff Karstens was also acquired from the Yankees and made 9 starts for the Pirates. He showed flashes of effectiveness and only went 2-6, but pitched better than his record.

BULLPEN:

Matt Capps had a solid year as the closer in 2008. He throws nothing but strikes and allowed 5 homers in 49 games. He's not a strikeout pitcher, but as far as closers go, there are many in baseball far worse than Capps.

Lefty John Grabow pitched very well in 74 games with a 2.84 ERA in 74 games. He struck out 62 in 76 innings and only allowed 60 hits. He can get out both rigties and lefties and gave up too many homers with nine.

Hard throwing Tyler Yates pitched reasonably well in 72 games. He can get wild, gives up a homer once in a while, but his power fastball makes him a useful component out of the pen.

Sean Burnett is a lefty specialist who pitched in 58 games. He's a contact pitcher who loses control of the strike zone and allowed a solid .171 batting average pitching to lefties.

Craig Hansen was acquired in the trade that sent Jason Bay to the Red Sox (and Manny Ramirez to the Dodgers); Hanson throws very, very hard and never really got a chance to pitch for the Red Sox; when he did, he was wild and pitched poorly. Hansen was horrible for the Pirates as well and was almost compulsively unable to throw strikes, walking 20 in 16 innings. The Pirates aren't going to be very good this year, so they should give Hansen at least the first half of the season and let him try to get himself straightened out with his mechanics and control and let him pitch.

Daniel McCutcheon was a formerly touted prospect for the Yankees and started eight games in Triple A for the Pirates after being acquired at mid-season. McCutcheon is a control pitcher who deserves a chance, at age 26, to hang around the big leagues.

LINEUP:

Ryan Doumit had split time over the past few years with Ronny Paulino, but Paulino was traded to the Phillies leaving the job for Doumit. The switch-hitting Doumit had a fine year at the plate in 2008 batting .318 with 15 homers, 69 RBI and a .357 OBP.

Adam LaRoche is no star, but he'll play solid defense, hit his 20-30 homers and drive in some runs. He could probably yield a decent return in a trade.

Freddy Sanchez won a batting title a few years ago, but he's a slap hitter with ocasional pop. He has terrible plate discipline, can play second base and third base and is making too much money for the kind of player he is. He's on the trading block, but they're not going to get much of anything for him; he's going to be a free agent at the end of 2009.

For some unfathomable reason, the Pirates signed Ramon Vazquez to a 2-year contract. Vazquez is a 32-year-old journeyman who played relatively regularly for the Rangers last season and batted .290 as a platoon player mostly at third base. There was no earthly reason for the Pirates to even sign Vazquez, let along give him a 2-year contract.

Jack Wilson was on the trading block and the Dodgers have had serious interest for awhile. The Pirates were asking an absurdly high price for Wilson and he's still with the Pirates. Wilson is 31, has no power, doesn't get on base, plus he's making a lot of money; getting his contract off the books should've been enough for the Pirates no matter what the Dodgers were offering.

Nyjer Morgan batted .294 in 58 games; he has some speed and he'll only play regularly until Jose Tabata is deemed to be ready.

Nate McLouth had his career year in 2008 hitting .276 with 26 homers, 23 stolen bases and winning a Gold Glove. (The fielding metrics I've read about have indicated that McLouth was not only undeserving of a Gold Glove, but was actually considered below average.) McLouth is 27 and just signed a 3-year contract extension for over $15 million. I'll be stunned if he repeats last season's hitting numbers. He's an overrated player.

Brandon Moss was acquired in the trade with the Red Sox and hit .222 in 58 games afterward. Moss has shown some pop in the minors and is considered little more than a fourth outfielder.

BENCH:

Eric Hinske is a good journeyman hitter who probably shouldn't unpack his suitcase or invest in any Pittsburgh real estate because once the Pirates are out of contention (on April 30th), contending teams will be looking at

Hinske's bat. He can play the corner infield and outfield positions and hits the ball out of the park.

Jason Jaramillo was acquired from the Phillies for Paulino. Jaramillo's a switch-hitter who batted .266 as the regular catcher for the Phillies Triple A club in Lehigh Valley. He's a backup.

Brian Bixler is a speedy backup infielder who made some on-field gaffes in the big leagues last season; he can steal a few bases.

Andy LaRoche was a highly touted third base prospect for the Dodgers who was acquired at mid-season. He was non-competitive to the point where he not only looked like he didn't belong in the big leagues, but he looked like he didn't belong in pro baseball. I'm convinced the Pirates weren't as enamored with LaRoche's talent as they were with the marketing possibilities of having brothers manning the infield corners. Not only didn't LaRoche hit, but he was clueless defensively as well. I've never seen much from LaRoche to be all that impressed with and he's already 25, so his days as a prospect are over; he has to start producing—if he can.

Steve Pearce has shown some power in the minors and has potential to be a solid backup outfielder.

Jose Tabata was a formerly "untouchable" Yankees prospect who lost his luster and was traded in the Nady deal. Tabata hit well after joining the Pirates organization and, at age 20, might get a chance to make the big club out of spring training.

PREDICTION:

The Pirates have some young pitching, but their offense is very weak. The high hopes that were present when Littlefield was fired have been all but extinguished with the embarrassing episode between Coonelly and Boras and the diminished return they received as they traded their remaining assets at mid-season 2008. They've done nothing to improve this off-season and have no chance to contend or even be respectable. This organization is a disaster.

PREDICTED RECORD: 64-98

National League West

1. San Francisco Giants
2. Los Angeles Dodgers
3. Arizona Diamondbacks
4. Colorado Rockies
5. San Diego Padres

San Francisco Giants
2008 Record: 72-90; Fourth Place, National League West

2008 Recap:

The Giants were expected to be the worst team in the National League as they continued to recover from the Barry Bonds hangover. Their offense was awful, but their starting pitching was pretty good led by Cy Young Award winner Tim Lincecum. Barry Zito got off to an atrocious start and pitched better over the second half of the season and Matt Cain continued pitching in perhaps the worst luck in baseball. Had there been one productive power hitter on the Giants roster, they might have won ten or so more games and once they got to that point, they would've been in contention for the division title in a bad division.

2009 ADDITIONS: SS Edgar Renteria signed a 2-year contract.
LHP Jeremy Affeldt signed a 1-year contract.
RHP Bob Howry signed a 1-year contract.
LHP Randy Johnson signed a 1-year contract.
INF Juan Uribe signed a minor league contract.
RHP Justin Miller signed a minor league contract.
1B Josh Phelps signed a minor league contract.
LHP Luis Pedromo was selected in the Rule 5 Draft from the St. Louis Cardinals.
OF Andres Torres signed a minor league contract.
RHP Brandon Medders signed a minor league contract.
RHP Francis Beltran signed a minor league contract.

2009 SUBTRACTIONS: RHP Tyler Walker refused an assignment to the minor leagues and elected free agency.
RHP Kevin Correia was non-tendered.
C Eliezer Alfonzo was non-tendered.
SS Omar Vizquel was not re-signed.
RHP Brad Hennessey was not re-signed.
RHP Vinnie Chulk was not re-signed.

2009 PROJECTED LINEUP: C-Bengie Molina; 1B-Pablo Sandoval; 2B-Emmanuel Burriss; 3B-Juan Uribe; SS-Edgar Renteria; LF-Fred Lewis; CF-Aaron Rowand; RF-Randy Winn

2009 PROJECTED STARTING ROTATION: Tim Lincecum; Matt Cain; Randy Johnson; Barry Zito; Jonathan Sanchez; Noah Lowry

2009 PROJECTED BULLPEN: Brian Wilson; Jeremy Affeldt; Bob Howry; Keiichi Yabu; Justin Miller; Billy Sadler; Patrick Misch; Jack Taschner; Brandon Medders; Alex Hinshaw

2009 BENCH: INF-Kevin Frandsen; 1B-Travis Ishikawa; OF-Dave Roberts; OF/1B-Nate Schierholtz; C-Steve Holm; INF-Rich Aurilia; 1B-John Bowker; INF/OF Eugenio Velez

2009 EXTRA PITCHERS/PROSPECTS: Luis Pedromo; Sergio Romo; Osiris Matos; Ramon Ortiz; Merkin Valdez; Francis Beltran; Geno Espineli; Joey Martinez; Kelvin Pichardo; Tim Alderson; Jesse English; Daryl Maday; Kevin Pucetas; Madison Bumgarner; Craig Clark; Ryan Paul

2009 EVERYDAY PROSPECTS: Matt Downs; Brad Boyer; Thomas Neal

ASSESSMENTS:
MANAGEMENT:

GM Brian Sabean has come under fire because of the shabby and ancient construction of the team over the past few years, but he had a choice: build around Barry Bonds with veterans and try to win immediately; or build for the future and deal with Bonds and the fans squawking about Bonds not having any support. Many other teams would've fallen further, faster than the Giants have since Bonds left; but they're actually well-prepared to turn things around as soon as 2009. They have a deep starting rotation; Sabean has improved the bullpen; and they're one bat away from being legitimate contenders. As currently constructed, the Giants may still wind up winning the war of attrition that the NL West looks like it's going to be and they have a lot more pitching in the minors and on the way up. There could be some difference-making bats available during the season and the acquisition of a Carlos Lee; a Jermaine Dye; or a Magglio Ordonez could put the Giants back into the playoffs far faster than anyone could've imagined considering the fallout after the Bonds years.

Bruce Bochy is one of the most respected managers in baseball on and off the field. Bochy can handle any situation and has the experience of getting occasionally overmatched teams into the playoffs. The Giants were expected to lose over 100 games last season, but they wound up at 72-90 and a major reason for that was because of Bochy's handling of the pitching staff and working with what little offense he had. Players like and respect Bochy and during his years managing the Padres, when his teams got the smell of a pennant race, they made the playoffs.

STARTING PITCHING:

There are few words to describe how brilliant Tim Lincecum was last season. After being considered too small to be able to make it through a season healthy (by myself included), Lincecum won the NL Cy Young Award with an 18-5 record; a 2.62 ERA; 182 hits allowed in 227 innings; 265 strikeouts and only 11 homers allowed and he did it with a shorthanded and shaky bullpen and a rotten offense. If he was on a team like the Cubs or Red Sox, he might have won 26 or 27 games and he's a dominant ace at the front of the Giants rotation.

For the second straight year, Matt Cain's record was far worse than it should've been given how well he pitched. Cain's numbers are excellent except for his won-lost record of 8-14. He pitched 218 innings and allowed 206 hits with 186 strikeouts. The Giants slightly improved offense and better bullpen should result in a possible reversal of fortune for Cain.

Randy Johnson was signed to a 1-year contract to win his 300th game near his Northern California home. Johnson is 45-years-old, but he started 30 games for the Diamondbacks last season; went 11-10 and pitched 184 innings with 173 strikeouts. He's not the Sandy Koufax-like force of nature he once was, but as a middle-of-the-rotation starter, he's a solid acquisition and he'll be motivated with his milestone victory within reach and one more chance to contend.

Barry Zito's numbers speak for themselves—badly: 10-17 record; 5.15 ERA; 102 walks and 120 strikeouts in 180 innings, and that's before getting to his bloated salary. Zito pitched better over the second half of the season and his velocity crept back up into the mid-to-upper 80s. The Giants have no choice but to keep putting him out there and hope he's able to keep them in games, but I'm not prepared to say Zito's finished. He has to learn to pitch with his diminished stuff, but it's not out of line to think that he can win 13 or so games.

Jonathan Sanchez went 9-12 in his first season as a fulltime starter.

Sanchez is a lefty with great stuff and struck out a batter per inning; he has the ability to be a 12-15 game winner.

Noah Lowry is returning from injuries to his hand and arm that kept him out for the entire season last year. With the depth of their rotation, the Giants can take it slow with the veteran Lowry and let him return to health and major league fitness.

BULLPEN:

Brian Wilson throws 100 mph and strikes out a batter per inning. He saved 41 games last season and had a bloated 4.62 ERA and allowed 7 homers, which is a lot for a closer. A better set-up crew should help him have some easier save opportunities and better numbers.

Lefty Jeremy Affeldt pitched for the Reds last season appearing in 74 games and was effective against both righties and lefties. Affeldt strikes out a batter per inning and throws strikes. He's a good pickup for the Giants to improve their bullpen.

Veteran Bob Howry was signed to a 1-year contract. Howry has closing experience and struggled a bit for the Cubs last season. He appeared in 72 games and allowed 90 hits and 13 homers. Howry throws strikes and has been a successful reliever in his career and a change of scenery might help him regain his form.

Keichi Yabu pitched in 60 games in relief and posted a 3-6 record and a 3.57 ERA. Yabu can lose the strike zone and got pummeled by lefties to the tune of a .355 average, but he only allowed 3 homers.

Justin Miller is the multi-tattooed righty who rejuvenated his career with the Marlins over the past couple of years; he pitched very well and was durable showing good control and a nice slider. He strikes out nearly a batter per inning and throws strikes.

Billy Sadler appeared in 33 games as a long reliever and struck out 42 in 44 innings.

Patrick Misch is a lefty who started seven games last season out of his 15 appearances. Lefties and righties hit him similarly well and he has good control.

Alex Hinshaw pitched very well as the lefty specialist last season. Hinshaw pitched in 48 games and logged 40 innings striking out 47 batters.

Brandon Medders was signed to a minor league contract from the Diamondbacks. Medders's control is terrible and he spent a chunk of last season in the minors.

Jack Taschner is a second lefty out of the bullpen and appeared in 67 games pitching 48 innings posting a high 4.88 ERA.

LINEUP:

Bengie Molina was the Giants top home run hitter with a measly 16. Molina isn't the same player he was earlier in his career with the Angels, but he can still handle a pitching staff and hit the ball out of the park. He drove in 95 runs and had 49 extra base hits out of his 155 hits.

Pablo Sandoval is one of the Giants top prospects and is listed on the depth chart as their probable third baseman, but I expect him to end up playing first base with Juan Uribe playing third. Sandoval doesn't look like much of a player at 5'11", 245, but he hits, has some pop and gets on base. He's 22 and everywhere he's played, he's put up the offensive numbers. In this Giants lineup, he deserves to play.

Emmanuel Burriss was the Giants top prospect at shortstop, but the signing of Edgar Renteria has relegated him to either the bench or to second base. Burriss batted .283 in 95 games with no power and 13 stolen bases. He's their best option at second base.

Juan Uribe is a veteran hacker who signed a minor league contract after playing for the White Sox for years. Uribe doesn't hit for average; doesn't get on base; but the way the Giants are currently constructed, Uribe is their best bet at third base to get some pop from the position.

Edgar Renteria had an awful year with the Tigers. He was excellent with the Braves two years ago and was out of shape and appeared disinterested with the Tigers. It could be seen that Renteria is just not an American League player (he struggled in his year with the Red Sox) or he could be on the downside of his career. He signed a 2-year contract with the Giants and I'd bet that he'll have a strong, rebound season.

Fred Lewis had a solid season in the impossible position of replacing Barry Bonds in left field. He hit 9 homers, stole 21 bases and had 11 triples.

Aaron Rowand was signed to a contract that indicated he was the main man in the Giants lineup, but he's not that kind of player. He was said to have shown up to camp out of shape last season which is disappointing for a player known for his fiery grit. Rowand is an excellent defensive center fielder and his power numbers dropped to about what's normal for him in a ballpark other than the bandbox of Citizens Bank Park in Philadelphia. Rowand hit 13 homers and drove in 70 runs; that's what the Giants should expect from him with maybe three or four more homers in 2009.

Randy Winn is a solid and underrated switch hitter who's never gotten the appreciation for being as good a player as he. Winn batted .306 last season with 10 homers, 64 RBI and 25 stolen bases with a .363 OBP.

BENCH:

Steve Holm is a catcher who batted .262 in 49 games as Molina's backup.

Kevin Frandsen missed almost all of last season with an achilles injury.

Rich Aurilia can play any infield position competently and has some pop in his bat; he's a well-liked veteran who's still a solid backup.

Travis Ishikawa put up big slugging numbers in Triple A last season and didn't do much in a brief trial in the big leagues. He could get a chance to win the first base job this season.

John Bowker played a lot of first base in 2008 and hit 10 homers in 111 games.

Speedy veteran outfielder Dave Roberts was hampered by knee injuries last season and missed most of the season. The Giants would love to be rid of Roberts, but his contract makes that a difficult proposition; the best they can hope for is if he's healthy and can contribute somehow this season.

Journeyman utilityman Eugenio Velez is a switch hitter who played a bit too much for his talent level last season, but had some big hits over the course of the year.

First baseman and outfielder Nate Schierholtz batted .320 in Triple A with 18 homers and 73 RBI; he has some pop so might get some at bats at first base this season.

PREDICTION:

The Giants need a power bat badly, but their starting pitching is good enough to keep them around the top of a weak division. Lincecum and Cain are an excellent 1-2 punch; with Johnson behind them and Zito still having the ability to contribute, pitching should carry them into contention. The bullpen is better with the additions of Affeldt and Howry and they have the minor league prospects to deal for a bat during the season. If Sandoval can produce offensively and they get *something* from the group vying for playing time at second base and third base, they'll score enough to keep their heads above water for the first two months of the season until some power bats come available.

I believe the Giants are going to battle it out with the Dodgers,

Diamondbacks and Rockies heading down the wire and their deep pitching staff will carry them to win the division title.

PREDICTED RECORD: 89-73

Los Angeles Dodgers
2008 Record: 84-78; First Place, National League West
Defeated Chicago Cubs in NLDS 3 games to 0
Lost to Philadelphia Phillies in NLCS 4 games to 1

*Note: At the time of this writing, Manny Ramirez is still a free agent. He and the Dodgers are discussing a deal, but the only thing keeping Manny from going elsewhere is that there doesn't appear to be anywhere else for him to go. He'll be listed as part of the lineup with the expectation that he'll eventually sign a contract to stay.

2008 Recap:

The team that the Dodgers began the season with bore little resemblence to the team that went to the NLCS. The mid-season acquistions of Manny Ramirez and Casey Blake awakened a slumping and slumbering team packed with declining star veterans and impudent rookies. Manager Joe Torre had his toughest job getting everyone on the same page and the team was staggering when the aggressive deadline deals were made to bring in Manny and Blake. With Manny carrying the team on his back with a display of power worthy of the greatest hitters in the history of the game, the Dodgers won the NL West with an 84-78 record, shocked the Cubs in a three game sweep in the NLDS before falling to the Phillies in the NLCS.

2009 ADDITIONS: 2B Orlando Hudson signed a 1-year contract.
LHP Randy Wolf signed a 1-year contract.
INF Mark Loretta signed a 1-year contract.
C Brad Ausmus signed a 1-year contract.
RHP Claudio Vargas signed a 1-year contract.
RHP Guillermo Mota signed a 1-year contract.
LHP Stephen Randolph signed a minor league contract.
RHP Jeff Weaver signed a minor league contract.
LHP Eric Milton signed a minor league contract.
LHP Shawn Estes signed a minor league contract.

OF Valentino Pascucci signed a minor league contract.
RHP Edgar Martinez signed a minor league contract.
RHP Charlie Haeger signed a minor league contract.

2009 SUBTRACTIONS: 2B Jeff Kent retired.
RHP Brad Penny was not re-signed.
RHP Takashi Saito was non-tendered.
RHP Greg Maddux retired.
INF Nomar Garciaparra was not re-signed.
C Gary Bennett was not re-signed.
RHP Derek Lowe was not re-signed.
RHP Mario Alvarez was non-tendered.
RHP Scott Proctor was non-tendered.
SS Angel Berroa was non-tendered.
OF Andruw Jones was released.
INF Pablo Ozuna was not re-signed.

2009 PROJECTED STARTING ROTATION: Chad Billingsley; Hiroki Kuroda; Randy Wolf; Clayton Kershaw; James McDonald; Eric Stults

2009 PROJECTED BULLPEN: Jonathan Broxton; Cory Wade; Hong-Chih Kuo; Guillermo Mota; Claudio Vargas; Scott Elbert; Yhency Brazoban

2009 PROJECTED LINEUP: C-Russell Martin; 1B-James Loney; 2B-Orlando Hudson; 3B-Casey Blake; SS-Rafael Furcal; LF-Manny Ramirez; CF-Matt Kemp; RF-Andre Ethier

2009 BENCH: INF-Blake DeWitt; OF-Juan Pierre; C-Brad Ausmus; INF-Mark Loretta; OF-Delwyn Young; OF-Jason Repko; INF-Chin-Lung Hu

2009 EXTRA PITCHERS/PROSPECTS: Shawn Estes; Jeff Weaver; Jason Schmidt; Nick DeBarr; Travis Schlichting; Scott Strickland; Stephen Randolph; Travis Chick; Edgar Martinez; Ramon Troncoso; Carmen Cali; Erick Threets; Francisco Felix; Javier Guerra; Blake Brannon; Victor Garate; Garrett White

2009 EVERYDAY PROSPECTS: Rene Rivera; Ivan De Jesus; Juan Gonzalez; Thomas Giles; Carlos Santana

ASSESSMENTS:
MANAGEMENT:

GM Ned Colletti was on the hotseat not just because the Dodgers were struggling at mid-season, but because he's signed so many high-priced free agents that turned out to be complete washouts. Jason Schmidt has barely pitched in his first two years with the Dodgers while earning $16 million a year, and I think I could've hit just as poorly as Andruw Jones did last season. Colletti was saved by the Red Sox desperation to dump Manny Ramirez and Ramirez's imitation of Babe Ruth over the last two months of the season carried the Dodgers to the division title, past the Cubs and into the NLCS; it was enough to save Colletti's job.

Manager Joe Torre did one of the best managing jobs of his career as he worked to get the prickly personalities; arrogant rookies; declining veterans; injury-riddled roster; and of course, Manny to work together as a team and win the division with a late hot streak. Torre did an excellent job getting the Dodgers past the Cubs until they ran out if magic against the Phillies. Torre is expected to be inundated with questions about his book, *The Yankee Years*, but Alex Rodriguez's positive steroid test and resulting scandal pushed Torre right out of the front of the newspaper and into the back where he belongs. There was talk that the Dodgers players weren't going to be able to trust Torre because he aired some dirty laundry in his book. (I read the book and there was nothing out of line printed as far as I could tell.) I don't think the Dodgers players are going to read the book or pay attention to the talk that they can't trust Torre; the gap between the manager at nearly 70-years-old and a mostly young roster is so vast that the concern about the another book is the least of Torre's problems handling the youngsters. If anyone can steer his club through any storm calmly, it's Joe Torre; he's got plenty of experience at it from the Yankee years.

STARTING PITCHING:

Chad Billingsley won 16 games last season and blossomed into a top of the line starter who gobbled innings. He struggled in the post-season and then compounded his troubles by slipping on the ice in his home state of Pennsylvania and breaking his leg. It's a question as to whether he'll be ready to pitch when the season starts. Billingsley has Cy Young Award potential at age 24.

Hiroki Kuroda showed flashes of brilliance in his first season in the big leagues. He went 9-10 with a 3.73 ERA and was almost unhittable when he was right (he was masterful in the NLDS against the Cubs); but he also struggled at times. Kuroda is a contact pitcher who throws strikes.

Former Dodger Randy Wolf returns to the team on a 1-year contract. Wolf had his first fully healthy season in five years and went 12-12 with the Padres and Astros. It was the acquistion of Wolf that helped spur the Astros to their hot streak that got them back into contention. Wolf is always an injury risk and I can't imagine that he'll be able to stay as healthy as he did last season given his history.

One of the best pitching prospects in all of baseball is 21-year-old lefty Clayton Kershaw. Kershaw struggled when he arrived in the big leagues last season, but it was easy to see why he's such a well-regarded prospect. He has a power fastball and a wicked overhand curve. Kershaw went 5-5 in 21 starts and struck out 100 in 108 innings. He was dominating Double A before his recall. Kershaw will undoubtedly experience some growing pains, but he's got future star written all over him and he might explode into his talent as early as this season.

When I first saw James McDonald in the playoffs, I said, "Where'd *this* guy come from?" The 6'5", 24-year-old McDonald has a 94-mph fastball; a slow curve and a changeup. He's not just going to be a success in the big leagues, he's going to be a star.

Lefty Eric Stults isn't exactly young (he's 29), but he throws strikes and has put up solid across the board numbers at every level. In comparing him with the veteran journeymen that the Dodgers are bringing to camp returning from injuries or on minor league deals—Jason Schmidt; Eric Milton; Jeff Weaver; Shawn Estes; Claudio Vargas—the Dodgers will be better off going with their younger pitchers because most of the above names either don't have much left or aren't going to be any better than Stults.

BULLPEN:

Jonathan Broxton takes over as the closer after Takashi Saito was let go. Broxton throws 100-mph, but sometimes let the pressure get to him in big games and overthrew, which resulted in his fastball flattening out and becoming easier to hit. Broxton saved 14 games and struck out 88 in 69 innings; he's going to be one of the top young closers in baseball if he keeps his head together.

Hong-Chih Kuo is a lefty who throws nearly 100-mph and can dominate when he's on his game. He struck out 96 in 80 innings last season and had a 2.14 ERA. He's been a starter before, but his home is in the bullpen. Kuo's also had a long injury history with two Tommy John surgeries, but if he's healthy, he's a great set-up man.

Young Cory Wade became one of Torre's favorite relievers. He had an excellent season with a 2.27 ERA in 55 games with excellent control. He did allow seven homers in 71 innings.

Former Dodger Guillermo Mota returns to the team with which he had his greatest success. Mota was part of the Dodgers shut down bullpen as the set-up man for an in-his-prime Eric Gagne and the club could've won the World Series if former GM Paul DePodesta hadn't made a series of nonsensical trades with the Dodgers in first place and rolling toward the playoffs. Mota has bounced around and had mostly poor results since then. It's hard to see him returning to the form he showed in his first go-around with the Dodgers at this point in his career.

Scott Elbert is a young lefty reliever who can get hitters from both sides of the plate out, racks up the strikeouts, doesn't give up many homers and throws strikes.

Claudio Vargas is a veteran who can start or relieve. He'll probably be a long man out of the pen.

LINEUP:

Russell Martin was said to be discussed in possible trades after the season, but he's still a Dodger. Martin batted .280 with 13 homers, 69 RBI; a .385 OBP and 18 stolen bases. Martin's only 26 and unless there's a problem with him that we don't know about, I wouldn't trade him.

James Loney batted .289 in 161 games, 13 homers and 90 RBI; he had some big hits in the playoffs and at age 25, Loney is heading toward stardom.

Orlando Hudson signed a 1-year contract with the Dodgers. Hudson's one of the top all-around second basemen in baseball, but has missed chunks of time with injuries to his hand and wrist over the past two years. Hudson's a Gold Glove second baseman and a good all-around player with power and is a great pickup in an incentive-laden deal.

Casey Blake returned to the Dodgers after testing free agency. Blake is a fine all-around player who can play third base, first base and the outfield. Blake has 20+ home run power and plays the game correctly as an example for the younger players to follow on how to behave like a pro.

Rafael Furcal had a back injury that kept him out of the lineup from May until late in the season. He batted .357 in 36 games and made it back for the playoffs. For a player with back problems at age 31, Furcal was in demand for several teams and there was a controversy as accusations flew that he'd accepted an offer to return to his original big league home with the Braves and then went back to the Dodgers after they upped their offer.

He was also pursued by the Athletics. The Dodgers had better hope that Furcal's back is healthy.

Manny Ramirez shoehorned his way out of Boston in an embarrassing and unprofessional way. He faked injuries; sleepwalked his way through games and played lazily as if he didn't care. It's a sad thing that Manny got his way and wound up in LA, but it was sort of justice that the huge money offers that agent Scott Boras promised him collapsed along with the economy. On the field for the Dodgers, Manny was incredible. He batted .396 with 17 homers and 31 extra base hits in 53 games; he had a .489 OBP and a .743 slugging percentage. Even at age 37, Manny is one of the top three hitters in baseball.

Matt Kemp was said to be discussed in trades in the winter (specifically to the Yankees in a deal for Robinson Cano). Kemp batted .290 (.369 against lefties) and hit 18 homers; he also struck out 153 times and his attitude is said to be a problem. Kemp has star potential if he matures.

Andre Ethier benefited from Manny's arrival more than anyone in the Dodgers lineup. Ethier got smoking hot with Manny in the lineup and ended the season with a .290 average, 20 homers and 77 RBI; he also had a .375 OBP and played a solid defensive right field.

BENCH:

Blake DeWitt was shifted to second base after Jeff Kent got hurt and played solid defense and hit reasonably well. He's got a little pop and gets on base. He's a solid all-around player.

Brad Ausmus was signed to a 1-year deal to be a backup for Martin behind the plate. Ausmus can't hit, but he's still solid defensively and calls a good game; he won't play very often unless Martin gets hurt.

Mark Loretta can play every infield position and was signed to a 1-year contract after playing for the Astros. Loretta batted .280 in 101 games last season and is a solid professional veteran.

Juan Pierre is on the trading block. He's unlikely to get much playing time unless someone gets hurt in the outfield and his skills (speed) is on the decline. Someone can use Pierre as a part-time player if the Dodgers will pick up part of his salary.

Delwyn Young is a young, backup outfielder who batted .246 in 83 games.

Chin-Lung Hu didn't hit at all when he got a chance to play for the injured Furcal, but he's put up impressive numbers in the minors in previous seasons.

Ivan DeJesus Jr. is a former top pick of the Dodgers and has been invited to spring training. He's 22 and batted .324 with a .419 OBP in Double A.

Jason Repko has been a solid player in the minors and at age 28, he'd be able to contribute as a bench player in the majors. Repko has pop, speed and on base ability.

PREDICTION:

Even with Joe Torre's ability to get any and every team into the playoffs, the Dodgers are going to have a tough time pulling off the feat this year. Their starting pitching is young with Billingsley, Kershaw and McDonald and I wouldn't expect much of anything from the veterans they're bringing in for the spring. They have enough power in their lineup to score runs, but the bullpen is a question mark. I think Broxton is going to be a good closer, but he could have some growing pains; there's no reasonable way to expect anything out of Mota; Kuo is an injury risk; and Wade is still young. The lineup will score some runs, but this club is an amalgam of young and old and injury risks and players still growing up. Torre's streak of making the playoffs is unbelievable and unprecedented especially in today's game; unfortunately for him, it's going to end in 2009.

PREDICTED RECORD: 85-77

Arizona Diamondbacks
2008 Record: 82-80; Second Place, National League West

2008 Recap:

The Diamondbacks made the aggressive off-season move to essentially add a second ace to their starting rotation in Dan Haren to go along with Brandon Webb. Haren and Webb lived up to their part of the bargain, but everything that went right for the Diamondbacks in their surprising run to the 2007 NL West title, went wrong in 2008. Their young hitters were inconsistent and struck out too much; the back end of their rotation was shaky; their fiery leader Eric Byrnes missed most of the season; and their mid-season trades to acquire veteran help were well-thought-out and designed to fill their holes, but they didn't work on the field. They faded out at the end of the season and lost the division title to the Dodgers.

2009 ADDITIONS: LHP Scott Schoeneweis was acquired from the New York Mets.
INF Felipe Lopez signed a 1-year contract.
RHP Jon Garland signed a 1-year contract.
RHP Tom Gordon signed a 1-year contract.
C James Skelton was selected in the Rule 5 Draft from the Detroit Tigers.
C Luke Carlin signed a minor league contract.

2009 SUBTRACTIONS: RHP Brandon Lyon was not re-signed.
2B Orlando Hudson was not re-signed.
LHP Randy Johnson was not re-signed.
OF Adam Dunn was not re-signed.
INF David Eckstein was not re-signed.
RHP Connor Robertson was traded to the New York Mets.
OF Chris Burke was non-tendered.
OF Jeff Salazar was non-tendered.

C Robby Hammock was non-tendered.
LHP Wil Ledezma was non-tendered.
INF Jamie D'Antona was released.
RHP Brandon Medders was non-tendered.

2009 PROJECTED LINEUP: C-Chris Snyder; 1B-Chad Tracy; 2B-Felipe Lopez; 3B-Mark Reynolds; SS-Stephen Drew; LF-Conor Jackson; CF-Chris Young; RF-Justin Upton

2009 PROJECTED STARTING ROTATION: Brandon Webb; Dan Haren; Jon Garland; Doug Davis; Max Scherzer; Yusmeiro Petit

2009 PROJECTED BULLPEN: Chad Qualls; Jon Rauch; Tony Pena; Scott Schoeneweis; Tom Gordon; Doug Slaten; Billy Buckner

2009 BENCH: C-Miguel Montero; 1B-Tony Clark; OF-Eric Byrnes; INF-Augie Ojeda; C-James Skelton; OF-Alex Romero

2009 EXTRA PITCHERS/PROSPECTS: Joe Coutlangus; Juan Gutierrez; Leo Rosales; Travis Blackley; Tony Barnette; Barry Enright; Dan Schlereth

2009 EVERYDAY PROSPECTS: Trent Oeltjen; Bryan Byrne; Pete Clifford; Evan Frey

ASSESSMENTS:
MANAGEMENT:

GM Josh Byrnes is one of the best executives in baseball. The Diamondbacks organization is bursting with prospects even with the trades they made to bring in veterans like Haren, David Eckstein, Jon Rauch and Adam Dunn; Byrnes was aggressive last season in trying to fill the Diamondbacks holes, but nothing worked. It wasn't anyone's fault, these things happen sometimes. Even with all of that and the financial troubles that have affected the industry (and resulted in numerous firings in the front office), the Diamondbacks can still contend based on their two Cy Young-quality starting pitchers and young lineup. Byrnes is aggressive in filling holes and acts quickly.

Just as there was little for Byrnes to do in straightening out the Diamondbacks last season, the same things that were working for manager Bob Melvin in 2007, weren't working in 2008. Melvin is a solid game manager for the most part and his players seem to like him and like playing for him; his personality isn't going to light the world on fire, but with all the young players the Diamondbacks are integrating into the big leagues, they're better off with Melvin than that would be with a raving maniac type who's going to make them nervous and afraid to fail.

STARTING PITCHING:

Brandon Webb led the league in victories with 22 and was expected to win the Cy Young Award before Tim Lincecum became a phenomenon. Webb is a true ace at the top of the rotation and one of the best pitchers in baseball. He pounds the strike zone with his heavy fastball, doesn't give up many homers, and gobbles innings; he's also not going to be 30 until May.

Dan Haren would be the ace on most of the other staffs in baseball, but with the Diamondbacks, he's their number 2 (or more accurately, 1A). Haren went 16-8 in 31 starts; he too gobbled innings and his control is even better than Webb's. Haren can also contend for a Cy Young Award at age 28.

Jon Garland was signed to a 1-year contract. Garland gives up a lot of hits and home runs, but finds a way to stay in games long enough to rack up wins. One thing that would concern me with Garland is the Diamondbacks porous defense. Garland is a pure contact pitcher who needs his fielders to catch the ball and that's something the Diamondbacks are not good at. Their bullpen and offense should give him an opportunity to win his 12-14 games, but that defense and his mediocrity will cause him to lose 12-14 games.

Doug Davis went 6-8 in 26 starts and missed time for treatment of cancer. Davis is a soft-tossing lefty who's the epitome of a .500 pitcher. He loses control of the strike zone and gets pounded if he's not on his game.

Max Scherzer is a hard-throwing righty who was a starter and reliever last season. Scherzer's probably more suited to the bullpen with his power fastball and slider. Scherzer struck out 66 in 56 innings in the big leagues.

Yusmeiro Petit is a chubby right-handed control pitcher who showed promise in 19 appearances (8 starts) in the big leagues last season. He throws strikes, gives up a lot of homers and, at age 24, should get a shot at the starting rotation at some point this season.

BULLPEN:

Chad Qualls became the closer after a long career as a set-up man with the Astros; Qualls was acquired to be a set-up man for Brandon Lyon and eventually supplanted him late in the season. Qualls is durable, throws strikes and will handle the closing duties well.

Jon Rauch was one of the better set-up men in baseball with the Nationals before he was traded to the Diamondbacks. Rauch was closing for the Nats when he was traded and got knocked around after joining the Diamondbacks. Rauch throws strikes and has an edge. With a full season in Arizona, he'll again be one of the better set-up men in baseball.

Scott Schoeneweis was acquired from the New York Mets and was one of the bullpen culprits in the Mets collapses in the past two years. Schoeneweis's contract is up at the end of the season, so he'll be motivated to have a good season and merely getting out of New York might help him revert to the solid reliever he's been for the majority of his career.

Veteran Tom Gordon signed a 1-year contract. Gordon has been injury prone in recent years, but when he's healthy, he's a workhorse. His stuff is greatly diminished, but he can still throw a good curveball and if he's used cautiously and not overworked, he can be a useful component out of the bullpen.

Tony Pena is a big righty who throws very, very hard and has excellent stuff. Pena was in 72 games last season and his stuff is far better than his results were with a 4.33 ERA and 80 hits allowed in 73 innings.

Doug Slaten is the lefty specialist who appeared in 45 games with 32 innings pitched. He's there for one reason and one reason only: to pitch to a lefty in a big spot and get him out.

Righty Billy Buckner pitched well in 10 games of relief in the big leagues in 2008; he got knocked around as a starter in Triple A Tucson.

LINEUP:

Chris Snyder had a productive offensive season (for him) with 16 homers and 64 RBI and a .348 OBP. 39 of Snyder's 79 hits were for extra bases and he did a good job handling the pitching staff splitting time with Miguel Montero.

Chad Tracy is listed as the Diamonbacks first baseman on their depth chart (with Conor Jackson moving to left field). Tracy's numbers were poor with 8 homers in 80 games with a .267 average and a .308 OBP. This production isn't enough to be an everyday player.

Felipe Lopez played a solid last month of the season with the Cardinals and it got him a contract as the starting second baseman for the Diamondbacks replacing Orlando Hudson. Lopez put up solid overall numbers last season with a .283 average and six homers while playing good defense. He then played excellent ball with the Cardinals, but that shouldn't be any indication that he's going to be able to continue that level of play. He's a stopgap at the position and nothing more.

Mark Reynolds's main attribute is that he hits the ball out of the ballpark relatively frequently. He's an atrocious defensive third baseman who struck out 204 times last season. His on base ability also leaves a lot to be desired. Reynolds is not a guy I'd build around and if I were Josh Byrnes, I'd hope that Reynolds got off to hot start and then I'd trade him.

Stephen Drew had an excellent all-around season offensively and defensively. Drew's emerging into a star at age 26. He hit 21 homers, had 44 doubles and 11 triples with a .291 average and 178 hits. He'll become more patient as he matures and will be one of the top shortstops in baseball before long.

Conor Jackson is moving to left field. Jackson is a fine hitter and batted .300 with 12 homers and 75 RBI with a .376 OBP and 10 stolen bases. What the Diamondbacks are going to do if Eric Byrnes is healthy enough to return is a question. They have several options such as trading Reynolds or Tracy and moving Jackson back to first base, but the return on either of those players isn't likely to be that high.

Chris Young is a durable, power-hitting, defensively solid center fielder. Young improved his plate patience and hit 22 homers with 85 RBI and 14 stolen bases. He has All Star potential.

Justin Upton is going to be a superstar and the ability to be even better than his brother B.J. of the Rays. Upton is still only 21 and improved drastically from his first big league opportunity as a 19-year-old in 2007. He strikes out a lot and only batted .250, but he did hit 15 homers in 108 games; he's still growing and maturing on and off the field and before long, he's going to be a superstar.

BENCH:

Miguel Montero was the subject of trade discussions possibly going to the Red Sox before they re-signed Jason Varitek; depending on how Varitek hits, the talks could be revisited. Montero has put up big numbers in the minors.

Respected veteran Tony Clark was reacquired from the Padres last season. He still has power from both sides of the plate; he's only a moderate threat at this point in his career and is kept around more for his leadership and to mentor the younger players than for his on-field play.

Eric Byrnes's intensity carried over to the entire team in 2007, but he got hurt in 2008 and missed a chunk of the season after striking out a tremendous amount and not hitting at all. Byrnes was the subject of trade discussions and might be moved if he proves he's healthy.

Augie Ojeda is a switch-hitter who played in place of the injured Hudson. He's a utility player with no power.

James Skelton is a young catcher who showed great on base potential in the minor leagues for the Tigers; the Diamondbacks selected him in the Rule 5 Draft and if they want to keep him, he'll have to stay on the big league roster all season. Those on base numbers may keep him on the roster if he shows anything in the spring.

PREDICTION:

The Diamondbacks haven't improved on paper from the 82-win team they were last season, but if the youngsters Upton, Young, Reynolds and Scherzer improve markedly, they'll be a much better team. The top two starters in the rotation are second to none; the back of the bullpen is solid. They still have a lineup that strikes out too much and if the young players only get slightly better, the Diamondbacks aren't going to go any further than they did last season. Lopez is a major downgrade from Hudson and I wouldn't expect much from Tracy. The NL West is going to be wide open a depending on who gets hot at the end, and any one of four teams could come out on top. The Diamondbacks are still very young and they're going to experience more growing pains as they win a couple of more games than they did last season, but finish out of the playoffs again.

PREDICTED RECORD: 84-78

Colorado Rockies
2008 Record: 74-88; Fourth Place, National League West

2008 Recap:

Following their magical final month-and-a-half of the 2007 season, the Rockies entered 2008 with their same management team, safe from firing for the near and distant future because of that stunning hot streak that took them to the World Series—and the team reverted back to what they've been for the majority of their existence, and that's not good.

The Rockies pitching and lineup, veteran and young, almost all took a step back. Injuries depleted the team of such stars as Matt Holliday and Jeff Francis and they stumbled back to the bottom of the NL West, which, other than brief spurts of good play here and there, has been their lot in life since their birth in 1993.

2009 ADDITIONS: RHP Huston Street was acquired from the Oakland Athletics.

LHP Greg Smith was acquired from the Oakland Athletics.

OF Carlos Gonzalez was acquired from the Oakland Athletics.

LHP Alan Embree signed a 1-year contract.

RHP Jason Marquis was acquired from the Chicago Cubs.

OF Matt Murton was acquired from the Oakland Athletics.

C Paul Phillips signed a minor league contract.

OF Dan Ortmeier signed a minor league contract.

RHP Matt Belisle signed a minor league contract.

LHP Randy Flores signed a minor league contract.

C Sal Fasano signed a minor league contract.

2009 SUBTRACTIONS: OF Matt Holliday was traded to the Oakland Athletics.

OF Willy Taveras was non-tendered.

LHP Brian Fuentes was not re-signed.

RHP Luis Vizcaino was traded to the Chicago Cubs.

INF Corey Wimberly was traded to the Oakland Athletics.

OF Corey Sullivan was non-tendered.

RHP Livan Hernandez was not re-signed.

RHP Matt Herges was not re-signed.

2009 PROJECTED LINEUP: C-Chris Iannetta; 1B-Todd Helton; 2B-Clint Barmes; 3B-Garrett Atkins; SS-Troy Tulowitzki; LF-Ian Stewart; CF-Ryan Spilborghs; RF-Brad Hawpe

2009 PROJECTED STARTING ROTATION: Aaron Cook; Ubaldo Jimenez; Jason Marquis; Jorge De La Rosa; Greg Smith; Jeff Francis

2009 PROJECTED BULLPEN: Huston Street; Manny Corpas; Taylor Buchholz; Alan Embree; Glendon Rusch; Randy Flores; Jason Grilli

2009 BENCH: C-Yorvit Torrealba; INF/OF-Jeff Baker; OF-Carlos Gonzalez; OF-Matt Murton; 1B-Joe Koshansky; OF-Dexter Fowler; OF-Seth Smith

2009 EXTRA PITCHERS/PROSPECTS: Josh Fogg; Jason Hirsh; Greg Reynolds; Jason Grilli; Ryan Speier; Juan Morillo; Steven Register; Cedrick Bowers; Craig Baker; Jhoulys Chacin; Connor Graham

2009 EVERYDAY PROSPECTS: Tony Blanco; Darin Holcomb; Thomas Field

ASSESSMENTS:
MANAGEMENT:

GM Dan O'Dowd's job is safe as he starts another rebuilding project because of that previously mentioned magical month in 2007. The Rockies are a team that has never been consistently good; they have an over .500 season here and there; they develop some good prospects; but they've never been able to translate that into consistent contention. The repeated excuse of limited payroll flexibility is always convenient. O'Dowd has been there for almost ten years and been allowed to build the team, tear it down and rebuild it over and over again without any clear, coherent strategy. Had the Rockies *not* had that hot streak and made it all the way to the World Series in 2007, ended with a record of around 86-76, and then stumbled and collapsed as they did in 2008, O'Dowd might've finally been fired; instead, he's safe for the near and distant future as he again deals veterans like Matt Holliday and patches the club together with another rebuilding project on the horizon.

Manager Clint Hurdle is a solid enough strategic manager and the players seem to like him. After last season's debacle, half the coaching staff was replaced and Hurdle's job has been rumored to be on the line depending on how the youngsters develop. Hurdle is unfairly attached to O'Dowd; if he's fired, I doubt he'd be out of work for very long; he might have to serve as a bench coach like Willie Randolph is, but he'll get another shot to manage if he is indeed dismissed.

STARTING PITCHING:

Ace Jeff Francis had an injury-plagued and terrible season last year and it was revealed just as pitchers and catchers reported to spring training that Francis's shoulder will require exploratory surgery and he'll likely miss the entire 2009 season.

Aaron Cook has always been a decent, if injury-prone pitcher who could be counted on to eat innings if he's healthy and was always better than his hard-luck record; he was signed to a long-term contract and suddenly became an All Star. The 30-year-old Cook went 16-9 with a 3.36 ERA and only allowed 13 homers in 211 innings; he's a pure contact pitcher who throws strikes. Given his history, it's hard to imagine him repeating those numbers and that durability, but as a sinkerballer, he may have figured everything out and could be reaching his prime years of production.

Ubaldo Jimenez has the ability to be one of the top young starters in baseball. He went 12-12 last season, but his across the board numbers were quite good. He pitched 199 innings, allowing 182 hits and only 11 homers; he can get wild (he walked over 100 batters), but he struck out 172. At the age of 25, he's got a bright future at the top of the Rockies rotation.

Veteran Jason Marquis was acquired from the Cubs because the Cubs were trying to slash some salary and were willing to take Luis Vizcaino for him. Marquis has a solid history of pitching well at Coors Field and his hitting ability will be enhanced by the hitter's heaven of Colorado. Marquis isn't great, but he'll pitch his 200 or so innings and win his 10-12 games. (Marquis is Jewish; is he going to fit in with the Christian-themed clubhouse in Colorado?)

Lefty Jorge De La Rosa had a good comeback season with a 10-8 record in 23 starts. De La Rosa numbers, other than his 4.92 ERA, were respectable. De La Rosa pitched 130 innings, allowed 128 hits and struck out 128. Given his career history, it's hard to believe he'll be as effective as he was last season.

Lefty Greg Smith was acquired from the Athletics in the trade that sent Holliday to Oakland. Smith's record was a hideous 7-16 with a 4.16 ERA, but his other numbers are impresive. He pitched 190 innings and allowed only 169 hits; he's a contact pitcher and allowed 21 homers, but that hits/innings pitched ratio show that he's got the stuff to turn his record around completely.

BULLPEN:

Huston Street was also acquired in the Holliday trade and will take over as the Rockies closer. Street is a relatively reliable short reliever whose diminished stuff led to concerns that he was hurt last season. Street struck out a batter per inning and saved 18 games. There were talks that the Rockies were going to spin Street off in another deal, but nothing came together and he's listed as their current closer. If he's healthy and they keep him, I think he can do a good job for them.

Hard-throwing Manny Corpas started last season as the closer after taking over for Brian Fuentes in mid-2007 and helping the team on their way to the World Series. Corpas struggled, gave up a lot of hits and home runs and lost the job back to Fuentes. He's the future closer of the Rockies; whether that's the near or distant future depends on what they do with Street.

Taylor Buchholz has found a home in the Colorado bullpen after years of struggling with the Phillies and Astros. Buchholz had a great year in 2008 with a 2.17 ERA in 66 games and excellent overall stats. The results of relievers tend to fluctuate, but Buchholz has a solid fastball, an excellent curveball and good control, so he should at least be a solid component in the Rockies pen.

Alan Embree was signed to a 1-year deal after leaving the Athletics. Embree served as a jack-of-all-trades for the A's and occasionally closed when necessary. He's had so many peaks and valleys to his career, that Embree might return to form even at age 39.

Glendon Rusch was acquired from the Padres last season and pitched reasonably well for the Rockies. The journeyman lefty could be a spot starter and to be a second lefty in the bullpen.

Jason Grilli appeared in 51 games and had a 2.91 ERA in 61 innings with only one homer allowed.

Former Cardinals reliever Randy Flores signed a minor league deal. Flores got rocked by both lefties and righties last season (a bad omen for a lefty specialist), but he's had a successful career and could make a comeback. The Rockies have had success in taking chances on pitchers like Flores.

LINEUP:

Chris Iannetta finally took the starting catching job from offensively challenged Yorvit Torrealba. Iannetta had a fine season with the bat hitting 18 homers in 104 games with a .390 OBP.

Todd Helton missed most of last season with back problems. His power is gone and he's on the downside of his career at age 35; he still gets on base, but the Rockies should try as hard as they can to find someone to take Helton's bloated contract (or most of it, anyway).

Clint Barmes's days as a prospect and regular player in the big leagues seemed over after injuries and lack of production made him into a utility player barely holding onto his roster spot, but the injury to Troy Tulowitzki gave Barmes a chance to rejuvenate his career, and he did. Barmes batted .290 in 107 games, hit 11 homers and stole 13 bases. It's possible that Barmes, penciled in as the starting second baseman, will stumble again now that he's got a secure spot, but if he can perform as he did last season, the Rockies should be thrilled.

Garrett Atkins is one of the better third baseman in baseball working in obscurity. Atkins batted .299 with 21 homers and 99 RBI in 2008. He can be counted on to hit the ball out of the park and drive in some runs.

A year ago, Troy Tulowitzki was drawing comparisons on and off the field to Derek Jeter; then the sophomore injuries started. More than anything else, Tulowitzki's injuries caused the Rockies to fall as far as they did. He batted .263 with 8 homers in 101 games and if the Rockies are going to turn things around, they need him to be the player he was in 2007.

The Rockies have a bunch of young outfielders and all might get a chance to play. The left fielder listed on their current depth chart is Ian Stewart who played a lot of third base last year as Atkins played first for the injured Helton. The 24-year-old Stewart has put up good power/on base numbers in the minors and hit 10 homers in 81 games with the Rockies.

Ryan Spilborghs takes over as the regular center fielder for Willy Taveras. Spilborghs batted .313 in 89 games with a .407 OBP. He may be holding the position until either top prospect Dexter Fowler or Carlos Gonzalez are ready.

Brad Hawpe had a solid year with 25 homers and 85 RBI and a .381 OBP. With the number of young outfielders the Rockies have in their system, Hawpe could be on the trading block as the season moves along and they try to slash some salary.

BENCH:

Yorvit Torrealba's best attribute as a catcher is that he handles the pitching staff, but he can't hit at all and the Rockies brought him back after a deal with the Mets fell through following the 2007 season. He's a backup at best and could be on the trade block.

Joe Koshansky had an excellent year at Triple A Colorado Springs in 2008. He hit 31 homers, drove in 121, batted .300 and had a .380 OBP. He strikes out a lot, but deserves a chance to play in the big leagues if Helton proves he's just about finished as his decline continues.

Jeff Baker had a good year as a utility player. Baker had 12 homers and 35 extra base hits in 105 games.

Much-traveled Matt Murton was acquired from the Athletics. Murton showed that he deserved to be in the big leagues in 2007, but was relegated to the minors for the Cubs last season as he got caught in a numbers crunch; he was then part of the trade that sent Rich Harden to the Cubs. Now he's with the Rockies and has struggled recently. I'd give him a legit chance to make the club out of spring training and find some at bats for him because he's got ability to at least be a part-time player.

Dexter Fowler is the Rockies best prospect. He destroyed the Texas League last season with a .335 average; 9 homers, 64 RBI; 20 stolen bases and a .431 OBP; he's only 23 and I'd give him a chance to win a starting job out of spring training. He's a Rookie of the Year candidate.

PREDICTION:

The Rockies have many positives going for them and if they're healthy, they can hang around the periphery of the weak NL West. Pitching will be the key because they have the bats to score runs and more young bats on the way. Their bullpen, which is annually a case of scouring the bargain bins, is usually solid. If Cook repeats last season and if Jimenez and Smith develop and they get a surprise contribution from an aging prospect like Jason Hirsh, the Rockies are a dangerous team. The injury to Francis is a bad place to start and they're still claiming poverty; but with the NL West as shaky as it is, the Rockies are as good a bet as any team to crawl to the top. I think they'll be among the other four teams struggling for supremacy as the season winds down and they'll be the one that falls first and ends respectably, but out of playoff position.

PREDICTED RECORD: 81-81

San Diego Padres
2008 Record: 63-99; Fifth Place, National League West

2008 Recap:

There's very little to say about the Padres other than that they were the worst team in baseball on and off the field in 2008. They did have some injuries to overcome, but even if they hadn't lost any manpower from the start of the season to the end, they were still no better than a 72-75 win team. They couldn't hit; couldn't pitch; couldn't do much of anything. What stuns me is how many people looked at that team and picked them to not only contend, but some picked them to go to the World Series!! They didn't even do a proper housecleaning as they only traded journeymen Tony Clark and Randy Wolf. 2008 was a disaster from top-to-bottom for the Padres.

2009 ADDITIONS: OF Cliff Floyd signed a 1-year contract.
C Henry Blanco signed a 1-year contract.
RHP Mark Worrell was acquired from the St. Louis Cardinals.
INF David Eckstein signed a 1-year contract.
RHP Jae Kuk Ryu was claimed off waivers from the Tampa Bay Rays.
RHP Kevin Correia signed a minor league contract.
INF Travis Denker signed a minor league contract.
INF Everth Cabrera was claimed in the Rule 5 Draft from the Colorado Rockies.
RHP Ivan Nova was claimed in the Rule 5 Draft from the New York Yankees.
OF Emil Brown signed a minor league contract.
INF Chris Burke signed a minor league contract.
RHP Chris Britton signed a minor league contract.
C Eliezer Alfonzo signed a minor league contract.

2009 SUBTRACTIONS: RHP Trevor Hoffman was not re-signed.
SS Khalil Greene was traded to the St. Louis Cardinals.
C Josh Bard was not re-signed.
LHP Shawn Estes was not re-signed.
OF Chip Ambres refused a minor league assignment and elected free agency.
RHP Charlie Haeger was non-tendered.
RHP Clay Hensley was non-tendered.

2009 PROJECTED LINEUP: C-Nick Hundley; 1B-Adrian Gonzalez; 2B-David Eckstein; 3B-Kevin Kouzmanoff; SS-Luis Rodriguez; LF-Chase Headley; CF-Jody Gerut; RF-Brian Giles

2009 PROJECTED STARTING ROTATION: Jake Peavy; Chris Young; Cha Seung Baek; Josh Geer; Kevin Correia

2009 PROJECTED BULLPEN: Heath Bell; Cla Meredith; Mark Worrell; Mike Adams; Chris Britton; Jae Kuk Ryu; Justin Hampson; Chad Reineke

2009 BENCH: C-Henry Blanco; INF-Edgar Gonzalez; OF-Scott Hairston; OF-Emil Brown; OF-Cliff Floyd; OF-Will Venable; 2B-Matt Antonelli; INF-Travis Denker; C-Eliezer Alfonzo

2009 EXTRA PITCHERS/PROSPECTS: Mark Prior; Scott Patterson; Oneli Perez; Ivan Nova; Mike Ekstrom; Everth Cabrera; Wade LeBlanc; Steve Garrison; Will Inman

2009 EVERYDAY PROSPECTS: Kyle Blanks; Chad Huffman; Kellen Kulbacki; Eric Sogard

ASSESSMENTS:
MANAGEMENT:

Padres fans can take heart in the knowledge that obnoxious, arrogant, condescending and inept CEO Sandy Alderson will be replaced as soon as Jeff Moorad takes control of the club from John Moores. Moorad, the former owner of the Arizona Diamondbacks who oversaw their reconstruction from on and off-field ruin, is the San Diego Padres savior. The Padres have been run in a clueless, haphazard and disorganized way since Alderson took over. He forced out solid manager Bruce Bochy because he didn't want to pay him; he tried to get rid of GM Kevin Towers (who was almost hired by Moorad to run the Diamondbacks) and when Towers's other opportunities fell through, he was forced to "get with the program" under Alderson.

Getting with the program meant being cheap; following the edicts of Alderson; allowing Alderson's own assistant Paul DePodesta to work outside of Towers's control as an entity in-and-of himself; and doing things that Towers presumably knew weren't in the best interests of the organization, but were done because Alderson wanted them done. The organization is barren and currently has little talent. Moores's divorce precipitated an attempted sell-off of any and all high-priced talent, but Moorad's purchase prevents the Padres from having to deal their two remaining All Star talents Adrian Gonzalez and Jake Peavy and the sooner the current management team is out of there, the quicker a reconstruction can begin; it probably won't be fast enough for the frustrated and angry Padres fans, who've seen their team ruined by Alderson and his minions.

Bud Black is still the manager of the Padres—after his inexperience cost the team a playoff spot in 2007 and the club was the worst in baseball in 2008—for one reason and one reason only: in 2009, the Padres are expecting to be worse than they were last season (if that's possible) and it made little sense to bring in another manager to lose 100 games when they're already paying Black.

Black is well-liked by the media, but he's a figurehead as the manager who was hired because he was happy to have the opportunity and do what he was told by the upper management. It's unfair to overtly blame him for the mess of 2008, but if he wants to get another managing job after he's cleared out by Moorad in the upcoming organizational high colonic, he's probably going to have to either manage in the minors for a couple of years or become a bench coach and replenish the reputation that made him a hot managerial prospect before he got the Padres job.

STARTING PITCHING:

The Padres did everything they could to trade ace Jake Peavy in the off-season, but Peavy's no-trade clause and reluctance to go to any of the American League teams and any other team on the East Coast hamstrung those efforts. The Cubs and Padres were close to a trade several times, but the flapping mouth of Towers as he tried to trade Peavy sabotaged any deal that looked like it had a chance to be completed. After Moorad agreed to buy the club, the Peavy trade was placed on the backburner and it's probably not going to happen now.

Peavy has some of the best pure stuff in baseball, but he gives everything he has on every pitch; has a stressful motion and is eventually going to get hurt. He missed part of the 2008 season with arm woes and his contract is going to start increasing his salary to $15 million in 2010. If I were Moorad, I'd have my new management team (whoever they are) explore trade options for Peavy anyway. He'll bring back a lot of young talent and it's better to let someone else worry about a physical breakdown.

Chris Young also missed time because he was hit in the face with a line drive. The 6'10" Young has the ability to dominate a game and with his sneaky motion, he's hard to hit. He runs out of gas as the season moves along and can't be counted on for more than 180 or so innings. He's signed to a reasonable contract and can be a 12-15 game winner on a good team.

Cha Seung Baek was acquired from the Mariners last season and pitched serviceably for the Padres after joining them. He has a good fastball but mediocre results for his career in the States. Baek is a back of the rotation starter at best who might carve out a career as a set-up man because he has good control and can strikeout a batter or two. Lefties hit him well, so perhaps he can be a guy to come in and get out some righty bats.

Josh Geer is a 25-year-old righty who started five games for the Padres after struggling at Triple A. Geer posted a 2.67 ERA in those starts and pitched over his head compared to his results in Triple A. Geer is a contact pitcher who probably shouldn't be in a big league starting rotation.

Kevin Correia was signed after being non-tendered by the Giants. Correia has excellent stuff and the ability to be a good starting pitcher. His results with the Giants were hideous last season, but he has a good fastball and there's something salvageable there; he'll be pitching for a bad team with a big ballpark, so perhaps he can gain something positive from joining the woeful Padres.

Mark Prior was re-signed after getting hurt again while trying a comeback. If the Padres want to believe that Prior's going to give them anything after all these years and all those injuries, I wish them all the luck in the world.

BULLPEN:

Heath Bell takes over as the closer after the unceremonious parting of the ways with Trevor Hoffman. On the field, Hoffman doesn't have much left and it makes sense to move on with Bell, but the Padres are going to be so terrible, what would've been the difference if they brought Hoffman back as the set-up man for Bell? He would've taken short money to stay and Hoffman is well-liked in the clubhouse and community and deserved a chance to stay in his preferred locale, but this was another example of Alderson's management style treating loyal players like worthless chattel to be squeezed for everything they're worth and cruelly dispatched.

Bell throws very hard and should be a solid closer. He strikes out a batter an inning and while his numbers weren't as dominant as they were in 2007, he'll get the chance to grow accustomed to the job under no pressure since there aren't going to be that many save opportunities with this team anyway.

Cla Meredith is a sidearming righty who appeared in 73 games. His numbers weren't all that good with 79 hits allowed in 70 innings; he also wasn't as good against righties as you'd think a sidearmer would be; but he's had success before and is a useful extra body in the bullpen.

Mark Worrell was acquired from the Cardinals in the salary dump of shortstop Khalil Greene. Worrell is another sidearmer who was dominant at Triple A for the Cardinals. He struck out 80 in 59 innings and allowed 45 hits with a 2.15 ERA.

Chad Reineke was acquired from the Astros in the trade of Randy Wolf at mid-season. Reineke started three games in the big leagues and showed some promise, but was very wild. His results in the minors for the Padres and Astros weren't very good and he's 27-years-old. I wouldn't expect much from him.

Mike Adams had a fine year with a 2.48 ERA in 54 games. He struck out 74 in 65 innings and had excellent control.

Jae Kuk Ryu was claimed off waivers from the Tampa Bay Rays. He didn't pitch much last season and could win a spot in the Padres bullpen.

Chris Britton has spent the last few years in the Yankees organization and didn't pitch much in the big leagues. Britton pitched very well in Triple A Columbus and had some big league success with the Orioles a few years ago.

Justin Hampson is a lefty who had a solid year with a 2.93 ERA in 35 appearances. He's a contact pitcher who only allowed one homer in 31 innings as the lefty specialist.

LINEUP:

Nick Hundley doesn't hit for average and doesn't get on base, but he's shown some pop in the minors. In the big leagues he batted .237 in 198 at bats. He's 25 and I don't know how much of a prospect he is as anything more than a big league backup catcher.

Adrian Gonzalez is an unknown superstar and once the Padres are under new management and begin to bring in some talent to surround him, he'll get the recognition he deserves. He's a power hitter, gets on base and is a Gold Glove caliber first baseman. Gonzalez was functioning alone in the Padres lineup and working in a cavernous ballpark, but still hit 36 homers. He struggled against left-handers, but at age 27, he'll learn to hit them and become a top-level superstar and MVP candidate.

Veteran David Eckstein signed a 1-year contract to compete for the second base job. Eckstein is only a stopgap until Matt Antonelli is ready. Antonelli was terrible at Triple A and in a brief trial with the Padres, but he's the second baseman of the future. Eckstein's days as an everyday player are over and he's a utility player to provide an example to the youngsters on how to get the most out of their ability and behave like a professional.

Kevin Kouzmanoff has the ability to be one of the better hitting third baseman in baseball. He 23 homers and drove in 84 last season, but his OBP was .299 and he struck out 139 times. The numbers he put up in the minors with the Indians were absurdly good and if he can develop into anything close to what those numbers indicate, he'll at least be a power/RBI guy for the sixth or seventh slot in a good lineup.

The Padres expressed interest in signing Omar Vizquel to be their shortstop, but he chose a minor league deal with the Rangers as a mentor to Elvis Andrus rather than sign with the hideous Padres. Veteran journeyman Luis Rodriguez played shortstop relatively regularly after Greene got hurt in 2008 and is listed on the depth chart as the starting shortstop. Presumably, he'll share time with Adrian Gonzalez's brother Edgar.

Chase Headley is one the Padres top prospects and has some pop and on base ability. Headley was a third baseman and is shifting to the outfield. Headley has 20+ home run power if he plays every day, and there's no reason for the Padres not to put him in the lineup every day and let him develop.

Jody Gerut made a comeback from injury-plagued years with the Indians and Pirates. The 31-year-old Gerut had a fine season with 14 homers and a .296 average in 100 games. Gerut's injury history makes him a question as to whether he'll be able to repeat those numbers. The Padres would be smart to trade him if he gets off to a good start this year.

Brian Giles blocked a trade to the Red Sox last season and it was more financially prudent to exercise his contract option than to just let him go. His power is just about gone from what it was earlier in his career, but he had an excellent season in 2008 at age 37. Giles batted .306 with 56 extra base hits and a .398 OBP. He'd be a good fit for a team that needs a lefty bat, but in order to trade him, the interested team would probably have to sign him to a contract extension. I can't imagine him having another year like that at age 38.

BENCH:

Cliff Floyd signed a 1-year contract and will see playing time in left and right field if he's healthy. Floyd's popular with other players and has a reputation as a leader, but despite great abilities and power, he's injury-prone and can't be counted on to play regularly.

Henry Blanco signed a 1-year contract to tutor young Hundley. Blanco is a veteran who can hit a little bit and will accept his role as a backup without complaint.

Scott Hairston hit 17 homers in 112 games (with only 31 RBI, which with 17 homers, is hard to do); he's a veteran backup outfielder.

Emil Brown signed a minor league contract after spending time with the Oakland A's. Brown has some power as a veteran off the bench.

Chris Burke is a veteran utility player who signed a minor league contract after having a disastrous season with the Diamondbacks in which he hit .194 in 165 at bats.

PREDICTION:

That this team has no hope to contend goes without saying, but they'll be lucky if they don't lose 110 games. The only positive thing the Padres have going for them is that Moorad is coming in and will clear out the current management in one clean sweep. They have a couple of youngish stars in Peavy and Gonzalez, and some background talent in Kouzmanoff and Headley. Bell has potential as a closer; but other than that, there's not much there. Black is in a hopeless situation and is pretty much building his resume for a future job somewhere. I'd expect Black to be fired early in the season just to make it *look* like they're doing something. Moorad can't arrive soon enough to save this dying franchise.

PREDICTED RECORD: 56-106

NATIONAL LEAGUE PLAYOFF PREDICTIONS:

NLDS:

Chicago Cubs vs Philadelphia Phillies

Cubs in Three

NLDS:

San Francisco Giants vs Florida Marlins

Giants in Five

NLCS:

Chicago Cubs vs San Francisco Giants

Cubs in Five

NATIONAL LEAGUE CHAMPIONS: CHICAGO CUBS

NATIONAL LEAGUE AWARDS:

MOST VALUABLE PLAYER: Hanley Ramirez, Florida Marlins

CY YOUNG AWARD: Johan Santana, New York Mets

ROOKIE OF THE YEAR: James McDonald, Los Angeles Dodgers

MANAGER OF THE YEAR: Bruce Bochy, San Francisco Giants